MW00388656

The
Fast Forward
MBA in Investing

THE FAST FORWARD MBA SERIES

The Fast Forward MBA Series provides time-pressed business professionals and students with concise, one-stop information to help them solve business problems and make smart, informed business decisions. All of the volumes, written by industry leaders, contain "tough ideas made easy." The published books in this series are:

The Fast Forward MBA in Financial Planning
(0-471-23829-5)
by Ed McCarthy

The Fast Forward MBA in Hiring
(0-471-24212-8)
by Max Messmer

The Fast Forward MBA in Business
(0-471-14660-9)
by Virginia O'Brien

The Fast Forward MBA in Finance
(0-471-10930-4)
by John Tracy

The Fast Forward MBA Pocket Reference
(0-471-14595-5)
by Paul A. Argenti

The Fast Forward MBA in Marketing
(0-471-16616-2)
by Dallas Murphy

The Fast Forward MBA in Investing

JOHN WAGGONER

John Wiley & Sons, Inc.

New York • Chichester • Weinheim • Brisbane • Singapore • Toronto

Published by John Wiley & Sons, Inc.
Published simultaneously in Canada.

No part of this publication may be reproduced, stored in a
retrieval system or transmitted in any form or by any means,
electronic, mechanical, photocopying, recording, scanning or
otherwise, except as permitted under Section 107 or 108 of the
1976 United States Copyright Act, without either the prior
written permission of the Publisher, or authorization through
payment of the appropriate per-copy fee to the Copyright
Clearance Center, 222 Rosewood Drive, Danvers, MA 01923,
(978) 750-8400, fax (978) 750-4744. Requests to the Publisher
for permission should be addressed to the Permissions
Department, John Wiley & Sons, Inc., 605 Third Avenue,
New York, NY 10158-0012, (212) 850-6011, fax (212) 850-6008,
E-Mail: PERMREQ @ WILEY.COM.

This publication is designed to provide accurate and authoritative
information in regard to the subject matter covered. It is sold
with the understanding that the publisher is not engaged in
rendering professional services. If professional advice or other
expert assistance is required, the services of a competent
professional person should be sought.

Library of Congress Cataloging-in-Publication Data:
Waggoner, John M.
    The fast forward MBA in investing / John Waggoner.
    p. ; cm.—(Fast forward MBA series)
    Includes index.
    ISBN 0-471-24661-1 (paper : alk. paper)
    1. Investments—United States.   I. Series.
HG4910.W248 1998
332.6—dc21   98-3803

Printed in the United States of America.

10 9 8 7 6 5 4 3 2 1

To
Nate and Hope,
my dearest treasures.

JOHN WAGGONER

John Waggoner, 42, is *USA Today*'s mutual fund columnist. He also covers personal finance, the stock market, and the economy.

Waggoner has been covering mutual funds and personal finance since 1983. Before joining the newspaper in September 1989, Waggoner was senior editor at *The Independent Investor,* an investment advisory newsletter covering stocks, bonds, taxes, and mutual funds. Prior to that, Waggoner was senior editor at The Donoghue Organization, a newsletter publisher specializing in mutual funds. Waggoner is author of *Money Madness: Strange Schemes and Extraordinary Manias On and Off Wall Street* (Irwin). He is also coauthor of *The Parents' Guide to Money,* an interactive CD-ROM published by Vertigo Development, and he has a question and answer column on investing at *USA Today*'s online site.

Waggoner has a B.A. and M.A. in English literature from Northeastern University in Boston. He lives with his wife, two children, and a large array of small, furry animals in Virginia.

ACKNOWLEDGMENTS

Books are the product of many people, and I can never thank those who have helped me enough.

I'd like to thank the kind people at Lipper Analytical Services (www.lipperweb.com) for their patience in helping me mine more data than most people see in a lifetime. In particular, Julie Friedlander, Scott White, and Melissa Daly have been essential to me in writing this book. And Michael Lipper has been most generous with his time and considerable expertise.

Similarly, Don Phillips and all the people at Morningstar have been generous with their time and data; I'm most grateful to all of them.

Debra Englander has been a most noble and helpful editor. Patient beyond belief, too. Evan Marshall, my agent, has supplied me generously with advice and support; Jeff Seglin, editor and friend, has kept me going with kindly good humor and praise.

Raymond Goldbacher, my editor at *USA Today,* performs daily feats of magic; his ideas and help and friendship have been an inspiration to me.

My mother, Dorothy Mundinger, has provided me with good advice, warm support, and great love all my life. Her gifts to me have been far greater than any investment ever could be.

And I'm grateful to my father, Miles Waggoner, for his kindly patience and affection.

Above all, my wife, Yvonne Surette, has endured a book-writing spouse with love and grace, pointing out where I needed to improve the manuscript and praising where I did not. I'd be lost without her. And my two wonderful children, Nathaniel and Hope, prove that there are some things that are absolutely beyond price.

J. W.

CONTENTS

This book was designed to be a primer on investments. That's easy enough: Investments are very specific objects indeed. You can describe them exactly and legally and in exquisite detail. In these days of global trade, very little is left vague about the instruments of finance.

But if you write about investments, you have a certain obligation to talk about investing, too: when certain investments are appropriate, and for whom, and when. So it's important to start with the most simple and familiar investments and work your way to the most complicated.

This book begins with the most familiar investments available: bank CDs, savings bonds, and money market mutual funds. They are the basic building blocks of a portfolio. After all, most people's investment money comes from the safety of the money market. We use money funds and CDs as staging areas for other investments, and for safe havens when other investments seem too risky.

The money market is important for another reason: It's the best barometer of Federal Reserve policy and the current state of the financial markets. Money market rates rise when the Fed thinks the economy is growing too quickly; they fall when the Fed thinks the economy is growing too slowly. Learn to monitor the money market, and you learn to monitor the Fed, too.

Thanks to the bull market in stocks that began in August 1982, money market investments seem quaintly tame and, well, boring. But I began writing about investing when the money market was interesting indeed. You could earn virtually risk-free returns of 12 percent or more. And stocks and bonds were just easing out of a decade-long period of misery. The money market may seem boring now, but it can become extremely interesting at any time.

Bonds, which can make even hardened MBAs roll their eyes and groan, are the subject of the next chapter. But bonds are the workhorse investments for investors with medium-term goals and retirees with the long-term need for income. Bonds are the vehicle that will help your 16-year-old get to college and help your grandmother live comfortably on her investments. They can help shield your stock portfolio from the worst days that Wall Street has to offer.

And like the money market, bonds can tell you volumes about the economy and Wall Street's view of its prospects. Rising bond yields mean the economy is cooking. But when bond yields rise too far, inflation could be in the pipeline. Similarly, falling rates are good news—provided they don't fall too far, too fast. So even if you don't invest in bonds, you need to understand the bond market.

From bonds we move to the current long-term investment of choice, the stock market. A portfolio of blue-chip stocks can boost your investment income; a portfolio of small, rapidly growing companies can boost your net worth and your blood pressure, too.

But many investors don't invest directly in bonds or stocks. Instead, they invest in bonds and stocks through mutual funds. So the next chapter explains what mutual funds are, how they work, and why they are so popular.

The next two chapters show how you can invest in both stocks and bonds through mutual funds. And, because most investors use stock and bond mutual funds in their long-term savings plans, we talk about different mutual fund investment strategies: how to create an income portfolio; how to create a growth portfolio; and how to use cash and bonds to protect your portfolio from meltdowns.

The final chapter is devoted to some of the most speculative investments available: precious metals, options, and futures. These are investments that are available, but come with high-risk premiums attached to them. Nevertheless, there are times when these investments are useful. You should know of them, but you should be wary of them, too.

So the book moves from the simple to the complex. Although it was written with the hope that you will read it from beginning to end, those of you who have some experience in investing may want to skip the first few chapters. No one will mind. And those of you who have never invested before should dive right in from the beginning. I'd be delighted if you did.

The
Fast Forward
MBA in Investing

Safe Stuff:
The Money Market

It's Monday morning, and you're contemplating the day in front of you. You've got to drop off the dry cleaning, get to work, and finish that big project. Come lunch time, you have to mail the bills and—that's right! Deposit that check for $67.24 you got from your dental insurance. You sigh. It's going to be a busy week.

No matter how busy the rest of your week is going to be, you can bet that your money will be just as busy. Once you hand your check to the teller at the bank, your $67.24 will become part of the money market—the sprawling, worldwide trade in cash among banks and major corporations. It could travel around the globe several times before you spend it.

Let's take a look at what could happen to your $67.24 over the next few days. The bank will send the check to the Federal Reserve for clearance. In most cases, the check will clear within 24 hours. (The bank can refuse to give you your money for up to 21 business days, depending on its policies and federal regulations, but that's another story.)

At the end of the next day, your bank will total how much it owes to other banks, companies, and individuals. It will figure out how much the Federal Reserve requires it to keep on deposit for emergencies. It will also tally up how much money has come into the bank, through deposits like your check, as well as through corporate payrolls and loan payments.

On this particular day, the bank has taken in $1 million more than it must pay out or keep in reserve. Your $67.24 is part of that $1 million.

The bank knows that this is just a temporary surplus: It has other obligations coming due in the next few months, such as certificates of deposit and dividend payments to shareholders. So it will need that $1 million soon.

But it's not about to let that $1 million collect dust for a month, either.

Now, it so happens that BigBank, the nation's second-largest bank, needs to make a $2 million short-term loan to BingCo, the nation's largest maker of high-performance ball bearings. It decides to borrow that $2 million from small banks like yours at a low overnight rate and lend the money to BingCo. The spread between the two loans is BigBank's profit. So your $67.24 is, at least temporarily, loaned to BingCo.

Just how long your $67.24 remains loaned to BigBank (and, in turn, to BingCo) is another matter. Your bank may decide it needs its $1 million back, and use it for its own loan portfolio. Or it may find that another bank is offering a slightly better rate than BigBank. And then your $67.24 would be off for another journey. By the time you spend it, your money might have been around the world—maybe more than once.

THE MONEY MARKET OFTEN GIVES BETTER RATES THAN A SAVINGS ACCOUNT

The money market is no longer just for the government, banks, and large corporations. A *money market mutual fund* is a registered investment company that is regulated by the U.S. Securities and Exchange Commission. It pools money from small investors and uses it to buy money market securities.

In 1972, the first money market mutual fund, the *Reserve Fund,* opened its doors. It took money from small investors, invested it in commercial paper, Treasury bills and other money market securities, and distributed the proceeds equally.

Now there are some 1,170 money funds with more than $1 trillion in assets. It's not hard to see why. The average bank checking account pays no interest. In fact, you will usually be charged an annual fee for your checking account, unless you keep a large balance. The average saving account pays a piddling 2 to 3 percent a year. And most bank money market accounts pay half the current Treasury-bill rate—a standard benchmark for money market interest rates.

After all, banks can pay any interest rate they want. They can even pay different rates to different investors. Money funds must divide their returns equally among their investors. Everyone gets the same return.

Money Market Mutual Funds Keep the Same Share Price Every Day

Most funds add up the value of their holdings every day, subtract their expenses, and divide by the number of shares outstanding to get a share price, or *net asset value.* (This is a bit of an over-simplification, as we will see in Chapter 4, but it will do for now.) Suppose you own 100 shares of Bull Moose Stock Fund. On Monday, the fund's share price is $41.53. Your account is worth $4,153. On Tuesday, the fund's share price is $41.49. Your account is worth $4,149, and you are $4 poorer.

Money funds work differently. In most cases, if you put $10,000 in, you'll get $10,000 out, plus interest. Let's say you invest $10,000 in a money market mutual fund. You have 10,000 shares, each valued at $1. A month later, your account has 10,041.67 shares, each valued at $1. The additional 41.67 shares is your interest. Why is this a big deal? Money funds are the only type of mutual fund whose structure is designed to keep its share price from rising and falling. In essence, it works much like a bank account or a credit union share account.

Now, there's one big caveat to this: Money funds don't have to stay at $1 per share all the time. They make heroic efforts to do so. But a money fund isn't guaranteed by the federal government, as a bank deposit is. If your fund's share price falls to $0.98 cents a share and you sell your shares, you will lose 2 cents a share, or 2 percent.

What Money Market Mutual Funds Invest In

- *Treasury bills.* These are short-term loans to the U.S. government, which guarantees timely payment of interest and principal.

- *Jumbo CDs.* Large bank certificates of deposit, typically above the $100,000 limit for Federal Deposit Insurance Corporation (FDIC) insurance.

- *Commercial paper.* Short-term loans to major corporations with extremely good credit ratings, such as General Motors Acceptance Corporation (GMAC), the financing arm of General Motors.

- *Repurchase agreement.* Overnight collateralized loans. To oversimplify: Bank A owns a $100,000 T-bill. It needs an overnight loan, but doesn't want to sell the T-bill. Bank B agrees to buy the bill, provided Bank A buys it back the next day for a slightly higher price. The purchase price is A's loan; the difference in price is Bank B's yield.

- *Eurodollar CDs.* Certificates of deposit issued by overseas banks, but denominated in dollars.

- *Yankeedollar CDs.* Certificates of deposit issued by U.S. branches of foreign banks.

- *Bankers' acceptances.* Short-term notes used to finance foreign trade.

How can this happen? Suppose your money fund buys an investment from a corporation or bank that, for one reason or another, goes into bankruptcy. Your money fund may have to write off its investment as a bad debt—which could push the share price below $1 per share. In the few times this has happened, the fund company has usually stepped in and purchased the bad securities from the fund, so no small shareholder has lost money.

In fact, a few fund groups, such as the Vanguard Group and Putnam Investments, now carry limited default insurance for their money funds. The insurance will pay the fund—not shareholders—if one of its holdings defaults. It won't pay if, say, market conditions cause the fund's holdings to be valued at less than $1. Other fund companies will probably get similar insurance soon.

But that's very limited insurance, and it won't protect shareholders in all situations. It's best to keep in mind that one money market fund—Community Bankers Money Market Fund—did see its share price fall below $1 per share in 1994. The fund had about 16 shareholders, all institutional investors. So no individuals lost money. But it served as a warning to investors that money funds don't come without risk. Somewhere in the prospectus of every money fund is a little warning that says, basically: This investment is *not* insured by the government, and *you could lose money.*

Don't forget this warning.

 Money Fund Yields Rise with Interest Rates

Like all mutual funds, a money market fund can't promise what returns it will bring in the future. But it's required to pass on higher returns to investors. So when rates on short-term money market investments rise, a money fund's yield will rise, too. (There's usually a three- to six-week lag as the fund's new, higher-yielding investments begin to make interest payments and older, lower-yielding investments get shuffled off to Palookaville.) Similarly, your fund's yield will fall when short-term interest rates fall.

 Money Funds Offer Check Writing

Typically, funds will require that your check be for $250 or more, so you can't pay your baby sitter with a money-fund check. But you can pay major debts, such as mortgages or big car-repair bills, straight from your money fund. Most funds will also wire money directly to your bank, if you prefer.

 Money Funds Offer Telephone Switching

Most—but not all—money funds will let you transfer into other funds within the same fund family with a simple telephone call. And if you belong to a large brokerage or discount brokerage, you can transfer money from a money fund into nearly any investment in the world.

Types of Money Market Funds (MMFs)

Money funds come in several varieties, depending on what types of money market securities they invest in. They are:

- *Treasury-only.* These funds only invest in T-bills, arguably the safest investment on earth. A sudden rise in interest rates could possibly force these funds to fall below $1 per share, but they are virtually immune to credit risk—the possibility that the issuer won't be able to pay interest and principal on its obligations.

  A few funds invest only in T-bills. These funds have an added attraction: The interest from these funds is exempt from state income taxes in 39 states. Interest from government obligations is free from state income taxes. In those 39 states, the state considers the income from the fund the same as the income from the obligation itself.

  Here are five such funds, according to *IBC's Money Fund Report.* Call them to see if your state is among the favored 39.

  Vanguard Money Market Reserves/Money Market Portfolio (800-662-7447).

  Dreyfus 100% U.S. Treasury MMF (800-782-6620).

  T. Rowe Price U.S. Treasury Money Fund (800-638-5660).

  Fidelity Spartan U.S. Treasury MMF (800-544-8888).

- *Government-only.* These funds invest in T-bills, as well as obligations issued by other agencies of the government. T-bills are backed by the full faith of the U.S. government. Other arms of the government, such as the Farmers Home Administration, issue money market securities that are not guaranteed by the U.S. government. On the other hand, it's very unlikely that Congress would let these agencies default, so they are considered moral obligations of the U.S. government. Typically, these securities yield slightly more than T-bills.

- *General-purpose.* These funds invest in a full range of money market investments, from commercial paper, to T-bills, to repurchase agreements. Typically, these are the most risky kinds of money funds—but they offer higher yields than Treasury-only money funds.

CHOOSING A TOP-PERFORMING MONEY MARKET MUTUAL FUND

If you're looking for high yields, look for a fund that charges low annual expenses. Like all mutual funds, money market funds take a percentage of the fund's assets every year to pay salaries, rent, and other costs. The average money fund charges about 0.70 percent, or 70 basis points. (One basis point equals 1/100 of a percentage point.)

That doesn't sound like much—until you figure that the average money fund yielded about 5 percent in April 1998. Giving 70 basis points to the fund's management reduces your yield by 12.2 percent. And, because 90 percent of the yield difference between money fund stems from expenses—not the manager's skill—it makes sense to look for funds with rock-bottom expenses.

Many fund companies waive expenses for their money market funds to make their yields tower above the rest. Typically, they stop waiving expenses when they get more money into the fund. Shareholders who fall for the tactic eventually get a fund with an average yield.

But some funds are committed to rock-bottom expenses. The *Vanguard Group* (800-662-7447), in Valley Forge, Pennsylvania, consistently offers top-performing money funds with low expenses. And several fund groups have money funds with low expenses for investors who can open an account with balances of $25,000 to $50,000 or even more. *Fidelity Investments* (800-544-8888) offers the *Spartan Money Market Fund;* Vanguard offers the *Admiral* group of extra-low-cost funds.

These two groups aren't the only ones committed to low expenses. *IBC's Money Fund Report* surveys all money funds every Wednesday and collects data on yields, expenses, and the funds' investments. The publication is aimed at institutions, which means you probably can't afford it. But IBC's excellent website (http://www.ibcdata .com) lists the top-yielding money market funds weekly at no charge.

If you are in a very high tax bracket, consider a tax-free money market fund. These funds invest in short-term municipal obligations. The interest on these investments—and the dividends the fund pays to you—are free from federal income taxes. And a few funds invest only in the money market securities of one state. If you live in that state, the interest is free from state, local, and federal income taxes.

The one drawback: The yields on these funds are very low. In the last week of June 1996, for example, the average taxable money market fund yielded 5.04 percent, versus 3.48 percent for the average tax-free money market fund. How do you know which is best after taxes?

- Find your federal tax bracket. Let's say you're in the 28 percent tax bracket.
- Subtract 28 percent, or .28, from 1. Answer: 0.72, or 72 percent.
- Multiply 0.72 percent by 5.04 percent. Answer: 3.63 percent.

Now you know how much you have left after taxes from your taxable fund. Since 3.63 percent is more than 3.48 percent, you'd be better off in a taxable fund.

 **TAP THE TREASURY WITH TREASURY BILLS**

The money market is the market for short-term debt, and few institutions have more short-term debt than the U.S. government. To meet its obligations, the Treasury borrows money by issuing short-term, interest-bearing IOUs called *Treasury bills*. A *Treasury bill* represents a short-term debt of the U.S. Treasury. It is negotiable, which means it can be bought and sold, and it's backed by the highest guarantee of the U.S. government.

What's so great about T-bills?

- *Safety.*   T-bills are backed by the full faith and credit of the United States, which means that the government must pay off T-bill holders before anyone else. If the FDIC, the federal agency that guarantees bank deposits, went bankrupt at the same time as the U.S. government, the Treasury would have to pay T-bill holders before it paid insured bank depositors. In practice, getting your T-bill paid off would be the least of your problems if the banking system was so bad that the FDIC and the federal government were bankrupt.
- *Liquidity.*   When something is easy to sell, it's called a *liquid investment*. T-bills, because they are so plentiful and so widely traded, are excep-

tionally easy to buy and sell. They are so liquid, in fact, that Wall Street refers to them as *cash*— a term that also refers to any safe investment that's easily liquidated.

- *Tax advantages.* Interest from T-bills is free from state and local taxes. You still have to pay federal taxes on your interest, however.

- *Yield.* T-bill yields are set at auction, so the rate represents the true market value of money at the time they are sold. Typically, T-bills yield a bit more than the average bank CD.

How the Treasury auction works is complicated. Investors can submit a *competitive bid* or a *noncompetitive bid.* If competitive bidders are successful, they get the yield they want. If not, their checks are returned. The Treasury honors all noncompetitive bidders. They get the average of all competitive bids.

Typically, those who submit competitive bids are large banks, bond dealers, or other big institutional players. The Treasury accepts the lowest-yielding bids first, then accepts higher bids until it has sold all its T-bills.

Let's consider a hypothetical T-bill auction. On this particular day, the Treasury must auction off $12 billion in T-bills. The Treasury gets $2 billion in noncompetitive bids and another $15 billion in competitive bids.

In the competitive auction, the bids stack up as follows:

- A government securities dealer puts in an order for $4 billion in T-bills. Its bid on the yield is 5.20 percent.

- A large bank puts in an order for $5 billion in T-bills. Its bid is 5.21 percent.

- A foreign bank puts in a $6 billion order. Its bid is 5.23 percent.

The Treasury sets aside $2 billion for the noncompetitive bidders, leaving it with $10 billion for competitive bidders.

The Treasury fills the government securities dealer's $4 billion order first, paying 5.20 percent on those T-bills. Next, it fills the bank's $5 billion order, paying 5.21 percent on those bills. Finally, it fills just $1 billion of the foreign bank's $6 billion order at 5.23 percent. Because it has now

Stellar Performer:
Vanguard Money Market Reserves
Prime Portfolio

The Vanguard Group of funds prides itself on its "cheap" reputation. But its money funds are worth cheering about.

By and large, most money funds are pretty much the same. Most of the difference between money fund yields are due to expenses, not to savvy management. Vanguard has the sense to realize that.

The Vanguard Money Market Reserves Prime Portfolio is a general purpose money fund that charges just 0.32 percent of the fund's assets for expenses, versus about 0.70 percent for the average money fund. That's about the cheapest in the mutual fund industry—about $32 a year on a $10,000 investment.

Those low expenses pay off over time: The fund has beaten the average money fund every year from 1986 through 1996.

Very wealthy investors can get an even lower expense ratio through Vanguard's Admiral U.S. Treasury Money Market Portfolio. The fund has a 0.15 percent expense ratio, or $15 for every $10,000 invested. Large accounts are easier and cheaper to service. So you have to write a big check to invest in the fund. Vanguard wants a $50,000 minimum initial investment for the Admiral U.S. Treasury Money Market Portfolio.

Those who don't have $50,000 kicking around in a savings account will still be well served by its Money Market Reserves Prime Portfolio. The vital statistics follow:

Vanguard Money Markets Reserve Portfolio

Minimum investment: $3,000 for a regular account, $500 for an individual retirement account, and $500 for a Uniform Gifts to Minors Account. Your account can fall below these levels after you have made your initial investment, but they will be subject to fees, following.

Account fees: $10 per year for nonretirement accounts with balances below $2,500, or retirement accounts with balances below $500.

Check writing: You can write checks against your account, provided the check amount is at least $250. Your money earns interest until the check clears.

Sales charge: None.

(Continued)

(Continued)

Performance (average annual returns as of December 31, 1997):

	Total return			
	1 year	3 years	5 years	10 years
Vanguard MM Reserve Prime	5.44%	5.52%	4.73%	5.86%
Lipper Money Market Funds Average	4.90%	5.05%	4.31%	5.40%

Telephone: 800-662-2739, 610-669-1000.
Website: http://www.vanguard.com.

SOURCE: *Lipper Analytical Services, Inc.*

---

sold all it needs, the Treasury returns the foreign bank's remaining $5 billion.

As you can see, if a competitive bid is not very close to the lowest bid, it runs a chance of being shut out. That's why most small investors submit a noncompetitive bid.

You don't have to wait long for a Treasury auction:

- The Treasury auctions three-month and six-month T-bills every week. Typically, it announces the auctions on Tuesdays, holds the auctions on the following Monday, and issues the new bills every Thursday. Most newspapers carry the results of the auction in their "Money Rates" column, buried deep in the stock-market listings.

- The Treasury auctions 52-week bills every 4 weeks. Normally, the Treasury announces the auction on Fridays; it holds the auction the following Thursday. The Treasury issues the bills the Thursday after the auction.

KEY CONCEPT **T-Bills Are Sold at a Discount**

T-bills come in minimum denominations of $10,000. But, like Series EE Savings Bonds, T-bills are sold at a discount from their face value. For example, suppose you want to buy a $10,000 T-bill. It sells at a discount rate of 5 percent, which

Stellar Performer: Schwab Money Market Fund

Schwab Money Market Fund isn't remarkable so much for its performance—which is, nevertheless, pretty good—as for the number of
places you can go to from there. For many investors, Schwab Money
Market Fund is the first stop before investing elsewhere. And through
Charles Schwab & Co., the nation's largest discount brokerage, you
can go just about anywhere.

For example, you can purchase hundreds of stock and bond
mutual funds through Schwab without paying a sales charge, thanks
to Schwab's immensely popular OneSource program. You can also
buy many funds that charge a sales fee through Schwab's Mutual
Fund Marketplace.

But that's not all. More aggressive investors can buy individual
stocks and bonds through Schwab, as well as options. And Schwab
will sweep your dividends and earnings back into the Schwab Money
Market Fund, if that's what you want. The particulars follow:

Schwab Money Market Fund

Minimum investment: $1,000 for a regular account, $1 for an
individual retirement account.

Account fees: None. The general purpose money fund has a
0.75 percent expense ratio, slightly higher than most money
funds. That's $75 a year on a $10,000 account.

Check writing: You can write checks against your account, provided the check amount is at least $250. Your money earns inter-
est until the check clears.

Sales charge: None.

Performance (average annual returns as of June 30, 1997):

	Total return			
	1 year	3 years	5 years	10 years
Schwab Money Market Fund	5.04%	5.12%	4.34%	New
Lipper Money Market Funds Average	4.90%	5.05%	4.31%	5.40%

Telephone: 800-525-8600.
Website: http://www.schwab.com.

SOURCE: *Charles Schwab & Co., Lipper Analytical Services, Inc.*

means you pay $9,500 for your T-bill. When it matures, the Treasury gives you $10,000.

This process is often confusing for first-time investors, because when you enter a noncompetitive bid, you have to send a check for $10,000—the T-bill's face value. If the T-bill's discount price in the noncompetitive auction is $9,500, the Treasury sends you a check for $500, leading some people to think that they have gotten their interest in advance. Nope. It's just the change. The interest comes when your T-bill matures for $10,000.

Astute readers—or at least those with an unusual interest in their calculators—will notice that the discount rate is actually lower than the T-bill's actual yield. If you invest $9,500 and you get $500 from your investment, your actual return is 5.3 percent. ($500 divided by $9,500 is 0.053, or 5.3 percent.) You should disregard the discount rate and look instead at the T-bill's yield when you're shopping for the highest yields in the money market.

 T-Bills Can Help You Defer Taxes to Another Year

Interest—like wages and salaries—is taxable the year in which you receive it. If you have a bank CD that earns $500 in interest in 1998, you owe taxes on that $500 on your 1998 tax return. That's true even if your CD matures in 2001.

However, with T-bills, your interest is taxable when your T-bill matures. So if you buy a one-year T-bill on January 1, 1998, and it matures January 1, 1999, your interest will be taxable in tax year 1999.

A GREAT DEAL: BUYING T-BILLS FROM THE FEDERAL RESERVE

You can buy T-bills from brokerages or banks. If you do, you'll have to pay your broker a commission—typically $29 to $50—for this service.

But you can also buy T-bills directly from the Federal Reserve. Best of all, it's free for those with $100,000 or less.

The Fed's program is called *Treasury Direct,* which allows you to buy Treasury bills (and notes and bonds, too) by entering noncompetitive bids at Treasury auctions. The Treasury will send your interest directly to your bank. It will also reinvest your maturing T-bills into T-bills of the same maturity automatically for up to two years.

To start a Treasury Direct Account, you'll need to fill out Form PD F 5182, "New Account Request," and send it, along with your investment, to the nearest Federal Reserve Bank. The addresses of the various Federal Reserve banks are at the end of this chapter.

USE BANK CDs TO TAP THE MONEY MARKET

Money funds aren't the only money market investment. Banks offer one type of investment that's absolutely awful, and another that's not bad.

The awful investment is the *money market deposit account,* sometimes called just a money market account (MMA). Basically, it's a savings account that offers a floating interest rate. What makes it so unattractive? In most cases, the rate is far below what a money fund offers. Money funds have to pay out the interest they earn, less expenses. Banks can pay whatever they want, and they usually don't want to pay much. As of the week of April 27, 1998, for example, the average bank MMA account paid 2.49 percent, versus 4.99 percent for the average money market mutual fund. That's a typical spread between the two.

But *bank certificates of deposit* (CDs) are a different matter. A CD is a contract between you and your bank. You promise to keep your money on deposit for a period of time, usually three months to five years. In return, the bank pays you a specific rate of interest. Typically, that rate is more than it will pay on savings accounts. And the longer you promise to keep your money on deposit, the more interest you will get from your CD. In most cases, CDs that mature in more than one year will yield more than a money market fund. For example, Figure 1.1 shows the average yields for CDs the week of April 27, 1998, according to *Bank Rate Monitor,* a newsletter that tracks CD rates across the nation.

The one drawback: If you take your money before the CD matures, or rolls over, you'll have to pay a penalty. The usual penalty is three months' interest, or all your interest, whichever is less. But

CD maturity	Rate, %
6 months	4.67
1 year	4.99
2.5 years	5.10
5 years	5.27

SOURCE: Bank Rate Monitor.

FIGURE 1.1 *Average CD yields.*

penalties can be whatever the bank wants, and
sometimes the early withdrawal penalty can be
quite stiff indeed. It pays to ask before you take
out the CD.

Compounding Counts

KEY CONCEPT   There are many different ways to compare CD yields, depending on whether the CD is
compounded semiannually (rare), monthly (common), or daily (common). For example, consider a
$10,000, 5-year CD with the stated annual rate of
5.5 percent. If interest is compounded:

- Semiannually, you'll have $13,117.
- Monthly, you'll have $13,157.
- Daily, you'll have $13,165.

The most no-nonsense way of comparing yields
is to ask the bank how much interest—in dollars—
the CD will earn over its lifetime. Compare that
figure with other dollar amounts that other banks
quote. They will gripe about this, but it's probably
the most honest way to compare returns from
CDs. Otherwise, ask for the average percentage
yield (APY).

And be sure to ask about any fees, particularly
if you're opening a money market account. A $5
monthly fee on a money market account will
reduce its yield from paltry to pathetic.

Shop Around for the Best Rates

KEY CONCEPT   When shopping for a CD, don't limit your
search to the local bank. One way to find them:
100 Highest Yields, a West Palm Beach, Florida,
newsletter that tracks bank CD rates across the
country. Call 800-327-7717 for subscription infor-

mation. You can also find top-yielding bank CD rates in *USA Today, Barron's,* and the *Wall Street Journal.*

When you open an out-of-state account, be sure to get an up-to-date yield quote. Banks can change their rates any time, and often do. Ask if the bank will guarantee the rate quoted until your check is received. *100 Highest Yields* recommends that you ask for an account form for your out-of-state account, and that you keep copies of it in a safe place. Be sure to keep your signature card, which is your proof of ownership should the bank fail.

Your broker may also be able to help you find CDs. Most major brokerage houses offer a menu of federally insured bank CDs from across the country. The brokerage gets its commission from the offering bank, so you don't have to pay for the service.

FEDERAL DEPOSIT INSURANCE: MORE THAN ENOUGH TO GO AROUND

In the past, when a bank failed, you became a creditor of the bank. In many cases, you would have to settle for 50 cents on the dollar or less if your bank went belly up. A bank failure was a real tragedy.

Fortunately, the Federal Deposit Insurance Corporation provides insurance for most banks and savings institutions in the nation. Technically, the Bank Insurance Fund (BIF), a part of the FDIC, insures most bank deposits. The Savings Association Insurance Fund (SAIF) insures savings and loan associations. But both are under the FDIC umbrella.

The FDIC insures accounts up to $100,000, which includes principal and interest. That should be enough for almost anyone. But if you need to have more than $100,000 covered by FDIC insurance, there are several ways to do so.

- *Spread your accounts to different insured banks.* The $100,000 FDIC insurance applies to accounts owned by the same people at different banks. If you go to CitiGroup and put $100,000 in a CD, then go to Chase Manhattan and put another $100,000 into a CD, you are fully insured for each account.

  But different types of accounts at the same bank don't get extra coverage. If you had a

$100,000 CD at Chase Manhattan and a $50,000 checking account at Chase Manhattan, you'd still only be insured for $100,000. The FDIC makes every effort to pay individuals in full. But in the unlikely event Chase were to fail, you would be standing in line with the bank's other creditors to collect $50,000—the amount not covered by insurance.

- *Spread your accounts to different types of ownership.* If you absolutely must have more than $100,000 in the same bank, make sure your accounts are in different ownership categories. For example, suppose Fred Bing had $100,000 in a CD at the First Bank of Bingleville. His wife, Fredrica, had $100,000 in a checking account. And they both had another $100,000 in a joint account. All $300,000 would be insured by the FDIC.

   Furthermore, if Fred had a $100,000 individual retirement account at the First Bank of Bingleville, it would be insured in full, too. So would Fredrica's IRA. The FDIC considers these accounts, as well as revocable and irrevocable trust accounts, to be separately insured.

There are still a few uninsured banks. Any insured institution should display an official SAIF or BIF logo. And some banks are covered by additional state deposit insurance.

Incidentally, the FDIC doesn't cover the contents of your safety deposit box, nor does it cover any securities you buy through the bank—mutual funds, stocks, bonds, and so forth.

KEY CONCEPT GIVE CREDIT TO CREDIT UNIONS

Another good place to look for high-yielding CDs is your local credit union. Credit unions were started in the United States around the turn of the century. Their purpose: to promote saving and make loans readily available to people of modest means. (Today we often forget that consumer loans and even mortgages were very difficult for the average person to get in the early part of this century.)

Unlike banks, which are run largely for the benefit of their stockholders, credit unions are run for their members. Basically, a credit union is a nonprofit, cooperative institution that is owned by its members. Technically, when you bank at a credit union, you don't have an account: You own shares in the credit union. Those shares entitle you to a vote in the credit union's affairs.

Because the credit union is controlled by those who use it, and because it doesn't need to think about turning a profit, it can often offer better rates on CDs or loans than a commercial bank. Typically, a credit union leans towards giving better loan rates or better CD rates, but not both. It depends on what its members are most interested in.

Like banks, credit unions are federally insured. The National Credit Union Share Insurance Fund insures credit union deposits up to $100,000. The rules for insurance are the same as at banks and savings and loan associations.

What's the catch? You have to be eligible to join a credit union. The federal government or the state defines a credit union's field of membership. Employers, churches, schools, or communities may offer credit unions. To find one in your area, call the Credit Union National Association at 800-358-5710.

WHY INVEST IN THE MONEY MARKET?

According to hoary Wall Street legend, someone once asked Albert Einstein what he thought was the most astonishing thing in the universe. His reply: "Compound interest."

And the rewards of compound interest, over great lengths of time, are astonishing indeed. A $1,000 investment at 10 percent interest a year will become $2,000 in 7.3 years and $10,000 in 24 years. It will become $1 million in 73 years.

The problem, of course, is that to get 10 percent interest these days, you either have to live in a country like Russia, which suffers from hyperinflation, or you have to be a loan shark. Both these strategies have more risks than the average money market investor wants to take. So here's our first rule about investing: *The potential rewards from your investment increase with the risk you take.*

The money market is not risk-free, but your chances of losing money in a T-bill, bank CD, or

a money market mutual fund are extremely
small. For that reason, the returns from money
market investments, such as three-year T-bills,
are typically small, too—just a little bit above or
below inflation in most years, as you can see in
Figure 1.2.

Inflation isn't the only element that cuts into
your yield. Taxes do, too. In fact, after inflation
and taxes, money market investments typically
lose money over the long term, as you can see
from Figure 1.3.

As we will see in other chapters, risky investments, such as stocks or commodities, don't automatically beat safe investments. But they have the
potential for enormous gains. Money market
investments don't.

Year	3-month T-bill yield, %	Inflation rate, %	Yield after inflation, %
1974	7.83	12.34	−4.51
1975	5.77	6.94	−1.17
1976	5.00	4.86	0.14
1977	5.26	6.70	−1.44
1978	7.22	9.02	−1.80
1979	10.04	13.29	−3.25
1980	11.58	12.52	−0.94
1981	14.01	8.92	5.09
1982	10.70	3.83	6.87
1983	8.62	3.79	4.83
1984	9.57	3.95	5.62
1985	7.49	3.80	3.69
1986	5.97	1.10	4.87
1987	5.83	4.43	1.40
1988	6.67	4.42	2.25
1989	8.11	4.65	3.46
1990	7.51	6.11	1.40
1991	5.41	3.06	2.35
1992	3.46	2.90	0.56
1993	3.02	2.75	0.27
1994	4.27	2.67	1.60
1995	5.51	2.54	2.97
1996	5.02	3.32	1.70

FIGURE 1.2 *The impact of inflation.*

How Long Will It Take to Double My Money?

You can use a mathematical shortcut to estimate how long it will take your money to double. It's called the *Rule of 72*, and it works as follows:

● Divide 72 by your interest rate to get the number of years it will take your money to double.

In this case, we use the rate as a regular number, not as its decimal equivalent. So if you were considering a CD that pays 6 percent interest, you'd divide 72 by 6 and get 12. In other words, it would take about 12 years at 6 percent interest to double your money.

The rule of 72 is approximate, not definitive. If you want to be more precise, you need to fire up your calculator. The basic formula for interest is:

$$\text{Interest} = \text{principal} \times \text{rate} \times \text{time}$$

Let's say you have a $1,000 investment. The bank is offering 5 percent simple annual interest for 1 year. So you would multiply $1,000 (your principal) by 0.05 (your rate) by 1 (the time—1 year). The answer, of course, is $50.

But as we all know, life is far more complicated. For example, suppose your bank is offering a 5 percent simple rate for 90 days. How much would you have after 90 days? To get the answer, you would multiply $1,000 (your principal) by 0.05 (your rate) by 0.25. The answer: $12.50.

How did we get 0.25 for the time portion of the formula? We divided 90 days by 360 days, which many banks use as the number of days in the year, because it's easier to calculate. Other banks use 365 days, (or 366, in a leap year). That's more precise, but gives you slightly less interest. For example, a $5,000 deposit at 6 percent interest will give you $75 in interest in 1 year, using 360 days in the year. Computed on 365 days in a year, you will get $73.97 in interest.

Another, more interesting problem is this: What will my money grow to after a certain number of years? The basic formula for annual compounding is:

$$\text{The future value of a deposit now} = P(1 + i)^n$$

In this case, *P* equals your principal, *i* equals your interest rate, and *n* equals the number of years you will have your money on deposit. Jump-start your calculator and walk through this problem:

(Continued)

(Continued)

The First Bank of Bingleville is offering a 6.5 percent interest rate on its 5-year CD. Interest is compounded annually. Ignoring (at least for the moment) any irritating bank fees, such as the one the bank charges to lend you a pen, how much money will you have in your account after five years?

- Start with the stuff inside the parentheses. In this case, add 1 to 0.065, which is 6.5 percent in its decimal form. You get 1.065.

- Now raise 1.065 percent to the 5th power. The answer is 1.37009. Whee! Aren't you glad we have calculators?

- Now multiply $5,000 by 1.37009. The answer—$6,850.45—is the amount you'll have after 5 years from a 6.5 percent CD, assuming simple compound interest.

Of course, many banks offer more frequent compounding—quarterly, monthly, weekly, or daily. (There's even continuous compounding, but it's not much different from daily compounding.) How do you figure that?

Simply use the same formula as for annual compounding, with one major difference: You must divide the interest rate by the number of compounding periods per year. For example, suppose you were considering the same CD as previously, but interest was compounded monthly. Hang on to your hat. Here we go. The formula for compound interest is:

$$\text{The future value of a deposit now} = P\left(1 + \frac{i}{12}\right)^n$$

- Starting with the information inside the parentheses, we will divide 0.065 by 12—our interest rate divided by the number of months in the year. The answer is 0.0054167.

- Now we add 1 to our previous answer. So we get 1.0054167.

- Next, we're going to raise 1.0054167 to the 60th power, because that's what calculators are for. Actually, we use the 60th power because there are now 60 compounding periods—12 months per year multiplied by 5 years. Our answer is 1.382817.

- Finally, we multiply 1.382817 by $5,000—the amount we are depositing in a CD. The answer is $6,914.09.

Of course, extremely practical people simply use compound interest tables, which can be purchased almost anywhere. And some people also use computers, because many popular software programs, such as Quicken and Microsoft Money for Windows, will help you calculate compound interest.

Year	3-month T-bill yield, %	Inflation rate, %	Yield after inflation, %	Yield after inflation and 28% taxes, %	Value of $10,000, after inflation and taxes
1974	7.83	12.34	−4.51	−6.70	$9,330
1975	5.77	6.94	−1.17	−2.79	9,070
1976	5.00	4.86	0.14	−1.26	8,956
1977	5.26	6.70	−1.44	−2.91	8,695
1978	7.22	9.02	−1.80	−3.82	8,362
1979	10.04	13.29	−3.25	−6.06	7,856
1980	11.58	12.52	−0.94	−4.18	7,527
1981	14.01	8.92	5.09	1.17	7,615
1982	10.70	3.83	6.87	3.87	7,910
1983	8.62	3.79	4.83	2.42	8,101
1984	9.57	3.95	5.62	2.94	8,339
1985	7.49	3.80	3.69	1.59	8,472
1986	5.97	1.10	4.87	3.20	8,743
1987	5.83	4.43	1.40	−0.23	8,723
1988	6.67	4.42	2.25	0.38	8,756
1989	8.11	4.65	3.46	1.19	8,860
1990	7.51	6.11	1.40	−0.70	8,798
1991	5.41	3.06	2.35	0.84	8,871
1992	3.46	2.90	0.56	−0.41	8,835
1993	3.02	2.75	0.27	−0.58	8,784
1994	4.27	2.67	1.60	0.40	8,820
1995	5.51	2.54	2.97	1.43	8,946
1996	5.02	3.32	1.70	0.29	8,972

FIGURE 1.3 *The impact of taxes.*

Use the Money Market for Short-Term Savings

You may not be able to make money in the long run from the money market. But there's no better place for your short-term savings—money you will need to spend in the next one to three years.

Consider the case of Jeff and Nancy. They want to buy a new house in three years. So far, they have saved $10,000 for a down payment. They need $15,000 for their down payment, and they plan to add $50 a month to their investment. Naturally, they want to earn as much as possible. If they wind up with more than $15,000 in 3 years, the extra money will help pay for the stuffed moose head that Jeff wants for the mantelpiece.

To reach $15,000 in 3 years, they will need to earn 9 percent annually on their investments. But a 3-year bank CD yields only 5.5 percent. A 1-year T-bill yields 5 percent. And a money market fund yields 4.8 percent. Nevertheless, a money market investment is their best bet. Why? Because if they lose money on a riskier investment, they won't have time to recoup their losses.

For example, suppose Jeff and Nancy decided to take a risk and buy the Vanguard Index 500 stock fund, which simply imitates the Standard & Poor's 500 stock index. Most years, they would have done very well with the fund: Between 1986 and 1996, the fund averaged a sizzling 15.04 percent gain.

But let's suppose it's October 1987 when Jeff and Nancy decide to invest in the Vanguard Index 500 fund. Unfortunately, that's the month when the stock market has its worst crash since 1929. The Vanguard Index 500 fund takes a bone-jarring 22 percent fall in October, and another 8.2 percent tumble in November. It rallies back for the rest of the three years. But by October 1990, their investment is worth just $12,321—even after putting $50 a month into the fund for 3 years. So Jeff and Nancy may not be able to buy the house. On the bright side, the moose head is out of the question.

Granted, that's an extreme example. Stock market crashes à la 1987 are thankfully rare. But you can't count on the stock market in the short term. And if you need a set amount of money by a specific date in three years or less, your best bet is the money market—even if you have to save a bit more each month.

Use Money Market Investments to Cushion Your Risk

Money market investments are also useful for cushioning your other investments from risk. Let's consider the Vanguard Index 500 stock fund once again. As was just mentioned, it tumbled 22 percent in October 1987. So a $10,000 investment in the fund would have swiftly become a $7,800 investment—a $2,200 loss.

But let's suppose you were leery of investing all your money in the Vanguard Index 500 fund, and decided to put $7,000 into the fund and $3,000 into a 3-month T-bill. The $7,000 in the Vanguard

Index 500 fund would have swooned to $5,460. But the $3,000 in the 3-month T-bill would have risen to $3,016. The total loss would have been $1,524 That's not a pleasant event, but it's better than losing $2,200.

Bear in mind, however, that keeping 30 percent of your money in money market investments will be a drag on your portfolio's performance in a bull market. For example, a $10,000 investment in the Vanguard Index 500 fund would have become $20,100 in the 5 years ending December 31, 1996. But if you had put $3,000 into a 3-month T-bill and $7,000 into a the Vanguard Index 500 fund, your investments would have been worth $17,765 during the same period.

But many people will accept somewhat lower returns for less worry. If you're one of those people, then the money market is for you.

 ## Watch the Fed for Short-Term Rates

The money market responds to short-term interest rates, which dance to a very different tune than long-term interest rates, such as those on mortgages or corporate bonds.

The Federal Reserve Board, the nation's central bank, is the prime mover of short-term interest rates. One of the Fed's main jobs is to keep the economy running smoothly—neither too fast nor too slow. If the economy is running too slowly, it runs the risk of falling into a recession. If the economy runs too fast, inflation could heat up.

Short-term interest rates are the Fed's main tool in controlling the economy. When the economy seems as if it's running too fast, the Fed has several tools it can use:

- *Reserve requirements.* The Fed sets the amount that banks must keep on reserve to cover emergencies. When the Fed raises reserve requirements, banks must take money out of circulation and place it on deposit with the Fed. That reduces the money supply, raises interest rates, and slows the economy. When the Fed lowers reserve requirements, that frees up money, lowers interest rates, and boosts the economy. The Fed has not used this powerful tool in many years, preferring to use the discount rate and its open market operations.

- *The discount rate.* The Fed makes temporary, secured short-term loans to Fed member banks through its Discount window—which, at one time, used to be a window at the Federal Reserve Bank. Few banks actually use the Discount window, because it's a sign they are having difficulties. But when the Fed raises or lowers the discount rate, it's a clear signal of which direction the Fed wants rates to go.

- *Federal funds.* The Fed most frequently nudges short-term interest rates higher through its powerful Open Market Committee, which meets every two weeks. When the Fed wants rates to go higher, it sells short-term money market instruments, such as T-bills, on the open market. This takes money out of circulation and drives short-term interest rates higher.

Let's look at an example. Suppose the Fed decides rates should rise to keep the economy from expanding too quickly. The Fed then offers $1 billion in 3-month T-bills for sale. Four major government securities dealers buy those T-bills. The Fed takes that money and, in effect, takes it out of circulation. That makes short-term loan money scarcer and drives up the price of money— that is, interest rates.

Higher rates, in turn, make it more expensive for companies to borrow and expand. The *prime rate,* which is the rate banks charge their most creditworthy corporate customers, often moves in lockstep with the discount rate and other short-term interest rates. (Many observers have noticed, however, that the prime rises much more quickly than it falls; see Figure 1.4.) And because many consumer rates, such as credit card rates, are tied to short-term interest rates, higher rates discourage consumer borrowing, too.

When the Fed wants rates to fall, it buys short-term money market instruments on the open market, putting more money into circulation and pushing rates down. As you might expect, this stimulates the economy.

The Fed doesn't put out a press release saying that the economy is moving too slowly and it will push interest rates down to give it a boost. But you can keep your eye on several indicators, such as the following:

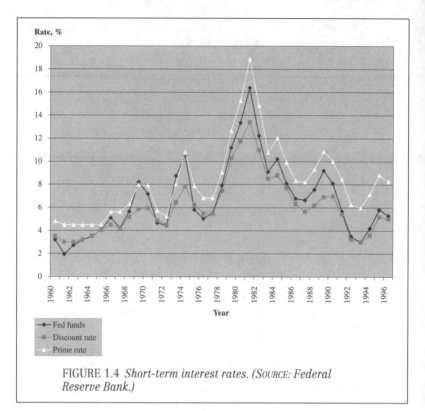

FIGURE 1.4 *Short-term interest rates. (SOURCE: Federal Reserve Bank.)*

- *The Fed Funds rate.* This is the short-term, open-market rate for loans between Federal Reserve member banks. It's published every day in most newspapers. Like many short-term rates, it's subject to goofy short-term fluctuations, especially around the end of the year. But watch the overall trend. If it's rising, other short-term rates will rise, too.

- *The minutes of the Federal Open Market Committee (FOMC).* The FOMC releases the minutes of its meetings six weeks after they have occurred. Typically, these are an exercise in deciphering FedSpeak, the maddening language of central bankers. But many newspapers will give very good explanations of what went on, and what that says about Fed policy.

- *The discount rate.* As previously noted, when the Fed changes the discount rate, it's generally very clear what the Fed wants.

 Use CDs to Lock In High Rates

Normally, you want to use CDs to lock in interest rates when they are high. Back in August 1984,

Three Steps and a Stumble

The discount rate is such a clear indicator of Fed policy that Wall Street has evolved the *three steps and a stumble* rule. It works like this: When the Fed has raised the discount rate three times in a row, the economy stumbles—in other words, slides into recession. It's not infallible, but it is one of the most reliable indicators of the economy.

for example, the average 6-month CD yielded a whopping 11.01 percent, according to *Bank Rate Monitor.* Long-term CDs yielded even more, and your best move would have been to lock in that rate for as long as you could.

Now let's move forward to August 1992, when short-term interest rates were exceptionally low. If you had gone to your bank for a 6-month CD then, you would have been quoted an average rate of 3.25 percent. At that rate, it would take more than 22 years to double your money. You'd be silly to lock in that rate for any period of time. Instead, your best move would have been to invest in a money market fund, which can pass on higher interest rates to you—when they start rising again, that is.

Naturally, this is a strategy that works best in hindsight. After all, when interest rates are rising, it's anyone's guess how much further they will rise. Even when rates were soaring in the early 1980s, some people were expecting them to go yet higher.

So in practice, most people lock in after rates have already peaked and are on their way down again. There's no shame in that.

Ladder Your CDs if You Don't Want to Predict Rates

If you want to leave forecasting to the economists and simply want a reasonably constant income from your investments, consider making a CD ladder—that is, buying CDs of different maturities. By

CD maturity	Rate, %
6 months	4.53
1 year	5.60
2½ years	6.18
5 years	6.67
Average yield	5.75

SOURCE: Bank Rate Monitor.

FIGURE 1.5 *CD portfolio rates, December 1994.*

doing so, you'll always have a few CDs maturing, which lets you lock in current rates. And you'll have some that are still at previous rates. Suppose, for example, you had $100,000 to invest in December 1994. You decided to put $25,000 into a 6-month CD, $25,000 into a 1-year CD, $25,000 into a 2½-year CD, and $25,000 into a 5-year CD. Figure 1.5 shows what your CD portfolio would have looked like then.

By June 30, 1995, your 6-month CD would have matured. And fortunately for you, rates on six-month CDs had risen slightly, to 4.91 percent. Figure 1.6 shows what your portfolio would have looked like on June 30, 1995.

As 1996 rolled in, you would have had two changes to make: Your 6-month CD would be due again, and so would your 1-year CD. Figure 1.7 shows what your new portfolio would look like.

As you can see, short-term savings rates had edged down. But the overall impact on your portfolio was fairly low. That's because you had locked

CD maturity	Rate, %
6 months	4.91
1 year	5.60
2½ years	6.18
5 years	6.67
Average yield	5.84

SOURCE: Bank Rate Monitor.

FIGURE 1.6 *CD portfolio rates, June 1995.*

CD maturity	Rate, %
6 months	4.74
1 year	5.04
2½ years	6.18
5 years	6.67
Average yield	5.66

SOURCE: *Bank Rate Monitor.*

FIGURE 1.7 *CD portfolio rates, December 1995.*

in last year's rate with your two long-term CDs. If interest rates would fall precipitously over the next two and a half years, your income would eventually fall. But it would be five years before you felt the full impact.

Of course, if interest rates would rise dramatically, it would be five years before you felt the full impact of that, too. But if rates rose very sharply, it would probably be worthwhile paying the early withdrawal penalty and investing in a new CD.

END POINT

Every year, *Forbes* magazine lists the nation's 500 richest people. It's safe to say that not one of them gained their wealth by savvy investments in the money market.

But many of them probably do have considerable amounts of money in the money market now. That's because they are more concerned with preserving their wealth, rather than growing it.

Money market rates of return are often too low to grow your investments to the level you will need over time. But that doesn't mean that you should spurn the money market. It's a great place to keep money that you will need to spend soon, or that you can't afford to lose. And, as we will learn later, the money market is an essential part of a diversified portfolio. Just don't expect to get rich from it.

To save the brokers' fees on T-bill transactions, contact one of the Federal Reserve Bank Branches listed in Figure 1.8, and open a Treasury Direct Account.

Alabama
1801 Fifth Avenue, North
P.O. Box 830447
Birmingham, AL 35283-0447
205-731-8702 (recording)
205-731-8708

Arkansas
325 West Capitol Avenue
P.O. Box 1261
Little Rock, AR 72203
501-324-8274 (recording)
501-324-8272

California
950 South Grand Avenue
P.O. Box 2077
Terminal Annex
Los Angeles, CA 90051
213-624-7398

101 Market Street
P.O. Box 7702
San Francisco, CA 94120
415-974-3491 (recording)
415-974-2330

Colorado
1020 16th Street
P.O. Box 5228
Denver, CO 80217-5228
303-572-2475 (recording)

District of Columbia
Servicing Center
Bureau of the Public Debt
1300 C Street, S.W.
Washington, DC 20239-0001
202-874-4000

Florida
800 West Water Street
P.O. Box 2499
Jacksonville, FL 32231-2499
904-632-1178 (recording)
904-632-1179

9100 NW Thirty-Six Street
P.O. Box 520847
Miami, FL 33152

305-471-6257 (recording)
305-471-6497

Georgia
Securities Service Dept.
104 Marietta Street, NW
Atlanta, GA 30303
404-521-8657 (recording)
404-521-8653

Illinois
230 South LaSalle Street
P.O. Box 834
Chicago, IL 60690
312-322-5369

Kentucky
410 South Fifth Street
P.O. Box 32710
Louisville, KY 40232
502-568-9240 (recording)
502-568-9238

Louisiana
525 St. Charles Avenue
P.O. Box 52948
New Orleans, LA 70152-2948
504-593-5839 (recording)
504-593-3200

Maryland
502 South Sharp Street
P.O. Box 1378
Baltimore, MD 21203
410-576-3500 (recording)
410-576-3300

Massachusetts
600 Atlantic Avenue
P.O. Box 2076
Boston, MA 02106
617-973-3800 (recording)
617-973-3810

Michigan
160 West Fort Street
P.O. Box 1059
Detroit, MI 48231
313-964-6157

FIGURE 1.8 *Federal Reserve Bank branches to contact for a treasury direct account.*

Missouri
925 Grand Avenue
P.O. Box 419033
Kansas City, MO 64141-6033
816-881-2767 (recording)
816-881-2883

411 Locust Street
P.O. Box 14915
St. Louis, MO 63178
314-444-8703

Minnesota
90 Hennepin Avenue
Minneapolis, MN 55401
612-204-6650

Nebraska
2201 Farnam Street
Omaha, NE 68102
402-221-5638 (recording)
402-221-5636

New York
160 Delaware Avenue
P.O. Box 961
Buffalo, NY 14240-0961
716-849-5158 (recording)
716-849-5000

33 Liberty Street
P.O. Station
New York, NY 10045
212-720-5823 (recording)
212-720-6619

North Carolina
530 East Trade Street
P.O. Box 30248
Charlotte, NC 28230
704-358-2424 (recording)
704-358-2100

Ohio
150 East Fourth Street
P.O. Box 999
Cincinnati, OH 45201
513-721-4794 ext. 334

1455 East Sixth Street
P.O. Box 6387
Cleveland, OH 44101

216-579-2490 (recording)
216-579-2000

Oklahoma
226 Dean A McGee Avenue
P.O. Box 25129
Oklahoma City, OK 73125
405-270-8660 (recording)
405-270-8652

Oregon
915 S.W. Stark Street
P.O. Box 3436
Portland, OR 97208-3436
503-221-5931 (recording)
503-221-5932

Pennsylvania
Ten Independence Mall
P.O. Box 90
Philadelphia, PA 19105
215-574-6580 (recording)
215-574-6680

717 Grant Street
P.O. Box 867
Pittsburgh, PA 15230-0867
412-261-7988 (recording)
412-261-7802

Tennessee
200 North Main Street
P.O. Box 407
Memphis, TN 38101
901-523-9380 (recording)
901-523-7171 Ext. 423

301 Eighth Avenue, North
Nashville, TN 37203-4407
615-251-7236 (recording)
615-251-7100

Texas
2200 North Pearl Street
Box 655906
Dallas, TX 75265-5906
214-922-6100
214-922-6770 (recording)

301 East Main
P.O. Box 100
El Paso, TX 79999
915-521-8295 (recording)
915-521-8272

FIGURE 1.8 *Continued.*

1701 San Jacinto Street
P.O. Box 2578
Houston, TX 77252
713-659-4433

126 East Nueva Street
P.O. Box 1471
San Antonio, TX 78295
210-978-1330 (recording)
210-978-1303 or 1305

Utah
120 South State Street
P.O. Box 30780
Salt Lake City, UT 84130-0780

801-322-7844 (recording)
801-322-7882

Virginia
701 East Byrd Street
P.O. Box 27622
Richmond, VA 23261
804-697-8355 (recording)
804-697-8372

Washington
1015 Second Avenue
P.O. Box 3567
Seattle, WA 98124
206-343-3615 (recording)
206-343-3605

FIGURE 1.8 *Continued.*

Coupon Clippers:
The Bond Market

You get home, take off your coat, and start sorting through the mail. And there, sitting on the table, is a notice from your mortgage company. Your mind races: You did pay the mortgage. You know you did.

You open the letter. Your friendly bank, which put up billboards all over town pleading with you to apply for a mortgage, is blowing you off. Another company in another state will be servicing your mortgage from now on. You've been a great customer, the letter says, and we will miss you, but don't bother us any more. The new company will contact you soon and tell you where to send your next check.

In all likelihood, this new company will simply be taking care of the administrative details of your mortgage: Calculating your escrow account, computing your new balances, sending out bills. A bank, mutual fund, or pension fund probably owns the mortgage itself, and is collecting the interest and principal on the loan that made it possible for you to buy your home. Most debts, like mortgages, can be bought and sold. In the case of your mortgage, your bank packaged your mortgage with hundreds of others and sold them all to investors.

The *bond market* is the market for long-term debt. A *bond* is an interest-bearing certificate of debt, representing a loan from the buyer of the bond to the issuer.

Mortgages are a big part of the bond market. But corporations need long-term loans, too, for new plants and new expansion. Cities, towns, and municipalities need long-term loans for roads, civic centers, and schools. And the U.S. government needs loans to build dams and highways, and for research, defense, and so forth (see Figure 2.1).

Rather than go to the bank for a long-term loan, most major institutions issue bonds. Typically, companies can get lower interest rates through the bond market than they can from a bank. When you borrow $100 million or more at a crack, shaving a quarter of a percentage point from your interest rate can translate into millions of dollars in savings over the life of a loan.

Although it doesn't get as much publicity as the stock market, the bond market is actually larger than the stock market. As of the end of 1997, the stock market's total value stood at $8.9 trillion, versus 9.8 trillion for the bond market. (The combined bond market and money market is called the *fixed income market,* because both bonds and money market investments make fixed income payments to investors.)

 A WORD ABOUT ENORMOUS NUMBERS

One of the most common errors in the financial press is mixing up billions and millions. After all, they're both enormous numbers and they both end in -illions. But every once in a while it's useful

Issuer	Outstanding debt, $ trillion
U.S. Treasury	$3.4
U.S. corporate	2.2
Municipal	1.4
Mortgage-backed	1.8
Federal agencies	1.0
Total	$9.8

SOURCE: The Bond Market Association. Data estimates as of December 31, 1997.

FIGURE 2.1 *Outstanding public and private debt, in trillions of dollars.*

to contemplate just how big the numbers are when talking about the financial system.

One way to put large numbers into perspective is to think of them in terms of time. Suppose, for example, we were talking about a million seconds. That's about 278 hours, or 11½ days. A billion seconds, however, is 1,000 million seconds. That's about 32 years. If you're lucky, you'll live a bit more than 2 billion seconds.

But forget about living a trillion seconds. A trillion is 1,000 billion. One trillion seconds is 32,152 years. Bonds may be around then, but we certainly won't be.

KEY CONCEPT BONDS, BIT BY BIT

Bonds have several integral components. Bonds originally were issued as certificates, and some still are. Many of the terms used to talk about bonds are derived from features of the certificate.

- *Face value.* The value on the face of a bond certificate. A $1 million bond has a face value of $1 million. This is the amount that the borrower will repay the holder of the bond when it comes due. Face value is also called *par value.*

- *Maturity date.* The date on which the company stops paying interest and repays the face value of the bond.

- *Coupon.* The value of a bond's interest payment. Old bond certificates had coupons around the side of the certificate. To get your interest payment, you had to clip the coupon and present it to the issuer.

- *Coupon yield.* The fixed interest rate that the bond pays to the holder of the bond. To find the coupon yield, divide a bond's interest payment, or coupon, by its face value. For example, a bond with a $90 annual coupon payment and a $1,000 face value has a 9 percent coupon yield ($90 divided by $1,000 equals .09, or 9 percent). A bond's coupon yield never changes.

So let's say you bought a U.S. Treasury bond with a $50,000 face value and a maturity date of December 31, 2028. Its semiannual coupon is $1,750, so its coupon rate would be 7 percent. Put simply, this means that you loaned Uncle Sam

$50,000. The Treasury will pay you 7 percent annual interest on your loan, in payments of $1,750 every 6 months. On December 31, 2028, the government will return your $50,000.

INTEREST RATES DETERMINE THE MARKET VALUE OF BONDS

If you hold your Treasury bond until it matures, you have virtually no risk. T-bonds are backed by the full faith and credit of the U.S. government, the same as T-bills. The government must pay T-bond holders before it pays anyone else, including employees, contractors, and even insured bank depositors.

If you decide to sell your T-bond before it matures, however, you may get more or less than the bond's face value. Interest rates—and the current state of the bond market—determine the price of your bond.

So how much will you get for your bond? Much of the answer depends on whether interest rates on comparable bonds are higher or lower than when you bought your bond. This brings us to our first rule of bonds.

BOND PRICES MOVE IN THE OPPOSITE DIRECTION OF INTEREST RATES

When rates rise, your bond's price falls. When rates fall, your bond's price rises. This causes most investors' eyes to cross, at least at first. Why should a bond become less valuable when interest rates rise?

Think of it this way. Suppose someone offered you an investment returning 7 percent and one returning 8 percent. Which would you choose?

Naturally, you'd choose the investment that returns 8 percent. Now, suppose you owned a bond with a coupon rate of 7 percent. Similar bonds now carry coupon rates of 8 percent. How do you think a buyer is going to react to your 7 percent bond? Not with enthusiasm. So how do you make your bond more attractive to a buyer?

You can't go back to the bond's issuer and ask for a higher interest rate. A deal, after all, is a deal. If you have a fixed-rate mortgage, your bank can't come to you and ask for a higher mortgage rate. And as the owner of a bond, you're in the same position as a banker. You can't ask for a higher rate on your bond.

Since you can't get a higher interest rate for your bond, you have to offer to sell the bond for less than its face value. In bond parlance, that's known as selling it *at a discount* from its face value.

Let's look at an example. Suppose you own a $50,000 Treasury bond that has a 7 percent coupon rate. As previously, you will get $1,750 in interest every 6 months, or $3,500 every year until the bond matures in 2028, at which point the Treasury will repay your $50,000.

Five years pass. You decide to sell your bond to pay for an addition on your house. Unfortunately for you, interest rates have climbed, and newly issued T-bonds now yield 8.5 percent.

To get your $50,000 bond to yield 8.5 percent, you will have to drop the bond's price until the bond's interest payment divided by its price equals 8.5 percent. Unfortunately for you, you'd have to drop the price to about $41,175 to get the bond to yield 8.5 percent. So you may have to settle for a gazebo instead of an addition. You would have to sell your $50,000 bond for a $8,825 loss.

If interest rates fall, however, the outcome is much happier. Let's say that you still have a $50,000 bond that pays $3,500 annual interest, or a 7 percent coupon yield. But we will assume that 5 years later, interest rates have fallen to 6 percent. Suddenly, you are a very popular person. A 7 percent bond when interest rates are at 6 percent is a thing of beauty. Bond traders will be willing to pay a premium for your bond—that is, an amount higher than its face value. By boosting the bond's price, you lower the bond's interest rate. Let's see how it works.

Let's kick the bond's price up to $58,550. At that price, its $3,500 interest payment will equal a 6 percent yield. You would make a $8,550 profit, or a 17.1 percent gain, on the sale of your bond. Heck, you might be able to add a garage, too.

These are rough estimates. For those who feel a close spiritual relationship with their calculators, a more exact formula for finding a bond's yield after a discount or premium is in the box.

Yields, Yields, Yields

As noted earlier, a bond's coupon yield is its interest payment divided by its face value. Bond traders refer to two other types of bond yields: current yield and yield to maturity. Let's take a look at them.

Current yield equals the bond's market price divided by its annual interest payment. Suppose you bought a bond for $41,175. It has 20 years to maturity and pays $3,500 annual interest. Its current yield would be $3,500 divided by $43,750, or 8.5 percent. *Yield to maturity* reflects the discount or premium you may have paid for the bond. The premium or discount is assumed to be paid over the life of the bond. In this case, the yield to maturity would be 8.64 percent. This is the yield typically quoted by brokers when you're shopping for a bond.

If mathematical formulas fill you with a strange excitement, hold on to your hat. Here's a way to get a rough idea of the yield to maturity for a bond bought at a discount. The formula is:

$$\text{Yield to maturity} = \frac{\text{coupon} + \text{prorated discount}}{(\text{face value} + \text{purchase price})/2}$$

Let's consider this $50,000 bond, which you bought for $41,175. It pays $3,500 annual interest and matures in 20 years.

1. Figure the amount of the discount. In this case, it's $50,000 minus $41,175, or $8,825. Divide the discount by the number of years before the bond matures. In this case, you divide $8,825 by 20 years to get $441. This is the prorated discount.

2. Add the prorated discount ($441) to the bond's coupon ($3,500). Your answer should be $3,941. Try to contain your excitement.

3. Now find the average of the bond's face value and its purchase price. In other words, add the bond's face value and its purchase price, and divide by two. In this case, you add $50,000 (the face value) to $41,175 (the purchase price) and divide by 2. The answer should be $45,587.50.

4. Finally, divide your answer in Step 3 ($3,941) by your answer in Step 4 ($45,587.50). The answer should be 8.645462023581 percent, which most normal people would round to 8.65 percent. That's your yield to maturity.

By now, you're probably saying to yourself, "But what if I purchase a bond at a premium? How do I calculate yield to maturity then? Here's how:

$$\text{Yield to maturity} = \frac{\text{coupon} - \text{prorated premium}}{(\text{face value} + \text{purchase price})/2}$$

(Continued)

(Continued)

Let's assume you bought a bond with a $50,000 face value for $55,300. It pays $3,500 annual interest and matures in 20 years.

1. Figure the amount of the premium. In this case, it's $55,300 minus $50,000, or $5,300.

2. Divide the premium by the number of years before the bond matures. In this case, you divide $5,300 by 20 years to get $265. This is the prorated premium.

3. Subtract the prorated premium ($265) from the bond's coupon ($3,500). Your answer should be $3,235. It is moments like this that make life worth living.

4. Now find the average of the bond's face value and its purchase price. In other words, add the bond's face value and its purchase price, and divide by two. In this case, you add $50,000 (the face value) to $55,300 (the purchase price) and divide by 2. The answer should be $52,650.00

5. Finally, divide your answer in Step 3 ($3,235) by your answer in Step 4 ($52,650). The answer should be 6.144349477683 percent, which just about anyone with sense would round to 6.14 percent. That's your yield to maturity.[1]

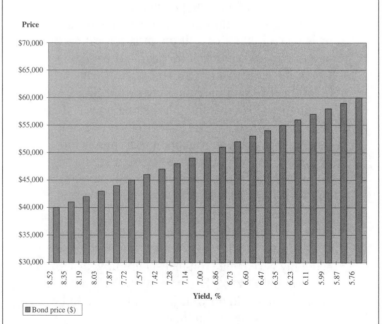

FIGURE 2.2 *Bond prices and yields move in opposite directions.*

(Continued)

(Continued)

Figure 2.2 shows how the price of a $50,000 bond with a 7 percent coupon rate would change as interest rates rose or fell. (As you can see, the bond's price falls as interest rates rise above 7 percent. When interest rates fall, however, the bond's price rises.)

INFLATION—OR THE FEAR OF IT— DRIVES THE BOND MARKET

Inflation is a period of rising prices for goods and services. The most common measure of inflation is the Bureau of Labor Statistics' Consumer Price Index (CPI), which measures the price of a fixed basket of goods.

Bond traders are peculiar people. They cry when unemployment falls. They weep when the economy soars.

Why? Because a rapidly rising economy typically breeds inflation, and bond traders hate inflation. Bond traders hate inflation because, as any pensioner could tell you, inflation erodes the value of a bond's fixed income payment.

For example, suppose you have a bond that pays you $5,000 a year. If the inflation rate is 2 percent a year, your $5,000 payment would be worth the equivalent of $4,102 after 10 years. If inflation rises to 5 percent a year, your $5,000 payment would have the purchasing power of just $3,070 in 10 years. That's a serious hit to your buying power. If you rely upon that money for expenses, you might have to tap your savings more heavily, go back to work, or call in your loans to your children.

Okay, you say, bond traders hate inflation. How does a rapidly rising economy breed inflation?

Let's look at an example. Let's suppose the economy is roaring. You feel secure in your job. Why shouldn't you? There are very few qualified people who could do your job. And their employers are anxious to keep them.

You have some money put away. You don't need to save it for a rainy day because, frankly, you see nothing but blue skies on the horizon. So rather that save it for a rainy day, you decide to buy a new Snazzmobile, which you have been eyeing at Happy Harry's new car lot.

But Happy Harry has noticed that many customers have gotten raises recently, and that they, too, covet a Snazzmobile. Harry wants a raise as much as you do. So he raises the price of a new Snazzmobile. And guess what? People pay that new price, and Harry is happy indeed. And that's one way inflation begins.

Of course, this kind of inflation can only occur when there are a limited amount of Snazzmobiles on the market. An economist would say that demand has exceeded supply, driving prices higher. It is also called *demand-pull* inflation.

Another type of inflation is called *cost-push* inflation, where the higher price of certain items, such as oil, can push up the prices of a variety of consumer goods, such as gasoline, heating oil, and plastic. At least part of the high inflation of the 1970s was cost-push inflation, sparked by the energy crisis.

So bond traders scour the economic news for signs of inflation. When economic news is good and inflation looks likely, bond traders demand higher yields to compensate for potential inflation. As was discussed earlier, that means pushing bond prices down.

 Bond Prices Depend on the Bond Market's Opinion of Inflation Trends

Unfortunately, you can't look at the current inflation rate and figure out where current interest rates should be now. The CPI measures past inflation. But the financial markets look forward, not backward. So traders are more concerned with what the inflation rate will be in the future, not where it is now. This, of course, is a matter of opinion, and those opinions are reflected in bond yields and prices. When traders think inflation will rise, they bid bond prices down and bond yields up. When they think inflation will fall, they bid bond prices up and bond yields down.

The word *speculation* comes from the Latin word meaning "to observe." Traders try to observe current events to help them forecast the future. Typically, bond traders look at a variety of current indicators of future inflation, including the following:

- *The economy.* Most broad measures of the economy, such as gross domestic product (GDP), are released too late and revised too often to be of great interest to the financial community. (GDP measures everything produced in the country, and it's a mighty big number indeed.) But many traders do look at the Index of Leading Economic Indicators, released monthly by the U.S. Commerce Department's Bureau of Economic Analysis, which gives a good idea of where the economy is headed.

- *Wages.* If you and everyone else you know is getting a big raise, interest rates might rise soon, too. Prices tend to rise when wages rise. Watch the unemployment rate as one measure of rising wages. It's released monthly by the Bureau of Labor Statistics. When unemployment dips below 5 percent, workers can usually demand higher wages. You can also watch the Labor Department's index of average weekly wages, which measures wages for hourly workers. Steadily climbing weekly wages could augur higher inflation.

- *Rising raw materials prices.* When raw metals, such as copper, aluminum, and steel, rise in price, manufacturers pass those costs on to consumers in the form of higher prices. One index to watch is the Producer Price Index (PPI), which measures the cost of raw materials and finished goods used in making other things. The PPI measures what it costs to make goods and, since those costs are passed on to the consumer, is a good way to look at the inflation pipeline. The Bureau of Labor Statistics releases the PPI monthly. Another indicator to watch is the Commodity Research Bureau (CRB) index, which measures the price of raw materials. If either index is rising, inflation may be on the way. The CRB is calculated daily, and most newspapers carry it daily or in their Sunday editions.

- *Rising short-term interest rates.* As noted in Chapter 1, the Federal Reserve Board's powerful Open Market Committee virtually controls short-term interest rates—the rates that determine money market yields. The Fed doesn't have direct influence over the long-term bond market, but the Fed's actions are a good indicator of where the Fed wants the economy to go—and what the Fed wants, it generally gets. If the Fed raises interest rates, it thinks the economy is rising too quickly, and wants to slow it down. If the Fed cuts rates, it thinks the economy is too sluggish and could be in danger of recession.

Although there is no hard-and-fast rule on the relationship between interest rates and inflation, you can look at the history of bonds to get some idea of the typical spread between bond yields and inflation. Over time, 30-year Treasury bond yields have typically been about 3 percentage points more than the current inflation rate. So when inflation runs at 3 percent, a 30-year T-bond should yield about 6 percent. It should be noted, however, that the spread between T-bills and inflation has been about four percentage points for the past decade (see Figure 2.3). The reason for this is still being debated, although it may be because bond prices have become much more volatile in the past 10 years.

Short-Term Bond Prices Are Hurt Less by Rising Interest Rates than Long-Term Bonds

Let's suppose your friend, Mr. Wimpy, asks you for $50 and promises to repay you on Thursday. You'd probably think little of it.

Now let's suppose Mr. Wimpy asks you for $50 and promises to repay you in 2028. You'd probably think a bit harder about it.

One reason, of course, is that there is far more uncertainty in the next 30 years than there is in the next few days. Mr. Wimpy may be broke in 30 years. He could run off to Brazil. His hamburger stand could go bankrupt. Any number of things could happen between now and 2028.

And the value of $50 in the year 2028 could be considerably less than it is now. In fact, if inflation averages just 3 percent over 30 years, $50 will have the buying power of $20.60 in 2028. This is the general reason why long-term bonds react more violently to changes in interest rates than short-term bonds do.

There's a mathematical reason for this, too. A bond's yield to maturity takes into account the dis-

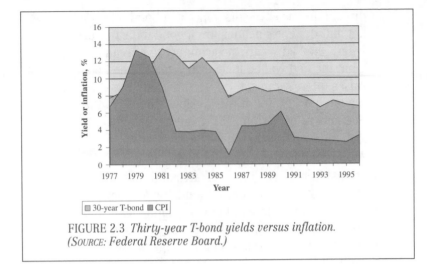

FIGURE 2.3 *Thirty-year T-bond yields versus inflation.*
(*SOURCE: Federal Reserve Board.*)

count or premium paid over time. Using the calculation for yield to maturity discussed earlier, we
see that it takes a larger discount or premium to
change a long-term bond's yield to maturity than
it does for a short-term bond. Figure 2.4 shows
how bonds of different maturities react to changes
in interest rates.

The Yield Curve

In Chapter 1, it was noted that risk increases with
return. The more risk you take with an investment, the greater the potential rewards. (Taking a
lot of risk doesn't guarantee a higher return, however, which is a notion that investors often forget.)

As has been seen, a long-term bond carries
more risk than a short-term bond. So long-term
bonds typically carry higher yields than short-term
bonds. For example, if a 1-year Treasury bill carries a 5 percent yield, it wouldn't be unusual for a
5-year Treasury note to yield 5.5 percent and a 30-
year bond to yield 6.2 percent (see Figure 2.5).

Bond investors typically look at a type of chart
called the *yield curve* to show how rates compare
in bond issues of different maturities. It's called a
yield curve because the chart typically shows an
upward curve, as seen in Figure 2.6.

The trick is to find a point on the yield curve
that matches your risk tolerance. Look at Figure
2.6. In this case, you get considerably more yield
from a two-year T-note than you do from a one-
year T-bill. So it makes sense to prefer the two-

Long-term bond prices are more volatile than short-term bond prices. The price of a $1,000, 7 percent bond with various maturity dates will rise or fall with changes in interest rates as shown.

Maturity	1 percentage point rate change	
	Rates rise	Rates fall
5 years	$953	$1,050
10 years	932	1,074
20 years	901	1,116
30 years	887	1,138

FIGURE 2.4 *Long-term bond prices versus short-term bond prices.*

year note over the one-year bill, particularly if you can hold the note to maturity.

Should you buy a longer-term bond? You'll get some extra yield by investing in a 5-year note, and a tiny bit more from extending out to 7 or 10 years. But you will get considerably more risk by moving from a 2-year note to a 10-year note. All things being equal, it's probably better to take the two-year note.

Going out further will bring you somewhat higher yields. For example, the 20-year T-bond yield in this example is 6.84 percent, and the 30-year T-bond yield is 6.76 percent. If you are a very conservative long-term investor, you *might* consider the 20-year bond. But it would make little sense to invest in the 30-year T-bond.

This is a typical yield curve. Normally, the yield curve flattens or falls after 15 years, meaning you get very little extra yield from long-term bonds, even though you get considerably more risk. For this reason, most of the activity in the bond market is in the two- to seven-year range. Although the yield on the 30-year T-bond is closely watched as an indicator, most investors buy bonds with maturities of 3 to 10 years. Most of those who buy 30-year bonds are speculating on interest rates.

The Inverted Yield Curve

DANGER!

Every once in a while, short-term bonds yield more than long-term bonds. This is called an *inverted yield curve,* and it's a red flag for investors everywhere. When short-term rates are

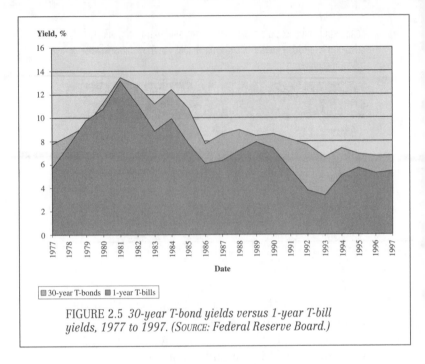

FIGURE 2.5 *30-year T-bond yields versus 1-year T-bill yields, 1977 to 1997. (SOURCE: Federal Reserve Board.)*

higher than long-term rates, Wall Street is expecting the Federal Reserve to raise interest rates—typically a precursor to an economic downturn. It's not an infallible indicator, but it's a good one. A highly inverted yield curve—where the yield on 3-month Treasury securities is 4.5 percent higher than 10-year Treasuries for more than a month—has preceded 6 of the past 9 recessions.[2]

 CREDIT COUNTS: BOND ISSUER CREDIT RATINGS

Bond issuers, like individuals, have credit ratings. The lower a bond issuer's credit rating, the higher the interest rate the issuer must offer to attract investors. Lenders want to be compensated for high-risk lending. So they demand higher interest rates from shaky borrowers.

As if bonds weren't confusing enough, you must also take credit quality into consideration. After all, bonds are loans. And as a bond investor, you are taking the same position as a lender. And lenders, perversely, prefer to lend to those who need the money the least. There's a better chance they will repay the loan than deadbeats will.

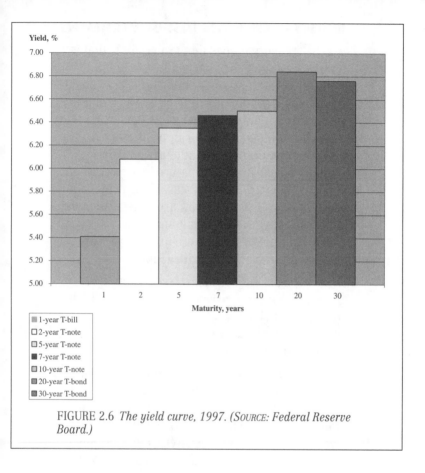

FIGURE 2.6 *The yield curve, 1997. (SOURCE: Federal Reserve Board.)*

Suppose you have $1,000 to lend. You have two people who are interested in borrowing the money: a millionaire and a journalist. If the millionaire were to welsh on the loan, you could repossess a Ming vase or some other bauble to get your money back. If the journalist couldn't repay the loan, however, you would probably have to settle for a 1984 Datsun.

Bond traders are little different from individual lenders. A big company with a great credit history, such as J.P. Morgan, the investment banking company, can borrow money in the bond market at low rates. Traders figure that J.P. Morgan can sell a division to make the interest and principal payment. Companies teetering on bankruptcy—or emerging from it—are another story. A bond secured by a 50-year-old cement factory is only going to interest the most speculative investors. To attract them, a shaky borrower has to offer high yields on its bonds.

THE BEST CREDIT: THE U.S. GOVERNMENT

The U.S. Treasury enjoys the best credit rating in the world: Its bonds are backed by the full faith and credit of the U.S. government, and are considered to have virtually no credit risk. After all, the government not only has enormous power to raise money through taxes, but it can print money, too—even though that's inflationary.

Treasury securities that mature in 1 to 10 years are called *Treasury notes.* Treasury securities that mature in more than 10 years are called *Treasury bonds.* Both pay interest semiannually.

Aside from their sterling credit quality, Treasuries have three other big attractions:

1. *Interest from U.S. Treasury securities is free from state income taxes.* If you live in a high-tax state, such as New York, Treasuries are particularly attractive. (To see how to compare taxable and tax-free yields, see page 8.)

2. *U.S. Treasury bonds are noncallable.* Most bonds have a provision that allows a company to retire the bonds before their maturity date if interest rates fall sharply. This is the *call provision:* When a company exercises its call rights, the bonds are *called away.* The issuer repays the principal to bondholders, who then must find somewhere else to invest their money. But Treasuries can't be called, so you can count on getting your interest payment until the bond matures.

3. *U.S. Treasury bonds are exceptionally liquid.* That is, it's quite easy to buy and sell them. You can buy T-bonds directly through the Federal Reserve for no fee, just as you can T-bills (See page 13). You can also buy them, for a fee, through most banks and virtually any brokerage house.

 Savings Bonds for the Timid

For the truly timid, there are U.S. savings bonds. Like Treasury notes and bonds, savings bonds are backed by the full faith and credit of the U.S. government. And interest from bonds is exempt from state and local taxes.

There the similarities end. Series EE savings bonds, currently the only kind of savings bond you can buy for cash, are sold at a discount. That is, you buy a bond for less than its face value and get its face value at maturity. The difference between the purchase price and the face value is your interest. Back in the old days, you would buy a savings bond for $50 and get $100 when it matured.

But savings bonds are far more complex than the old-fashioned savings bonds of a decade or two ago. First, all Series EE bonds (and all of the older E bonds that still pay interest) have market-based interest rates. Here's how it works:[3]

- Series E/EE bonds and savings notes issued before May 1995 get market-based yields if they've been held for at least five years and if such rates are higher than their guaranteed minimum yields. (Market yields are based on 85 percent of the average of 5-year Treasury-note yields).

- Series EE bonds issued on or after May 1995 do not have a guaranteed rate of return. EE bonds issued May 1997 or later earn interest based on 90 percent of the average yields on 5-year Treasury securities for the preceding 6 months. These bonds increase in value every month and interest is compounded semiannually. The new rate is announced each May 1 and November 1.

- EE bonds issued May 1995 through April 1997 earn short-term market-based rates during the first 5 years after issue and long-term market-based rates from 5 years through 17 years. The rate the bonds earn is adjusted to market-based rates every six months. New rates are announced each May 1 and November 1.

EE savings bonds stop earning interest after 30 years. Final maturity of the older Series E bonds varies. Series E bonds issued from May 1941 through November 1965 stop earning interest after 40 years. Series E bonds issued from December 1965 through June 1980 stop earning interest after 30 years.

Savings bonds have some interesting advantages. In some cases, interest from savings bonds is exempt from federal taxes, if you use them to pay qualified college expenses. The provisions are littered with bizarre exceptions, but they still may apply to you. The rules are as follows:

- Bonds must be held in the name of a parent to qualify. If you put the bond in the child's name, the child won't get the tax break. Interest may be excluded from federal income tax when the bond owner pays qualified college costs in the same year as the bonds are redeemed. Room, board, and books are *not* qualified educational expenses.

- The bond owner must have been at least 24 years old by the first day of the month in which the bonds were purchased. If the parent is below the age of 24, grandparents or just about anyone else can buy bonds in the parent's name. The purchaser won't get the exclusion, but the parent may.

A full exclusion is also only available if the taxpayer's adjusted gross income (which must include the interest earned on redeemed savings bonds) is under certain limits in the year the bonds are redeemed. For the 1997 tax year, the income limits were as follows:

- For single taxpayers, the tax exclusion begins to be reduced with a $50,850 modified adjusted gross income and is eliminated for adjusted gross incomes of $65,850 and above.

- For married taxpayers filing jointly, the tax exclusion begins to be reduced with a $76,250 modified adjusted gross income and is eliminated for adjusted gross incomes of $106,250 and above. Married couples must file jointly to be eligible for the exclusion.

Savings bonds also enable you to defer taxes on your interest for a long time—50 years, in some cases. The government doesn't consider accrued savings bond interest as taxable until you cash your bond. So you can defer taxes on the earnings from your Series EE savings bond for 30 years.

If you like, you can then use your Series EE bonds to buy Series HH bonds, which pay semiannual interest. Series HH bonds mature in 20 years. If you roll your Series EE bonds into Series HH bonds, you can defer the taxes from the interest you earned on your EE bonds for another 20 years.

**Beat Inflation with
Inflation-Adjusted Bonds**

The government has recently introduced inflation-adjusted bonds, which are designed to give you a steady return after inflation. The drawback: The yield is somewhat low, at least compared with traditional Treasury securities. But if you're a conservative investor concerned about inflation, inflation-adjusted bonds might be a good idea.

The Treasury's inflation-protection bonds are fairly simple. The Treasury adjusts the bond's price for inflation, and bases the bond's coupon payment on the adjusted price. So if you have a $1,000 bond and inflation rises 1 percent in the first 6 months, the bond's price will rise 1 percent to $1,010.

Let's say this bond pays 3 percent annual interest, paid semiannually. The first half of the year, you would get a $15.15 interest payment—1.5 percent multiplied by $1,010. Now let's suppose the inflation rate rises to 3 percent over the next 6 months. The bond's value would rise to $1,030, and the bond's yield would rise to $15.45, or 1.5 percent multiplied by $1,030. Inflation-adjusted bonds have proved extremely popular in Europe and Canada, and for good reason. After all, a 6 percent yield from a regular bond sounds better than a 3 percent yield on an inflation-adjusted bond. But you're typically losing 3 percent or more to inflation every year. Best of all, inflation-adjusted bonds don't get hurt by the bond market's never-ending paranoia about inflation.

The bonds have one tax drawback, however. As with most bonds, the interest that inflation-adjusted bonds pay is taxable as income in the year you receive it. But the price adjustment to the bond is taxable as income in the year you receive it, too—even though you won't get the interest until the bond matures.

 **Government and Agency Bonds Provide
a Slightly Higher Yield**

The U.S. government issues many other bonds, although they are not backed by the government's full faith and credit guarantee. For this reason, they often yield a bit more than Treasuries.

Because the government would be extremely embarrassed if one of these issues failed, however, they are sometimes called *moral obligations* of the government. The likelihood that one of these issues would actually default is extremely remote. In most cases, savvy bond investors can pick up a bit of extra yield through a U.S. government agency obligation with only negligible extra risk.

U.S. government and agency bonds are issued by the following entities:

- Federal Farm Credit Bank System.
- Federal Credit Financial Assistance Corporation.
- Federal Home Loan Bank.
- Federal Home Loan Mortgage Corporation.
- Federal National Mortgage Association.
- Student Loan Marketing Association.
- Financing Corporation.
- Resolution Trust Corporation.

 Everyone Loves Ginnie Mae

Wall Street so loves the Government National Mortgage Association (GNMA) that it has bestowed a pet name upon it: Ginnie Mae. And Wall Street has a good reason to like Ginnie Mae. The company helps make some of the best bonds in the country.

Ginnie Mae takes thousands of mortgages backed by Federal Home Administration and Veterans Home Administration insurance, packages them together, and sells them to investors in the form of GNMA bonds. Investors get the interest and principal payments from the mortgages.

What's so interesting about that? Well, first of all, mortgages tend to pay higher yields than Treasury bonds. So by and large, GNMA securities offer higher yields than Treasury bonds with comparable maturities.

Second, the U.S. government guarantees timely payment of interest and principal, just as it does for Treasury securities. So GNMA securities are just as creditworthy as T-bonds.

Why does GNMA do this? Investors have an insatiable appetite for safe, high-yielding bonds. So by selling the bonds, GNMA insures that there's plenty of mortgage money available for home buyers. And lenders can make the loans, collect fees for originating them, and then sell them off, reducing some of their risk if interest rates rise or fall.

The big drawback to Ginnie Maes: When you pay a mortgage, you pay a bit of principal each month along with your interest. So when you invest in a Ginnie Mae certificate, you get a few dollars' worth of principal back at each interest payment. You have to be careful to reinvest your principal, or you could inadvertently spend your principal.

Also, people often move, refinance, or prepay mortgages, in which case your return of principal can be significant. Typically, a sharp drop in interest rates will produce quite unbondlike behavior in a Ginnie Mae: Its price will fall. Bond traders don't want to own a security that will deliver great messy gobs of principal to be reinvested every month. In general, Ginnie Maes fare best when interest rates remain flat.

Interest rates rarely remain flat, so it's almost impossible to predict when a GNMA will mature. If you do buy a GNMA, it's best to do it through a mutual fund that invests exclusively in Ginnie Maes (see Chapter 5).

Ginnie Mae isn't the only mortgage-backed bond on the market. The Federal National Mortgage Association (Fannie Mae) and the Federal Home Loan Mortgage Corporation (Freddie Mac) also issue mortgage-backed bonds. Because these bonds aren't backed by the full faith and credit of the U.S. Government, they often offer higher yields than Ginnie Maes.

GIVE CREDIT TO CORPORATE BONDS

Let's suppose that BingCo, our fictional manufacturer of high-performance ball bearings, needs to build a new plant. The price tag: $10 million.

BingCo doesn't want to pay cash for the plant, because it needs the cash for its day-to-day operations. So it decides to borrow the money and repay it over 30 years. BingCo doesn't want to go to a bank because bank rates would be too high. It decides instead to go to Farley, Grundoon & Wombat, a prestigious Wall Street securities dealer and investment banker, to underwrite the bond. Farley, Grundoon & Wombat meets with BingCo and negotiations begin for the bond's underwriting.

As underwriter and dealer, Farley, Grundoon & Wombat will sell BingCo's bonds to the public. They will also structure the terms of the bond, including its initial price, its coupon rate, and its call provisions. The company will file a prospectus for BingCo's bonds with the Securities and Exchange Commission. The prospectus is the legal document that spells out all the terms of the offering to investors, including the *indenture agreement,* which spells out the bondholders' rights in case the company defaults.

Farley, Grundoon & Wombat may decide to buy the entire issue outright from BingCo and assume all responsibility for selling it. This is called acting as a *principal.* Obviously, BingCo would like this very much, because the company would get the full proceeds from the bond sale all at once. And if Farley, Grundoon, & Wombat couldn't sell the bonds, that would not be BingCo's problem.

But Farley, Grundoon & Wombat could also act as agent, which means it would simply pledge to do its best job in selling the bonds to the public. In any event, Farley, Grundoon & Wombat will charge investors a higher price for the bonds than it paid BingCo and will gain an *underwriting spread*—its reward for doing the job. If bonds remain unsold, BingCo will have to figure out how to deal with the shortfall.

DO A CREDIT CHECK BEFORE YOU BUY

DANGER! Now suppose you're interested in one of the bonds that Farley, Grundoon & Wombat has underwritten for BingCo. Your main question: Just how creditworthy is BingCo? Although companies typically pledge collateral as backing for the bonds, no one wants to have to wait in the creditors' line to get his or her money back from a bond default.

Fortunately, four Wall Street companies rate companies' creditworthiness for you: Standard & Poor's, Moody's Investor Services, Fitch Investors Services, and Duff & Phelps Credit Rating Co. All use letter ratings, and are fairly comparable. Here are Standard & Poor's bond ratings, as well as the comparable ratings from the other agencies:[4]

AAA. An obligation rated AAA has the highest rating assigned by Standard & Poor's. The obligor's capacity to meet its financial commitment on the obligation is extremely strong. Comparable grade from Moody's Investor Services: Aaa. Comparable grade from Fitch and Duff & Phelps: AAA.

AA. An obligation rated AA differs from the highest-rated obligations only in small degree. The obligor's capacity to meet its financial commitment on the obligation is very strong. Comparable grade from Moody's: Aa. Comparable grade from Fitch and Duff & Phelps: AA

A. An obligation rated A is somewhat more susceptible to the adverse effects of changes in circumstances and economic conditions than obligations in higher-rated categories. However, the obligor's capacity to meet its financial commitment on the obligation is still strong. Comparable grade from Moody's, Fitch, and Duff & Phelps: A.

BBB. An obligation rated BBB exhibits adequate protection parameters. However, adverse economic conditions or changing circumstances are more likely to lead to a weakened capacity of the obligor to meet its financial commitment on the obligation. Comparable grade from Moody's: Baa. Comparable grade from Fitch and Duff & Phelps: BBB.

Obligations rated BB, B, CCC, CC, and C are regarded as having significant speculative characteristics. BB indicates the least degree of speculation and C the highest. While such obligations will likely have some quality and protective characteristics, these may be outweighed by large uncertainties or major exposures to adverse conditions.

BB. An obligation rated BB is less vulnerable to nonpayment than other speculative issues. However, it faces major ongoing uncertainties or exposure to adverse business, financial, or economic conditions that could lead to the obligor's inadequate capacity to meet its financial commitment on the obligation. Comparable grade from Moody's: Ba. Comparable grade from Fitch and Duff & Phelps: BB.

B. An obligation rated B is more vulnerable to nonpayment than obligations rated BB, but the obligor currently has the capacity to meet its financial commitment on the obligation. Adverse business, financial, or economic conditions will likely impair the obligor's capacity or willingness to meet its financial commitment on the obligation. Comparable grade from Moody's, Fitch, and Duff & Phelps: B.

CCC. An obligation rated CCC is currently vulnerable to nonpayment, and is dependent upon favorable business, financial, and economic conditions for the obligor to meet its financial commitment on the obligation. In the event of adverse business, financial, or economic conditions, the obligor is not likely to have the capacity to meet its financial commitment on the obligation. Comparable grade from Moody's: Caa. Comparable grade from Fitch and Duff & Phelps: CCC.

CC. An obligation rated CC is currently highly vulnerable to nonpayment. Comparable grade from Moody's: Ca. Comparable grade from Fitch: CC. Duff & Phelps has no comparable grade.

C. The C rating may be used to cover a situation where a bankruptcy petition has been filed or similar action has been taken, but payments on this obligation are being continued. Comparable grade from Moody's and Fitch: C. Duff & Phelps has no comparable grade.

D. An obligation rated D is in payment default. The D rating category is used when payments on an obligation are not made on the date due even if the applicable grace period has not expired, unless Standard & Poor's believes that such payments will be made during such grace period. The D rating also will be used upon the filing of a bankruptcy petition or the taking of a similar action if payments on an obligation are jeopardized. Comparable grade from Fitch: D, DD, or DDD. Duff & Phelps has a DD rating.

Plus (+) or minus (–). The ratings from AA to CCC may be modified by the addition of a plus or minus sign to show relative standing within the major rating categories.

R. This symbol is attached to the ratings of instruments with significant noncredit risks. It highlights risks to principal or volatility of expected returns that are not addressed in the credit rating. Examples include obligations linked or indexed to equities, currencies, or commodities; obligations exposed to severe pre-payment risk, such as interest-only or principal-only mortgage securities; and obligations with unusually risky interest terms, such as inverse floaters.

For the average investor, the ratings by Standard & Poor's and others are a pretty good guide. A study by the National Bureau of Economic Research showed that just 6 percent of top-rated bonds defaulted from 1900 through 1943—a period that included the Great Depression.[5] Defaults by top-rated bonds are exceptionally rare nowadays.

How do you find a bond's rating? Your broker should tell you a bond's current rating before you buy a bond. You can also find the bond ratings yourself through Standard & Poor's or Moody's Investors Services in your local library.

 Play the Credit Curve

It was seen earlier that long-term bonds usually—but not always—yield more than short-term bonds. That's because the bond market usually figures that a long-term bond has more risk than a short-term one. And the greater the risk, the greater the potential reward.

Similarly, bonds with low credit ratings tend to offer higher yields than high-quality bonds. They also offer greater chances for price appreciation—or for price loss. Even small differences in credit quality will often translate into differences in yield. For example, bonds with an AAA rating from Standard & Poor's typically yield a quarter of a percentage point or so more than a Treasury bond. Why? Because as good as an AAA bond issuer is, it's not as good as the U.S. Treasury.

So for most income-oriented investors, buying a top-rated corporate bond is a great way to pick up a bit more yield for almost no extra credit risk. Even an A-rated bond is probably a good buy for an investor who is willing to hold the bond to maturity.

Talking Trash

Those who like a bit more risk—and the potential for more reward—try to buy low-rated bonds that have the potential to be upgraded. Typically, when a bond's credit rating improves, more investors decide the bond is worth buying. As this happens, the bond's price is bidded up.

Naturally, the more room a bond has for improvement, the more potential it has for price appreciation. Consider Chrysler's bonds in 1990. The company was virtually bankrupt; the U.S. government had to step in and lend it money so it could keep operating.

When Chrysler was teetering on the brink, its bonds traded for as little as $700 per $1,000 of face value. As the company's financial picture improved, however, Chrysler's bonds did, too. An investor who had bought a Chrysler bonds in 1990 and waited a year would have made a 30 percent return on the bond's price—and collected interest, too.

Bonds that are rated BB or below are considered non-investment-grade bonds, meaning most conservative investors won't touch them. Wall Street calls them *high-yield bonds;* most other people call them *junk bonds.*

You can get returns from junk bonds that are close to stock-market returns. That's because you would be taking risks that are close to those you take in the stock market. Let's take a look at some of the issues tracked by Federal Filings Business News, a company that tracks the high-yield bond market (see Figure 2.7).

The *bid price* is the highest amount someone will pay for a security. It is what they bid to buy it, and what you get when you sell it.

The *ask price* is the lowest price at which someone will sell a security. It is the price they are asking for the security, and what you pay when you buy it.

The difference between the two is called the *bid-asked spread.*

Using the information from Figure 2.7, on this particular day—October 16, 1997—we see the price action for several junk-bond issues. Let's look at the listing for Cityscape. Its notes mature in 2004; their coupon is a juicy 12.75 percent.

	Description		Bid	Ask	Change	Comments
Bruno's	10.5%	Nts-05	50	51	−0.75	
CAI Wireless	12.25%	Nts-02	36.5	37.5		
Cityscape	12.75%	Nts-04	82	83	−1.5	Moody's downgrade; put on negative watch by S&P.
Harrah's Jazz	14.25%	Nts-01	29.5	30.5	−0.5	
Trump A.C.	11.25%	Nts-06	98.25	98.34		

SOURCE: *Federal Filings. Data as of October 16, 1997.*

FIGURE 2.7 *Bond trades.*

Currently, dealers are bidding 82, or $820 per bond, for Cityscape's bonds. The asking price is 83, or $830.

On this day, bondholders have gotten some bad news. Moody's has downgraded the bond; Standard & Poor's is considering doing the same. Bond traders have knocked the price by 1.5, or $15 per bond.

As you can see, this is the risk with junk bonds. If the bond's credit deteriorates, so does the bond's price. If the company defaults on its interest or principal payments, then the bond's price will fall further still.

Junk bonds had their worst year in 1990, when many savings and loan institutions and insurers sold their bonds—as did many mutual funds, too. Topping off all that selling was a modest recession. Junk bonds are exquisitely sensitive to economic downturns, because a poor economy means the issuer has a much greater chance of going bankrupt—or at least of defaulting on the bonds.

You can buy individual junk bonds through most full-service brokers. But it's not an area for amateurs. Owning a bankrupt bond is about as much fun as Dutch elm disease.

BOND BUYER TALK

Every kind of market has its own language, and the bond market is no different. First, there's the matter of how bond prices are quoted. Most taxable bonds carry a face value of $1,000. Traders knock a decimal place off bond prices when they quote them. So a bond quoted at $90 means one that's selling for $900. A bond quoted at $101 means one that's selling for $1,010.

Like stocks, fractional bond prices are quoted in eighths. But in the world of bonds, we're talking one-eighth of $10, or $1.25. So a bond quoted at $77¾ would cost $777.50.

Now let's take a look at how bonds are listed in the newspaper. Companies typically have several bonds outstanding, so the newspaper will list bonds by their issuer, their coupon rate, and their maturity date. An Exxon bond with a 5.75 percent coupon that matures in 2015 would be listed like this:

Exxon 5¾   15

Typically, newspapers list a bond's yield, the volume of bonds traded, their closing price, and the change for the day.

The *yield* is the current yield, or coupon divided by price. In this case, the bond's coupon would be $57.50. If the bond's price were quoted at $109, or $1,090, the bond's current yield would be 5.3 percent—$57.50 divided by $1,090.

Volume is the number of bonds traded, not the dollar value. So if the volume were listed as 70, it would mean that 70 bonds traded.

Price is the closing price of the day; *change* is its change from the closing price the previous day.

 **MUNICIPAL BONDS: ALL THIS AND TAX-FREE, TOO**

Corporations and the U.S. government aren't the only big players in the bond market. Cities, states, and municipal organizations, such as airports and toll roads, are big borrowers, too. The bonds they issue are called *municipal bonds,* and, except in fairly special circumstances, the interest from muni bonds is free from federal income taxes. In some cases, interest may be free from state and local taxes, too.

Like corporate bonds, municipal bonds involve credit risk—that is, the risk that the issuer won't be able to make timely interest and principal payments. So the best way to classify municipal bonds is by their issuer—and, by implication, their credit risk. The two major classifications are:

- *General obligation bonds.* These bonds are backed by the issuer's taxing power. If the issuer comes close to default, it can raise taxes to make up the shortfall. These bonds are generally considered to be among the safest of all municipal bonds.

- *Revenue bonds.* Typically, these bonds are issued to build bridges, toll roads, hospitals, airports, and other large projects. The issuer pledges part or all of the fees from these projects to pay off the bonds. For example, if a state wanted to build a toll road, it would pledge a part of the toll receipts to repay the bonds. Because large projects sometimes fail, you need to investigate these bonds somewhat more carefully than general obligation bonds.

There are, of course, many different subvarieties of muni bonds, too. For example, *special tax bonds* are backed by a special tax designed to pay bondholders. *Public housing bonds* are backed by the rents from public housing projects, but generally have the backing of Housing and Urban Development (HUD), a government agency. The same ratings agencies that grade taxable bonds grade tax-free bonds, too. The ratings companies use the same ratings for municipal bonds as they do for taxable bonds (see pages 54–55).

Many municipal bonds are now insured by private, third-party insurers, such as the Municipal Bond Insurance Association (MBIA) and the American Municipal Bond Assurance Corporation (AMBAC). These companies are strong, well-capitalized insurers. Ratings agencies rate insured bonds on the strength of the insurer, not the underlying company. The slightly lower yield you get from an insured muni is probably well worth the reduction in risk. On the other hand, if you pay taxes, you should be happy that your municipality is getting a break on its interest rate. After all, you're ultimately paying the bill.

 DO THE MATH TO SEE IF MUNIS ARE RIGHT FOR YOU

So what's not to like about munis? Because they are free from federal taxes, muni bonds usually

| Maturity | Bond yields, % | |
	Muni	Treasury
2 years	4.06	5.750
5 years	4.39	5.875
10 years	4.81	6.125
30 years	5.47	6.375

SOURCE: Bloomberg Business News. Yields as of October 17, 1997. Muni yields for AAA-rated, insured revenue bonds.

FIGURE 2.8 *Muni yields versus treasury yields.*

carry lower yields than comparable Treasury bonds. The yield spread between Treasuries and munis varies, but a muni bond yield is typically 80 to 90 percent of a comparable Treasury bond yield.

See Figure 2.8 for an example of how muni yields compare with Treasury yields.

How do you tell whether you're better off with a muni? How do you know which is best after taxes? Let's compare the five-year muni yield in Figure 2.8 with the five-year Treasury yield:

1. Find your federal tax bracket. Let's say you're in the 28 percent tax bracket.

2. Subtract 28 percent, or .28, from 1. Answer: 0.72, or 72 percent.

3. Multiply 0.72 percent by the Treasury security yield, which is 5.875. Answer: 4.23 percent.

Now you know how much you have left after taxes from your taxable fund. Since 4.39 percent is more than 4.23 percent, you'd be slightly better off in a taxable fund.

Figure 2.9 shows the taxable equivalent yields for the bonds in Figure 2.8, assuming the investor is in the 28 percent tax bracket.

| Maturity | Bond yields, % | | |
	Muni	Treasury	Taxable equivalent
2 years	4.06	5.75	4.14
5 years	4.39	5.88	4.23
10 years	4.81	6.13	4.41
30 years	5.47	6.38	4.59

SOURCE: Bloomberg Business News. Yields as of October 17, 1997. Muni yields for AAA-rated, insured revenue bonds.

FIGURE 2.9 *Taxable equivalent yields.*

Maturity	Bond yields, %		
	Muni	Treasury	Taxable equivalent
2 years	4.06	5.75	3.47
5 years	4.39	5.88	3.55
10 years	4.81	6.13	3.70
30 years	5.47	6.38	3.85

SOURCE: *Bloomberg Business News. Yields as of October 17, 1997.*

FIGURE 2.10 *Muni yields versus taxable yields.*

As you can see, only the 2-year muni bond would be a worse investment for someone in the 28 percent tax bracket. The comparison would improve greatly for someone in the 39.6 percent tax bracket, as shown in Figure 2.10.

If you live in the state where a municipal bond is issued, you have an extra advantage: The interest from those bonds is free from state and local taxes, too. If you want to compare taxable and tax-free bonds, be sure to add your state, local, and federal tax rates together in Step 1.

One word of caution: If you sell a muni bond for a profit, you will owe taxes on your capital gains. So for investors who really hate to pay taxes, it makes little sense to make interest-rate plays with munis.

 **ZERO-COUPON BONDS HELP
LOCK IN A LONG-TERM RATE**

Some bonds pay no interest whatsoever until they mature. Because these bonds have no coupon payments, they are called *zero-coupon bonds*.

Although some companies issue zero-coupon bonds, major brokerage houses manufacture most of them from Treasury Separate Trading Registered Interest and Principal (STRIP) bonds. STRIPs are a special Treasury issue designed to be made into zero-coupon bonds.

STRIPs, like savings bonds, are sold at a deep discount from their face value. For example, you could buy a 30-year STRIP that yields 7 percent for about $323. The same STRIP would cost about $250 if its yield were 10 percent.

STRIPs are a great way to lock in current rates for up to 30 years. And they are also a very efficient way to plan for future goals. For example, suppose you know you need $50,000 in 20 years. A 20-year STRIP yielding 7 percent costs $416. So you could invest $20,800 ($416 multiplied by $50) now and be assured of $50,000 in 20 years.

Two drawbacks:

1. You will owe taxes on the interest from your zero-coupon bonds the year it is earned, even though it may not be paid for decades. For this reason, it's best to keep zero-coupon bonds in a tax-deferred savings account, such as an Individual Retirement Account.

2. If you decide to sell your bonds before they mature, you could get considerably less or more than you counted on. Prices on zero-coupon bond prices are much more sensitive to changes in interest rates than regular bonds.

BUY CONVERTIBLE BONDS FOR PRICE APPRECIATION

Investors who want more price appreciation and less yield can try taking a spin in a convertible.

Convertible bonds can be converted to common stock when the stock's price rises above a certain level. In return for the conversion feature, convertible bonds typically offer a lower coupon rate than regular bonds.

Let's take a look at a convertible bond offered by BingCo, the entirely enterprising yet entirely fictitious ball-bearing company. BingCo's bonds can be converted to stock when the stock price rises above $50 per share. The bonds have a face value of $1,000.

If BingCo's stock rises to $50 per share, you can convert your bond to 20 shares of BingCo stock. If the stock rises above $50 per share but you decide not to convert, your bond's price will probably rise because the bonds' conversion feature makes them more attractive.

Naturally, there's a formula for this, too. The following formula shows the point at which a convertible bond's price is at parity with a regular bond's price:[6]

$$\frac{\text{Par value of bond}}{\text{Conversion price}} = \frac{\text{Market price of bond}}{\text{Market price of stock}}$$

So let's look at your BingCo convertible. It's has a $1,000 par value and a $50 conversion price.

The market price of the stock is $55. What's the bond worth?

1. The par value divided by the conversion price is $20.

2. Now we multiply 20 by $55, the conversion price, and we get $1,100. That should be the market price of the stock.

Of course, the market isn't as neatly efficient as all that, and sometimes traders can pick up huge bargains in the convertible market, in part because it's often overlooked.

 USE BONDS TO INCREASE YOUR INVESTMENT INCOME

Chapter 1 discusses a sample portfolio of CDs of different maturities—a technique called *laddering*. Had you formed your portfolio at the beginning of 1997, Figure 2.11 shows what your choice of money market returns would have looked like.

That's a decent yield for a risk-free portfolio. But a $100,000 investment would give just $5,660 a year in income. To get a $50,000 income at these rates, you'd need about $885,000.

But now suppose you used bonds instead of CDs. Your portfolio would have yields as shown in Figure 2.12.

A $100,000 Treasury portfolio would generate $6,280 in income, versus $5,140 for the CD portfolio. That's a 22 percent increase. And as long as you held on to your bonds to maturity, you would not be taking on more risk.

But if you added lower-quality bonds, or if you decided to sell your bonds, you would be taking on risk. And, as was seen earlier in this chapter, more risk opens the door to greater returns—and

CD maturity	Rate, %
6 months	4.75
1 year	5.03
2½ years	5.25
5 years	5.54
Average yield	5.66

Source: *Bank Rate Monitor.*

FIGURE 2.11 *Money market returns.*

CD maturity	Yield, %	Treasury maturity	Yield, %
6 months	4.75	2 years	6.08
1 year	5.03	3 years	6.21
2½ years	5.25	5 years	6.35
5 years	5.54	7 years	6.46
Average yield	5.14	Average yield	6.28

Source: Bank Rate Monitor, Federal Reserve Board.

FIGURE 2.12 *Bond yields.*

greater losses. Let's look at the return side first (see Figure 2.13).

Figure 2.13 shows that bonds have given better returns over the past 15 years than T-bills. (We should bear in mind that the past 15 years have seen a dramatic drop in interest rates, and one of the best bond markets in a generation.)

These better returns are due, in part, because bonds are riskier than T-bills, which are basically risk-free if held to maturity. But as can be seen from Figure 2.14, bond prices can fluctuate widely from quarter to quarter, even if the interest is

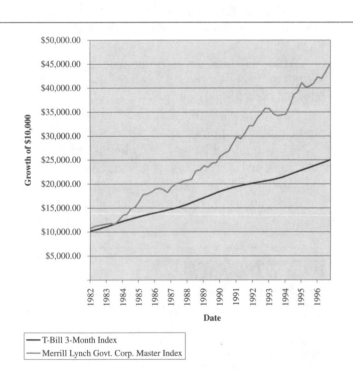

—— T-Bill 3-Month Index
—— Merrill Lynch Govt. Corp. Master Index

FIGURE 2.13 *Bonds versus T-bills, September 30, 1982, to September 30, 1997. (Source: Lipper Analytical Services, Inc.)*

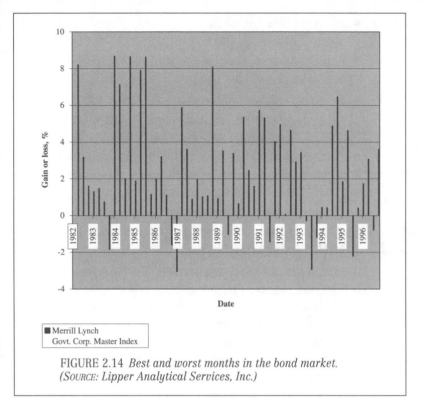

FIGURE 2.14 *Best and worst months in the bond market.*
(*SOURCE: Lipper Analytical Services, Inc.*)

reinvested. The worst quarter: a 7.96 percent loss in the first quarter of 1980. The best: a 17.88 percent gain the following quarter.

 ## USE BONDS TO TEMPER STOCK MARKET VOLATILITY

You can also use bonds to offset stock losses. Income from bonds will help cushion the blow of a major market meltdown. And historically, bonds often do well when stocks falter.

Why? As was discussed earlier, the bond market thrives on bad news. Nothing makes the bond market happier than a good recession. The stock market, however, is optimistic by nature. It likes a robust, expanding economy.

Throughout most of history, it has made sense to keep some bonds in your overall portfolio. When stocks fare well, bonds will lag. But when stocks do poorly, bonds will rise—and will ease some of the pain of a major stock market meltdown.

In recent years, however, stocks and bonds have moved in lockstep. The reasoning for this is somewhat convoluted, but let's give it a shot:

- Interest rates fall when the economy slows down. That's good for bonds.
- Falling interest rates tend to stimulate the economy. That's good for stocks.
- So stocks rally when the economy slows down.

Nevertheless, the recent correlation between bonds and stocks may be ephemeral. For most of the past century, a 60 percent mix between stocks and bonds has provided a comfortable, although unexciting return. It may continue to do so.

USE TREASURY BONDS AS PROTECTION AGAINST DEFLATION

If inflation is the bond market's enemy, *deflation* is the bond market's friend. Deflation is a period of declining prices of real assets, such as food, real estate, and precious metals.

When prices are falling, a fixed income payment will buy more goods each year. So in those few periods of declining prices—the Great Depression was the last such major period—Treasury bonds become extremely valuable.

Why Treasury bonds? Deflationary periods are often extremely difficult economic times, as anyone who survived the Depression will tell you. Corporate bonds become much more vulnerable to default.

Just how likely is deflation? Not terribly. The U.S. monetary system has a built-in inflationary bias, since currency is no longer convertible to gold. But you never know.

END POINT

It's quite possible to make a great deal of money in the bond market. For example, if you buy bonds when interest rates are extremely high and sell them when rates are low, your returns will be quite similar to those from the stock market.

But predicting interest rates is a loser's game. Economists can't do it; bond traders can't do it; you probably can't, either. Use bonds if you need extra income. Use them if you need to hedge your portfolio against stock market downturns or deflation. But if you're looking to grow your portfolio, look to other investments instead.

Stock Answers:
The Stock Market

It's 7:00 A.M., and your General Electric alarm clock wakes you up. You go down the hall and make some of the Starbucks coffee that your sister Sarah gave you for Christmas. You shave with a Gillette razor, and wash your hair with Procter & Gamble shampoo. An hour later, you hop into your Volkswagen and head off to your job making high-performance ball bearings.

Every working day, thousands of shares of stocks of each of those companies—General Electric, Starbucks, Gillette, Procter & Gamble, and Volkswagen—are traded on the nation's stock exchanges. In all likelihood, you own some of each, either directly, in a brokerage account, or indirectly, through a mutual fund or pension fund.

The stock market is a catch-all term for the thousands of stocks traded every day on more than a half-dozen exchanges across the country. As the old Wall Street saw goes, it's actually a market of stocks and not a stock market. There are stocks of huge, well-known companies, like General Motors and IBM. There are stocks of tiny, specialty companies like Mallinckrodt, which makes chemicals for the medical industry. And there are stocks of hundreds of companies in between. In total, all the stock in the nation is worth about $9 trillion.

The stock market itself is a source of endless fascination. The media loves to watch up-and-coming money managers—and down-and-out ones, too. Every day, you hear the closing figures for the Dow Jones Industrial Average (DJIA) or the NASDAQ Composite Index. Most newspapers devote page after page to stock listings; magazines trumpet stories with such titles as "Seven Stocks to Buy Now" and "Tomorrow's Megastocks."

To a casual observer, the stock market's day-to-day gyrations make little sense. One day the Dow Jones Industrial Average is up 30, another day it's down 15. Because of that, many people dismiss the stock market as nothing more than gambling.

Wall Street's public relations departments, of course, see the stock market as an efficient, dispassionate system for determining the prices of companies and their earnings prospects. A 200-point plunge is a "correction"; a 600-point surge is a "technical rally."

In fact, the stock market is neither entirely random nor coolly calculating. Gambling is, indeed, random. But intelligent investing is much more than chance. And those well-groomed men and women on Wall Street can be every bit as loony as anyone else—in the short term. That's what makes the stock market so interesting.

To invest successfully in the stock market, you need to be patient. You need to be willing to do your own research and make your own decisions. And you need to be willing to brave some losses. If not, then you're better suited to bonds or money market investments. But if so, you can have a lifetime of interesting, though occasionally painful, investing.

A BIT OF HISTORY

The stock exchange began in the late 1700s, when traders met beneath a buttonwood tree in Manhattan to trade government bonds. U.S. currency was not entirely trustworthy in the early days of the Republic, so all trades were made in Spanish milled dollars, better known today as pieces of eight. To this day, stocks are still quoted in eighths of a dollar, although most stocks are now quoted in sixteenths, as well. At some future date, most stocks will be traded in decimals instead of fractions.

In 1792, 24 brokers and merchants signed an agreement standardizing stock commissions. This is generally viewed as the beginning of the New York Stock Exchange (NYSE). The first stock traded: Bank of New York.

Organizations tend to become more formal the larger and older they get, and the NYSE was no exception. In 1817, the NYSE moved indoors permanently. After many different moves, including to the back of a coffee house, it settled at 60 Broad Street in 1903, where it remains today.

But not all stock trading stayed with the NYSE. Some people still traded stocks outdoors on the curb. The so-called Curb Market flourished for many years until 1921 when it, too, moved inside. Trading stations on the original trading floor looked like the streetlights outside. In the 1940s, the Curb Market dropped its old name and became the American Stock Exchange (AMEX). Today, the AMEX is the second-largest auction market in the country, but the smallest national stock exchange. It will soon merge with the NASDAQ stock market.

Even though the Curb went inside, there was still a lively trade in small stocks between brokerage houses. Initially called the Over-the-Counter Market, it eventually became formalized into the National Association of Securities Dealers Automated Quotation (NASDAQ) system. It's now considered to be the third national stock exchange.

In addition to the NYSE, the AMEX, and NASDAQ, there are several regional exchanges as well. These include the Boston, Midwest (Chicago), Pacific (Los Angeles and San Francisco), and Philadelphia exchanges. Some small companies are listed only on regional exchanges. But many regional exchanges also list large national companies.

 WHEN YOU OWN STOCK, YOU OWN A PIECE OF THE COMPANY

A *stock* is a certificate of ownership in a company. When you buy a share of stock, you own a proportionate amount of that company. For example, if the company has 50,000 shares outstanding and you own 5,000 shares, you own 10 percent of the company. If you own a majority of the company's

stock, you control the company. And in theory, if
the company decided to go out of business and liquidate all its assets, all shareholders would get a
proportionate amount of the company's assets
after it had paid its debts. (As a practical matter,
most companies that liquidate their assets have
nothing left after they have paid their debts—that's
why they are going out of business.)

When a company issues stock, it's selling ownership of the company for cash. Here's what happens when a company decides to sell stock, or go
public, in Wall Street terms:

1. The company hires an underwriter, an investment banker such as Goldman Sachs. The underwriter often teams up with other investment
   bankers to form an underwriters' syndicate.

2. The underwriters and the company negotiate
   on the size and price of the stock offering. That
   is, they decide how much of the company will
   be in public hands, and how much will be left
   in the hands of the owners. The underwriters
   arrive at a price by looking at how Wall Street
   prices other, similar companies and how recep-
   tive the market is for a new offering.

3. When the underwriters and the company reach
   agreement, the underwriters purchase the
   entire block of stock from the company. Sometimes, underwriters will sell an issue on a *best
   effort* basis, which means they will simply try to
   sell as many shares as they can. Obviously, this
   means that the underwriters have many reser-
   vations about the stock, and you should, too.

4. In most cases, however, the underwriters then
   sell the stock to the public at a slightly higher
   price than they paid to the company. To do so,
   they must file a prospectus with the Securities
   and Exchange Commission. This is a legal document that details the company's current financial condition, what it plans to do with the
   proceeds of the sale, and any other information
   that would make a material difference as to
   whether an investor would buy the stock.

5. Whether or not the underwriters get the price
   they want for the stock, the money from the
   underwriting is the company's to keep. It may
   spend the money more or less as it likes, within
   the confines of the prospectus—the legal docu-

ment that gives potential investors material information about the company and its plans.

What is the company giving up in return? Plenty. Publicly traded companies must disclose far more financial information than privately traded companies do. It must file an annual report with the SEC, for example. Any time it makes a business decision that will have a material affect on its prospects, it also must file with the government. And it must report when key insiders buy or sell shares of its stock.

Furthermore, a public company must gear itself toward pleasing stockholders, rather than pleasing its management. Critics have noted that this sometimes makes management short-sighted, inclined to favor moves that will increase short-term profits rather than long-term goals.

Finally, going public opens the possibility that an outsider could accumulate enough stock to oust the current management and take over the company. This isn't always a bad thing. But it rarely makes the old management happy.

KEY CONCEPT — Shareholders Have Rights, Too

Stockholders have certain rights that the company must respect. As a stockholder, you get to vote in the company's annual meeting, either in person or by proxy. If you attend in person, you get a chance to meet key officers and, sometimes, to question them. Because companies like to keep their shareholders happy, you have a good chance of getting a free meal or a keepsake of your visit.

Most people, however, vote by *proxy.* That is, they sign a document indicating how they would vote on key issues. The document allows another person to vote on their behalf in a corporate election. A *proxy fight* occurs when a company tries to take over another by winning a majority of proxy votes. Typically, the acquiring company attempts to vote the current management out of office in favor of a management team friendly to the acquiring company.

Most corporations work on the basis of one share, one vote. If you have 500 shares, you have 500 votes. But some share classes have different voting rights. It's not uncommon for officers and directors to have a special class of stock with more voting clout than common stock, for example.

You'll find details of the stock's voting privileges in the prospectus.

Stock ownership also entitles you to receive *dividends,* which are a cash payout of the company's earnings to shareholders. The company's board of directors decides how much it will pay in dividends each year; most companies pay out dividends quarterly.

 Don't Overlook Dividends

Each evening, when the news anchors announce the day's closing figure for the Standard & Poor's 500 stock index, they're only telling part of the story. The S&P 500 (as well as the Dow Jones Industrial Average and most other stock indexes) is a *price* index. That is, it shows only how the price component of the index has fared.

But just looking at price action ignores *dividends,* and that's a lot to ignore. Suppose you had invested $10,000 in the S&P 500 at the beginning of 1962. Without dividends, your $10,000 would have grown to $153,843. But if you had reinvested your dividends, your $10,000 would have grown to $555,280.

Why the huge disparity? First of all, companies paid much higher dividends in the 1960s and 1970s. Indeed, for a long time, the rule on Wall Street was to buy stocks when their dividend yields—the dividend divided by the current stock price—were higher than bond yields. But dividend yields have been shrinking since the early 1980s. In 1997, the dividend yield was below 2 percent, an all-time low.

Second, dividends cushion the blow when stocks tumble. For example, during the dreadful 1973 to 1974 bear market, the S&P 500 price index fell 46 percent. But the S&P 500 with dividends reinvested fell 42.3 percent.

Finally, dividends have the magic of compounding. Even if your stock goes nowhere, your dividends accumulate over time. It's money that works while you sleep.

Splits Don't Have to Be Good, But They Often Are

Periodically, a company will vote to split its stock. Although this has no effect on the value of the stock, it often helps to push up a stock's price.

A *split* simply means that a company increases the amount of its shares, without increasing the value of your holdings. Suppose you own 100 shares of BingCo common stock, currently trading at $200 a share. Your BingCo stock is worth $20,000.

BingCo declares a two-for-one split. On the day of the split, two things happen:

1. You now have 200 shares of BingCo stock, instead of 100.

2. Your stock is now worth $100 a share.

In short, you have twice as much stock, but its share price is half of what it was before the split. Your BingCo stock is still worth $20,000. You simply have twice as many shares.

Companies typically split their stock to make it more affordable to small investors. But stocks often rise after a split. Why? No one is exactly sure. Sometimes, companies raise their dividends after a split. But mostly it's because low-priced stocks are easier to sell to the public than stocks whose prices are in the hundreds of dollars per share. After all, many people can afford to buy a round lot—100 shares—of a stock selling at $10 a share. That's a $1,000 purchase. But not many people can afford 100 shares of a $200 stock. That's a $20,000 purchase.

In rare cases, a company will have a reverse split—which often means it's in its final days. Suppose a company's stock sells for $0.50 a share. It might have a 1-for-5 reverse split, meaning that investors will get 1 share valued at $2.50 for every 5 shares they own. The idea is to boost the stock's price so it seems more respectable. Don't be fooled. Bail out.

KEY CONCEPT — ALL KINDS OF STOCKS

Most of the stocks traded are *common stocks,* which represent ownership in a company. But there are other kinds of stocks as well, including the following:

- *American Depositary Receipts* (ADRs) represent shares of foreign stocks on deposit with a U.S. bank. ADRs let you buy overseas companies without having to conduct business on a foreign stock exchange.

- *Preferred stock* usually pays a higher dividend than common stock. And if the company must choose between paying the dividend on the common stock or the preferred, it must choose the preferred. (That's why it's called preferred stock.) But most preferred stock doesn't carry voting rights.

- *Adjustable-rate preferred stock* pays a dividend that is adjusted every quarter. Typically, the dividend is pegged to a benchmark, such as three-month Treasury-bill rates.

- *Convertible preferred stock* can be converted to common stock under certain conditions.

- *Real estate investment trusts* (REITs) represent ownership in portfolios of commercial or residential property. REITs must get 75 percent of their income from real estate, and 95 percent of their net earnings must be distributed to shareholders.

- *Closed-end mutual funds* are funds that issue a set number of shares and trade on the stock exchanges. For more on closed-end funds, see Chapter 4.

- *Master limited partnerships* are publicly traded versions of limited partnerships, private investment vehicles that buy and sell illiquid investments, such as oil and gas drilling rigs, apartment complexes, or commercial office buildings.

 STOCKS ARE TRADED BY AUCTION AND BY DEALER

When you buy a stock, you're not giving any money to the company that issued the stock. The company has already gotten its money from the underwriter. Instead, you are buying from another investor.

So how is the price decided? Basically, stocks trade in two ways: by auction and by dealer. Both are simply ways to match a buyer with a seller.

The New York Stock Exchange and the American Stock Exchange are auction markets. At the NYSE, orders flow from around the world to the floor of the exchange, where they are routed to a specialist—a person whose sole job is to make sure that buyers and sellers of one particular stock are matched up. The specialist keeps a record of who is bidding for a stock, and who is trying to sell. When no one else will buy or sell the stock, the specialist must do so. His or her job is to provide an orderly market in that particular stock. The AMEX uses a similar system.

The NASDAQ, however, is a market of dealers. Essentially, the NASDAQ is a computerized system that allows brokers to see what dealers are bidding and asking for stocks at any given moment. The broker can then choose the best bid for the client.

- Don't forget: *Bid* means what a dealer would bid for a stock—in other words, what you would get if you sold it. *Ask* means the price at which a dealer would sell stock—that is, the price at which you would buy it.

For many years, stocks were exclusively traded as *certificates,* elaborately engraved pieces of paper that represented your investment. If you didn't trust your broker to hold your stock for you, you could keep the certificates in your own strongbox. Today, most companies don't issue paper certificates. Instead, your investment is an electronic notation at your broker's office. You can buy or sell your stock with a telephone call.

 THERE'S A BROKER FOR EVERYONE

Until May 1, 1975, brokerages had uniform minimum stock brokerage commissions. On that day, a ruling by the Securities and Exchange Commission ended uniform minimum commissions. Since May Day, as Wall Street now calls it, brokerage houses can compete for customers by offering cut-rate commissions. The SEC rule gave birth to a thriving discount brokerage industry.

So you currently have the choice of going to a full-service brokerage, such as Merrill Lynch, or to a discount brokerage, such as Charles Schwab & Co. If you go to a full-service broker, you can expect a wide range of services. Merrill, for example, offers financial planning, company research, mortgage loans, annuities, options, and virtually every other financial service you would need. Its brokers are expected to give advice about what stocks to buy and what stocks to sell.

For all of this, you'll pay a full-service price—typically about 3 percent of the purchase price. If you bought 200 shares of a stock selling for $15, for example, you could expect to pay $95 to $105 at a full-service broker. Full-service brokers include Merrill Lynch, Salomon Smith Barney, and Prudential Securities.

A discount broker, on the other hand, offers a limited line of services and gives you no advice whatsoever. But if you know what you want to buy, a discount broker is the way to go. Typically, a discount broker's minimum commission will be $25 to $40, depending on the brokerage company. The largest discount brokerage is San Francisco–based Charles Schwab & Co. Next in line is Fidelity Brokerage, based in Boston. But other discount brokerages, such as Jack White & Co., Muriel Siebert, and Waterhouse Securities are also hot contenders in the discount brokerage field.

Discount brokerages have gone even further, if you care to trade online and skip talking to a live person altogether. You can trade for as little as $9.50 online—a significant savings for the small investor. Some of the more well-known Internet brokerage traders are the following:

- Accutrade, http://www.accutrade.com.
- American Express Direct, http://www. americanexpress.com.
- K. Aufhauser & Co, http://www.aufhauser.com.
- E-broker, http://www.ebroker.com.
- Olde Discount Stockbrokers, http://www.oldediscount.com.
- PCFN, http://www.pcfn.com.
- Quick & Reilly, http://www.quick-reilly.com.
- Regal Discount Securities, http://www. regaldiscount.com.
- eSchwab, http://www.eschwab.com.

KEY CONCEPT **ORDERING YOUR STOCK**

Normally, when you buy a stock, you put in an order *at the market:* That is, you want the broker to buy the stock as soon as possible at the current market price. You can also consider the following more specific orders:

- *Limit orders.* With a limit order, you specify the highest price you'll accept for the stock. If IBM is currently selling at 100, for example, you might put in a limit order for $98 in the hope of buying it in a temporary dip. If the price never hits $98, however, you won't get any IBM. Probably the most famous limit order was during the crash of 1929, when some enterprising clerks put in bids for stocks at $1—there being no other bids, the clerks got the stocks.

- *Stop orders.* These are typically standing orders to sell stock as soon as it goes below a certain price. Customers who have huge gains and want to protect against a big drop will sometimes put in stop orders.

- *Fill-or-kill orders.* The order has to be filled immediately and fully at a particular price, or it's cancelled. An *immediate-or-cancel* order is much the same, except that it may be partially filled.

Normally, an order is considered to be good all day, unless you specify a particular holding period. You can also specify a *good-till-cancelled* order, which means the order stands until you cancel it.

WHAT YOU CAN TELL FROM NEWSPAPER LISTINGS

For many years, you had to call your broker to get a stock quote. Today, you can get the previous day's prices in your daily newspaper. A newspaper typically lists the following information:

- *Company name.* This is often in a very abbreviated form.

- *Highest price in the past 52 weeks.* A stock that's on a big climb will be at or near its 52-week high. Upward price momentum is good, but the stock may also be peaking.

- *Lowest price in the past 52 weeks.* If the stock is near its 52-week low, it may be a bargain. But many cheap stocks deserve to be cheap, and can get cheaper.

- *Ticker symbol.* Each stock has a ticker symbol to identify it. If you want to buy the stock, it helps to have its ticker handy so your broker can find it quickly. Stocks traded on the NYSE usually have three-letter tickers. But a few stocks that have been traded for a long time have one-letter tickers: T for AT&T and F for Ford, for example. NASDAQ stocks have four-letter tickers, such as MSFT for Microsoft. And American Depositary receipts have five-letter tickers.

- *Dividend yield.* This is the stock's annual dividend divided by its current price. A stock that sells for $45 a share and has paid a $1.04 dividend per share would have a 2.3 percent dividend yield. Stocks with very high dividends typically have seen their price fall sharply. For example, if this same stock fell in price to $12 a share, its dividend yield would be 8.7 percent.

- *PE ratio.* This is the price-to-earnings ratio. It shows the company's current price divided by its past 12 months' earnings per share. Suppose a company's stock trades for $132 per share and has earned $4.52 per share in the past 12 months. Its PE is 29. The PE ratio tells you how much investors are willing to pay for a company's earnings. Typically, dependable, boring companies like utilities and banks have low PEs; young, growing companies have high PEs.

- *Volume.* This tells you how much of the stock has been traded in a day. A stock that's rising on high volume is usually in a solid uptrend. Conversely, a stock that rises on little volume might not have much backing the move.

- *Hi/Lo/Close.* This tells you the stock's intraday high, low, and closing price. Stocks that close on their high are usually in a strong uptrend; those that close on their lows are usually headed lower.

- *Net change.* This tells you how the stock has performed for one day.

The stock table footnotes will tell you other important information, such as whether a stock has paid its dividend, or whether trading was halted for the day. Don't overlook them!

WHAT YOU CAN TELL FROM STOCK MARKET AVERAGES

You have probably heard about the Dow Jones Industrial Average. You may even know its current level. But what about the Standard & Poor's 500? The NYSE Composite? The NASDAQ Composite? The Wilshire 5000?

The Dow was the first stock market index. It was created in 1884 by Charles Dow, a founder of the *Wall Street Journal.* The original Dow was composed of 11 stocks, mostly railroad stocks. Dow simply took the closing prices of those 11 stocks, added them together, and divided by 11. (That's why they are called the Dow averages). In 1896, Dow created a new average, composed of 12 industrial stocks (see Figure 3.1). It's the ancestor of today's Dow Jones industrial average (see Figure 3.2). Meanwhile, he brought the number of stocks in his original average up to 20, and dubbed it the Rail Index. We know it today as the Dow Jones Transportation Average. The Dow Utility Average appeared in 1929, long after Dow's death in 1902.

The Dow averages still remain an average, rather than an index. But they don't just tally up the stock prices and divide by 30 to determine the Dow Jones Industrial Average any more. To account for splits, replacements, and other problems, the prices are divided by a special divisor rather than the exact number of stocks. The *Wall Street Journal* prints the divisor every day, for those who are inordinately fond of their calculators.

Although the Dow is the best-known stock index, it's probably not the most accurate. After all, there are thousands of stocks listed on the New York Stock Exchange alone; how can 30 stocks represent the stock market?

Company	What became of it
American Cotton Oil	Distant ancestor of CPC
International American Sugar	Evolved into Amstar Holdings
American Tobacco	Broken up in 1911 antitrust action
Chicago Gas	Absorbed by Peoples Gas, 1897
Distilling & Cattle Feeding	Whiskey trust evolved into Quantum Chemical
General Electric	Going strong and still in the DJIA
Laclede Gas	Active; removed from DJIA in 1899
National Lead	Today's NL Industries
Tennessee Coal & Iron	Absorbed by U.S. Steel in 1907
North American Utility	Combine broken up in 1940s
U.S. Leather (preferred)	Dissolved in 1952
U.S. Rubber	Became Uniroyal, now part of Michelin

SOURCE: *Dow Jones & Co.*

FIGURE 3.1 *The original Dow Jones Industrial Average stocks.*

Company	Percentage of DJIA
Merck & Co.	5.62%
J.P. Morgan	5.49
International Business Machines	5.40
Walt Disney	4.94
Minnesota Mining & Manufacturing	4.28
American Express	4.24
Procter & Gamble	4.07
Chevron	3.94
General Electric	3.77
United Technologies	3.66
Johnson & Johnson	3.48
Aluminum Co. of America	3.42
AT&T	3.35
Coca-Cola	3.34
Hewlett-Packard	3.29
Goodyear Tire & Rubber	3.22
Exxon	3.12
Eastman Kodak	3.03
General Motors	2.95
Du Pont	2.84
Travelers Group	2.60
McDonald's	2.45
Caterpillar	2.33
Sears, Roebuck & Co.	2.33
Boeing	2.33
Philip Morris	2.32
International Paper	2.24
Union Carbide	2.10
Wal-Mart Stores	2.06
AlliedSignal	1.87

SOURCE: *Bloomberg Business News.*

FIGURE 3.2 *The current Dow Jones Industrial Average stocks.*

Standard & Poor's, the venerable stock and bond rating company, decided it had an answer in 1957. It combined two earlier indexes into the Standard & Poor's 500 Stock Index (S&P 500). The index has 385 industrial stocks, 15 transportation stocks, 56 financial stocks and 44 utility stocks.

Unlike the Dow, each stock in the S&P 500 is weighted by its market capitalization—that is, the number of shares outstanding multiplied by its current market price. The bigger the stock, the greater the impact on the S&P 500. The 10 largest components of the S&P 500 index in January 1997 are shown in Figure 3.3.

Stock	Percentage of S&P 500
General Electric	3.21%
Microsoft	2.18
Coca-Cola	2.15
Exxon	2.00
Merck & Co.	1.76
Intel	1.63
Royal Dutch Petroleum	1.48
Philip Morris	1.46
Procter & Gamble	1.42
AT&T	1.41
Total	18.69%

SOURCE: *Bloomberg Business News.*

FIGURE 3.3 *The 10 largest components of the S&P 500 index, January 1997.*

But the Dow and S&P 500 aren't the only indexes by a long shot. Some of the more widely used indexes are the following:

- *NASDAQ Composite Index.* Measures the moves of all NASDAQ-traded stocks. Like the S&P 500, it's a capitalization-weighted index Because the NASDAQ has many technology companies, some use it as an measure of speculation. But that's not really fair: The NASDAQ is an exceptionally broad exchange.

- *NYSE Composite index.* Measures the moves of all NYSE-traded stocks. It, too, is a capitalization-weighted index.

- *AMEX Composite Index.* Measures the moves of all AMEX-traded stocks. It's capitalization-weighted, too.

- *Standard & Poor's 100 Stock Index.* Measures the moves of the 100 largest stocks in the S&P 500 for which there are options listed on the Chicago Board Options Exchange.

- *Wilshire 5000 Stock Index.* Measures the moves of 5,000 U.S. common stocks on all three exchanges; the broadest measure of stock prices.

 **WHAT YOU CAN—AND CAN'T— LEARN FROM THE INDEXES**

Charles Dow compared his indexes to putting sticks in the sand to determine whether the tide is going in or going out. And that's a good analogy. A stock index can't help you predict when the next bull or bear market will be. But it can give you some idea of whether it's a bull market or a bear market now, and that's useful information.

Market technicians use a variety of terms to describe patterns in stock charts—a head-and-shoulders pattern, for example, has a smaller peak (the left shoulder) a larger, rounded peak (the head), and a smaller peak (the right shoulder). These may be helpful if you are trading large baskets of stocks on a day-to-day basis. But the human mind is designed to see patterns, often despite whether they are really there. For most investors, reading patterns from charts smacks of reading entrails.

But if you want to take the market's current pulse, it helps to study the indexes. A few quick indicators follow.

PE Ratio of the S&P 500

Standard & Poor's calculates the average PE ratio of the stocks in the S&P 500 and has tracked it over time. It has proven to be a reasonably reliable indicator of whether the stock market is too high or too low.

The average PE for the S&P 500 since 1950 has been 14.6. Normally, stocks are considered to be expensive—and therefore vulnerable to a tumble—when the S&P 500's PE is above 20.2. Ned Davis Research, a company that produces stock research for large institutional clients, says that the Dow's median level is 7.3 percent lower 6 months after the S&P 500's PE rises above 20.2. (*Median* means that half the periods are higher, half lower.)

Stocks are considered to be bargains when PEs fall below 9.3. According to Ned Davis Research, the Dow typically is 27.5 percent higher 24 months after the S&P 500's PE dips below 9.3.

The catch: The PE is the price divided by earnings. If earnings soar, prices can rise even when the S&P 500's PE is soaring. In 1993 and 1994, for example, the S&P 500's PE was well above 20.3 percent. But earnings soared, and so did the S&P 500.

Rate of Change of the S&P 500

In most cases, the S&P 500 doesn't rise a great
deal more than 30 percent in a 12-month period.
And it doesn't fall a great deal more than 9 percent in a 12-month period.

One fairly simple set of rules, again formulated
by Ned Davis, is the following:

- If the S&P 500 falls by more than 9 percent in
  a 12-month period and then rises above a
  9 percent loss, consider buying.
- If the S&P 500 rises by more than 30 percent
  and its 12-month gain then falls below 30 percent, be careful.

It's a commonsense way of looking at the stock
market: Buy when prices are low but rising; don't
buy when the market has had big gains and is
falling. Most newspapers print the S&P 500's 12-
month change every day.

Be Careful When the Dow Is the Only Rising Index

In a true bull market, the majority of stocks are
rising. Many are posting new highs. But as a bull
market gets old, fewer and fewer stocks rise. Only
big, well-established stocks keep rising, because
they are considered to be safe and extremely liquid by Wall Street pros and foreign investors alike.
Typically, these stocks, too, start to decline and a
correction then begins.

As you recall, the Dow consists of 30 big, well-
established stocks. If the S&P 500 and the Wilshire
5000 are falling, but the Dow is posting gains, be
careful: The bull market is probably running out of
steam.

Don't use these indicators as reasons to go in
and out of the market. Trying to predict peaks and
valleys is a fool's game—and, potentially, a costly
one. If you had missed the 50 best months in the
stock market from 1926 through 1987, your
would have missed all the gain for the period.
Instead, use the indicators as a way to test your
own bullishess (or lack of it) against reality. Most
people find the urge to buy at the top hard to
resist—and the urge to sell at the bottom is even
harder. If you're dying to buy more stock, but several of the preceding indicators are flashing a

warning signal, then perhaps you should wait, or
buy just half the amount you'd like.

THE EFFICIENT MARKET

KEY CONCEPT

One particularly popular theory on how
to pick stocks on Wall Street is the *efficient market*
theory. This theory starts with the notion that
most information about a company is widely available, and is available pretty much at the same
time for everyone (overlooking illegal insider trading). Because the stock market is a fearsomely efficient discounter of current information, the
current price of a stock reflects all the current
knowledge about the company's prospects. Any
short-term gain one makes is entirely arbitrary (or
random) and so most stock portfolios, over time,
will revert to the mean. In other words, after all is
said and done, the best stock-pickers will match
the return of the stock-market averages, less
expenses. It's a sort of financial determinism.

Others are less sure. After all, there's a long list
of men and women who have, in fact, beaten the
market averages for extended periods of time. And
if the market is so darn efficient, how does one
explain the 508-point, 1-day decline in the Dow
Jones Industrial Average on October 1987, or the
520-point, 1-day decline in the Dow in October
1997? Furthermore, anyone who has observed
Wall Street for any period of time knows that the
stock market tends to go to extremes of optimism
and pessimism that have little basis in rationality.

THE GROWTH SCHOOL OF INVESTING

Peter Lynch is one of Wall Street's living legends.
Lynch ran the Fidelity Magellan fund from 1977
through 1990. In those 13 years, he drove the
fund to a 2,500 percent gain—one of the best
records in any fund in history.

Lynch's basic tenet: Stock prices follow earnings. Sure, many goofy things will happen to a
stock in the short term. A rumor on Wall Street
can knock it down a few points. An international
crisis can send it tumbling, too. But if the company's earnings rise 8 percent, the stock will probably rise 8 percent, too.

Let's take a look at one of Lynch's favorite
stocks, Fannie Mae. The company is more for-

mally known as the Federal National Mortgage Association. But stock traders quickly took its initials—FNMA—and turned it into Fannie Mae. The company helps stabilize the mortgage market by buying, selling, and guaranteeing mortgages.

Fannie Mae stock rocketed from an average $2.78 a share (on a split-adjusted basis) in 1986 to $33.64 per share in 1986, up about 11 times. Lynch would say that the stock's growth makes perfect sense: Its earnings grew even more (in percentage terms), soaring from $183 million in 1986 to $2.7 billion in 1996.

Lynch's dictum—stock prices follow earnings— is at the heart of the growth school of investing. Growth-stock investors look for companies whose earnings they think will soar. That, in turn, will lead to higher stock prices down the road.

And, in fact, academics would say that there's a reasonable explanation for Lynch's theory. After all, most companies pay out a portion of their earnings in dividends each year. So one could argue that a person who buys a stock is actually purchasing a stream of future dividends. This is plausible for companies like Coca-Cola, which have paid dividends for years and are likely to do so for years to come.

But what about companies that have never paid a dividend, such as Microsoft or Intel? Analysts will argue that these companies probably will pay out a dividend someday. And because a company's ability to pay dividends hinges on its earnings, they try to forecast earnings to see what the fair market value of a stock might be.

 ### The Importance of Reading Earnings

A thorough discussion of stock analysis is beyond the scope of this book. But there's no great harm in looking at other people's earnings estimates. And they are easily available from a variety of sources.

- Your broker.
- I/B/E/S, a service that collects earnings estimates and publishes consensus estimates for thousands of stocks. Although this is an institutional service, your broker should be able to get you the I/B/E/S estimates for most stocks. Zach's Investment Research offers a similar service.

- *Value Line Investment Survey* offers earnings estimates for about 1,700 stocks. Most well-stocked libraries carry it.

A fair number of investors simply buy stocks when the stocks' actual earnings outstrip the consensus. They then sell the stocks when earnings don't live up to expectations. This approach, called *earnings surprise,* has some merit, although so many people now use the system that earnings surprises produce almost instant price changes in the underlying stocks. You have to be pretty quick on the trigger now to lock in gains from earnings surprises.

A few words of warning about earnings estimates. First, few analysts issue *sell* signals on a stock. Instead, they describe the stock in various shades of lukewarm action, including *hold* or *buy on weakness.* Second, earnings estimates become more accurate the closer they are to the present. A five-year forecast is somewhat like a five-year weather report. But an estimate made in the second quarter for fourth-quarter earnings is probably pretty close to the mark.

Use others' earnings estimates as a beginning point, not an ending point. Flag companies whose earnings have been steadily improving over a period of time. Companies that are on an earnings roll tend to stay on an earnings roll for a fairly long time. You can find corporate earnings histories in companies' annual reports. If you have a computer, you can get many corporate documents through the Securities and Exchange Commission's EDGAR system (http://www.sec.gov). And most companies have their own websites, too. If not, try that trusty old standby, the library. You can get a wealth of corporate information from sources like the *Value Line Investment Survey* and *Standard & Poor's Outlook.*

But even if you are a rank amateur at stock-picking, you can use other starting points that are just as valuable. As Lynch says, you have an edge that most people don't. Look around you. You probably know your company's industry better than most people on Wall Street do. It's a good bet your average Wall Street analyst doesn't shop at Wal-Mart or buy tires at Sears. Is there a hot new product or a new innovation that will take the industry by storm? Or look for turnaround situations. Has your company (or your company's competitor) hired new management that seems to be electrifying the workforce? If so, then you have a good candidate for a growth stock.

Pricing a Growth Stock

If analysts have an earnings forecast, they can use a price-to-earnings analysis to try to determine what a stock's price should be. The formula they use is fairly similar to the present value projections bond traders use to determine the price of a bond. Here, however, they use a price-to-earnings ratio based on earnings estimates, called a *forward PE*. (A PE based on the previous 12 months' earnings, such as you would see in a newspaper, is called a *trailing PE*.) After all, you're investing in a stream of future earnings, not past earnings.

In a very simple example, let's compare BingCo, the fictional maker of ball bearings, with its archrival, Amalgamated Bearings. BingCo's earnings, currently $1.50 per share, are projected to grow at 7 percent a year for the next 10 years. But Amalgamated Bearings is on a roll: It's projected to grow at 15 percent a year, thanks to its thriving skateboard business. Its current earnings are also $1.50 per share.

If these assumptions are true, we know that BingCo's earnings will be $2.95 in 10 years. Amalgamated Bearings' earnings will be $6.07 per share. Companies in the ball-bearing industry typically sell for 10 times forward earnings. Using those growth rates, we could figure that:

- BingCo could sell at $29½, or 10 times its forward earnings. That would be about 20 times its current earnings.
- Amalgamated Bearings could sell at $60⅝, or 10 times its forward earnings. That would be about 40 times its current earnings.

Naturally, nothing is that simple. Many investors would never pay 40 times current earnings for stock on the grounds that it simply seems too high. Or other factors, like a change of management at BingCo, could affect the prospects for either stock. This isn't an exact science. But it's one way to try to figure out the prospects for a stock.

The advantage to growth investing: A good growth stock will outperform most other stocks during a bull market. The disadvantage: Growth stocks, particularly small growth stocks, get clobbered in a bear market. But growth investors figure that the outperformance in the good times makes up for the wretched performance in the bad times.

Dividend Achievers

Not all growth stocks are high-flying technology companies that soar for three years and go bankrupt in the fourth. Some very stodgy companies produce impressive, consistent earnings growth year after year. How can you find them? One telltale sign is that they have raised their dividends every year for the past 5 to 10 years. These companies may not make CD-ROM players that double as toasters. But if you're looking for good, consistent earnings growth, this may be a good list from which to start.

A company decides every year how much of its earnings it wants to pay out in dividends. A company that cuts its dividend usually sees its price plunge: It's an admission that the company is earning less this year than it has in the past.

Conversely, a company that raises its dividend is telling shareholders (and Wall Street) that it can do so with no sweat. Furthermore, it's implying that it will be able to maintain that level in the future, since most companies seriously avoid dividend cuts. By raising dividends every year, management raises the financial bar it must jump over in succeeding years. It also shows that management likes to share the company's fortunes with shareholders. That's a good company to invest in.

Moody's Investors Services offers *Moody's Handbook of Dividend Achievers,* which lists more than 300 companies that have raised their dividends every year for the past 10 years. You can buy the book from Moody's by calling 800-342-5647, or check your local library. It's not an infallible list, but the dividend achievers are one of the best starting points.

CONSERVATIVE INVESTORS LOOK FOR VALUE

If a growth investor figures that Wall Street rewards good stocks, a value investor thinks Wall

Street sometimes punishes good stocks, too. And if you can find a stock that the herd on the Street has beaten up and left for dead, it can sometimes come back to life in a most gratifying manner.

A truly hard-nosed value approach would look for stocks whose prices are at or below *book value,* which is an approximation of the company's liquidation value. To find book value, add up the following items from a company's annual report:

- Par value of common stock.
- Capital surplus.
- Retained earnings.

Then subtract any *intangible assets.* These are bookkeeping notions, such as *goodwill,* which tries to approximate the value of a brand name. The value of patents also falls under the intangible category. Finally, divide this amount by the total number of shares outstanding.[1] You can get all this information from the company's annual report.

But most value managers retain some flexibility, looking for stocks that have, for some reason, lagged similar stocks. The advantage: Value stocks tend to be less volatile than growth stocks, because they have already been beaten down. After all, if you can buy a stock at or close to its liquidation value, how much could you have to lose? And in fact, many value stocks are takeover candidates because they are so cheap. So when the rest of the stock market falls, value stocks often hold up well.

Value stocks also tend to have higher dividend yields than growth stocks do. Growth investors tend to be riveted on price appreciation. But value stocks often sport decent dividend yields, mainly because their prices have fallen. That dividend yield is a cushion in a downturn, and helps make the pain of waiting for the stock to rise a bit easier.

The disadvantage: A low-priced stock can stay low for a very long time. You can't just buy all the stocks that are hitting new 52-week lows. Instead, you need to hope for a catalyst that will turn the company around, such as new management or a new product. Or you need to hope that Wall Street is not taking certain corporate assets, such as real estate or patents, into account.

THE DOGS OF THE DOW

Here's a commonsense strategy that helps you buy high-quality companies when their prices are low—a good idea at any time.

The *Dogs of the Dow* theory says you should buy the 10 Dow stocks with the highest dividend yields. You hold the dogs for 12 months, then buy the next litter of dogs. The strategy has earned 24.2 percent a year over the 5 years ending 1997, versus 22.3 percent for the Dow itself.

This strategy has a lot going for it. A high dividend yield doesn't usually mean that the company has decided it wants to share more of its earnings with shareholders than usual. Instead, it means that the dividend has stayed the same, but the stock price has fallen steeply.

If these were random stocks picked by throwing darts at the newspaper, the strategy would make little sense. But the Dow consists of 30 stocks of the best companies in the nation. If you buy them when they're down, you have a good chance of making decent gains over the next 12 months.

A variation of the Dogs of the Dow theory is the *Puppies of the Dow* theory. You buy the 5 lowest-priced stocks of the 10 dogs. The strategy has resulted in a 20.9 percent average annual return since 1973.

Traditionally, you should buy the 10 doggiest Dow stocks as of December 31. But there's no particular magic to December 31. If you like, find the most recent Dow dogs and hold them for 12 months. Your results over time should be similar to those who buy in December. The Dow dogs for 1998 are shown in Figure 3.4.

Buying all 10 Dow dogs—or even the 5 Dow puppies—can be an expensive proposition. You might consider buying a Dow dogs unit investment trust, described in Chapter 4.

WALL STREET ACCORDING TO GAARP

People in the growth and value camps usually have opposing views. Growth investors say that value investors are still waiting for the Erie Canal to turn around. Value investors are still giggling about Digital Equipment Corporation, which has yet to recover from the 1987 stock market meltdown.

Company	Yield, %	Small dog?
Philip Morris	3.54	Yes
J.P. Morgan	3.37	No
General Motors	3.29	Yes
Chevron	3.01	No
Eastman Kodak	2.91	Yes
Exxon	2.68	No
Minnesota Mining & Manufacturing	2.58	No
International Paper	2.32	Yes
AT&T	2.15	No
Du Pont	2.10	Yes

SOURCE: *Dogs of the Dow Online, http://www.dogsofthedow.com, January 18, 1998.*

FIGURE 3.4 *1998 Dow dogs.*

But both camps have excellent points about stocks. Earnings really do determine stock prices. And it really does help to buy stocks when their prices are temporarily depressed. The fusion of these two camps is the *growth at a reasonable price* (GAARP) theory.

GAARP investors would say that they like companies with strong and growing earnings. But they would buy the stock when its industry group is temporarily out of favor, or if the company has a slight earnings stumble that won't be repeated again.

DIVIDEND REINVESTMENT PLANS (DRIPs)

Probably one of the best deals to ever emerge from Wall Street is the dividend reinvestment plan (DRIP). DRIPs work as follows:

- You buy your first shares of the company from a broker.
- You enroll in the company's dividend reinvestment plan.
- When the company pays its dividends, it credits your account with additional shares of stock equal to your dividends. Typically, there's no charge for this.

That's it. So what's the big deal? Many companies will let you buy additional shares of stock on a regular basis with no commission. Some companies will even let you make your initial purchase for no fee. And you can reinvest your dividends in additional stock for no charge, either. That's a tremendous savings.

If you start a new DRIP every year, you can have a fully diversified portfolio in 10 years. Over time, your portfolio of DRIPs can become a great core holding—at virtually no cost.

MARGIN CAN AMPLIFY GAINS AND LOSSES

Stocks—as well as bonds and most mutual funds— are *marginable securities.* This means that your broker will lend you money secured by your stocks.

To get a margin loan, you must open a margin account and, in most cases, pass a credit check by the brokerage. Once your account is open, your broker will give you a loan equal to 50 percent of the value of the securities in your margin account. The advantages:

- You can use the loan for anything—from a new car to the purchase of more stock.

- The interest rate, typically 1 to 3 percentage points above a benchmark called the *broker call rate,* is typically lower than the rate for an unsecured loan. You don't have to repay the loan until you close the account or you receive a margin call, which will be explained later.

Most people use margin to increase their buying power, however. For example, if you have a margin account and $10,000 to invest, you can buy $20,000 of any marginable stock. Suppose you think BingCo is going to $60 per share from its current $50 per share. You decide to make a bet on margin. You buy:

- 200 shares of BingCo with your money.
- 200 shares of BingCo with borrowed money.
- Your total purchase is 400 shares, which has a value of $20,000.

Several months later, BingCo is selling for $57 a share. Your account looks like the following:

$22,800	For 400 shares of BingCo stock.
−$10,000	For margin loan.
=$12,800	Value of your investment, or equity.

You have made a $2,800 profit on a $10,000 investment, or a 28 percent gain. (This is ignoring, of course, the fact that you're paying interest on your loan). If you had not taken the margin loan, you would have made $1,400 on 200 shares, or a 14 percent gain.

The drawbacks: You will feel twice the pain when your stock falls in value. Suppose BingCo falls to $45 per share. Your account now looks like the following:

$18,000	For 400 shares of BingCo stock.
–$10,000	For margin loan.
=$ 8,000	Value of your investment, or equity.

Your stock has fallen 10 percent, from $50 to $45. But your investment has fallen 20 percent, from $10,000 to $8,000.

If you have really made a bad call, you could get an even worse one: the *margin call.* Brokers take the value of your equity and divide it by the total value of the account to see if it meets the minimum maintenance requirements. In the preceding example, the broker would divide $8,000 by $18,000 to get 44 percent.

If your equity falls below 25 percent, you'll get a margin call. Your broker will ask you to bring your account's equity back up to about 35 percent of your account value. If you decline, your broker will liquidate your position.

You can also use margin in a different way—to make a bet that a stock's price will fall. This is called a *short sale.*

To sell a stock short, you borrow shares from your broker, sell them on the open market, and hope to repurchase the shares later at a lower price. The difference is your profit. For example, suppose you think BingCo is due for a tumble. You borrow 100 shares from your broker and sell for $50 a share. Your broker holds the proceeds.

If the stock falls to $40 a share, you can repurchase 100 shares and return them to your broker. The difference—$10 per share, or $1000—is yours to keep, less commissions.

The problem, of course, is that the stock could rise. If the stock in the preceding example rises to $60 per share and you have to close your position, you would lose $10 a share, or $1,000. Short sales, like margin purchases, are subject to minimum maintenance requirements, too. Before you get too eager to sell short, remember this: There's

DRP Newsletters and Stock Purchasing Services

The American Association of Individual Investors regularly lists companies with dividend reinvestment plans. It also lists publications and services that keep tabs on dividend reinvestment plans. This list is kindly reprinted from the June 1997 *AAII Journal*.[2] It includes newsletters, directories, and websites, as well as services that offer an alternative route (bypassing a brokerage firm) for buying the initial shares of companies that do not sell initial shares directly to the public.

Directories and Newsletters

The DirectInvestor: 900-225-8585. Faxes a current list with phone numbers of stocks that offer initial shares directly to the public. $2.50 per call.

Directory of Companies Offering Dividend Reinvestment Plans: Evergreen Enterprises, P.O. Box 763, Laurel, MD 20725-0763, 301-549-3939. Directory with plan details. Updated annually; $32.95.

Directory of Dividend Reinvestment Plans: Dow Theory Forecasts, 7412 Calumet Avenue, Hammond, IN 46324-2692, 800-233-5922. Directory with plan details. Updated annually; $15.95. Monthly newsletter: *DRIP Investor;* $79 per year.

Guide to Dividend Reinvestment Plans: The Moneypaper Inc., 1010 Mamaroneck Ave., Mamaroneck, NY 10543, 800-388-9993. Directory with plan details. Updated quarterly; $27. Monthly Temper Enrollment Service helps you enroll in DRIPs; $45. Includes the *Guide* and *The DRP Authority,* a newsletter, for one year.

The Individual Investor's Guide to Dividend Reinvestment Plans: American Association of Individual Investors, 625 N. Michigan Ave., Suite 1900, Chicago, IL 60611, 800-428-2244. Directory with plan details. Updated annually; provided free to AAII members each June; $10 per extra copy; $12.50 for nonmembers.

Standard & Poor's Directory of Dividend Reinvestment Plans: Standard & Poor's Client Relations, 25 New York, NY 10004, 800-852-1641. Directory with plan details. Updated annually; $39.95.

(Continued)

(Continued)

Direct Purchase Information and Newsletters

Direct Stock Purchase Plan Clearinghouse: 800-774-4117. Telephone source for plan prospectuses of firms that offer initial shares directly to the public.

First Share: 304 Mitchell Mountain Road, Westcliffe, CO 81252, 800-683-0743. A cooperative for buying the first share of stock of over 200 companies. $18 per year.

NAIC Low Cost Plan: National Association of Investors Corp., 711 W. 13 Mile Rd., Madison Heights, MI 48071, 248-583-6242, http://www.better-investing.org/store/lcp.html. Initial share purchasing service for 150 companies. $39 per year plus one-time setup charge of $7.

Websites

Net Stock Direct: DRPs search with contact information, list of direct purchase firms, and request plan brochures. http://www.netstockdirect.com.

John Greiner's DRP Guide: List of DRPs with details. http://www.cs.cmu.edu/~jdg/drip.html.

No-Load Stocks Info: List of DRPs with plan details. Links to companies offering initial shares directly. http://noload.base.org.

no limit to how high a stock can rise. But a stock can only fall 100 percent, to zero.

BEAR MARKETS CAN CLAW HOLDINGS

DANGER!

Experts disagree on the exact definition of a bear market. But a drop in the Dow Jones Industrial Average of 20 percent or more would suit most people. We have suffered through nine bear markets since the end of World War II. The median bear market since 1900 has beaten down the Dow by 27 percent and lasted 390 trading days, according to Ned Davis Research.

What causes a bear market? An economic downturn is one prime cause: Four of the nine postwar bear markets started just before a recession. But others can start because of exogenous events—wars, trade sanctions, or world tensions.

A look back at the nine major post–World War II bear markets follows.

May 1946 to May 1947: Down 23.2 Percent

The U.S. economy was in a postwar funk. Soldiers were returning home from World War II and the job market was glutted. Labor was striking manufacturing industries. Inflation was soaring as rationing ended. People worried that the Great Depression, ended by the war, would resume. When the economy began growing again, the bull market resumed and the bear market ended.

December 1961 to May 1962: Down 27 Percent

If you ever wonder how much attention Wall Street pays to Washington, here's your answer: plenty. The stock market had been in a frothy, speculative market in 1961 as Wall Street cheered Kennedy's handling of a steel strike. Then the steel companies raised prices, and Kennedy said, "My father always told me that all businessmen were sons of bitches, but I never believed it till now."

Stocks plunged the next three months, ending only when Kennedy helped get a tax cut past Congress.

February 1966 to December 1966: Down 25.2 Percent

The Federal Reserve Board, worried about the roaring economy, nudged interest rates higher starting in late 1965. By 1966, 5-year Treasury notes yielded more than 5 percent for the first time in decades. They were dubbed *magic fives,* because most savings accounts yielded just 2.5 to 3 percent. People lined up around the block at Federal Reserve Banks to get them. Many investors sold stocks to buy magic fives.

Helping to push stocks down was heavy spending on the Vietnam War and the Great Society poverty programs. The stock market tumbled for eight months until the Fed pushed rates down again in 1967.

December 1968 to May 1970:
Down 35.9 Percent

The stock market was red-hot in 1968, a time called the *go-go years*. But investors figured the economy would weaken in 1969, and it did. Inflation was rising, and the Fed once again pushed interest rates higher. On April 22, 1970, Ross Perot lost $450 million on paper when the stock of his company, Electronic Data Systems, crashed in a jittery market. Stocks finally rose in May 1969, as investors sensed that the recession was ending.

January 1973 to December 1974:
Down 45 Percent

What a rotten time to be in the stock market. The prime rate hit 9.5 percent in August 1973, a record. The Arab oil embargo began in October 1973. President Nixon resigned over the Watergate scandal in August 1974.

Slowly, investors turned more positive about the economy in the beginning of 1975, and the stock market crawled out of its worst bear market since the Great Depression. But the damage from the 1973 to 1974 bear market was tremendous: Brokerages went out of business, banks failed, and investors fled stock mutual funds for more than a decade.

September 1976 to February 1978:
Down 26.9 Percent

Start with the election of Jimmy Carter. Add a new round of oil-price hikes to an already inflation-weary economy, and you have another bear market, just one year after the last.

April 1981 to August 1982:
Down 24 Percent

Federal Reserve Chairman Paul Volcker declared war on inflation. He nearly killed the stock market and the economy at the same time. The prime rate soared to 21.5 percent, the economy crumbled, and the stock market withered. But ultimately, Volcker's harsh medicine worked: Inflation tumbled throughout the 1980s, and a great bull market was born in August 1982.

August 1987 to October 1987: Down 36 Percent

The red-hot bull market went stone cold on October 19, 1987, when the Dow plunged 508 points—a record in point terms that would hold until October 1997. The culprit: steeply rising interest rates, which began to fall again on the day of the October crash.

July 1990 to October 1990: Down 21 Percent

Iraq invaded Kuwait. Oil prices rose. Interest rates soared, and the United States prepared for war. The bear market ended when the Fed began to push short-term rates down in late 1990.[3]

END POINT

Why all this talk about bear markets? To scare you. Quite frequently, you'll hear investment advisors say that stocks invariably produce better returns over the long term than do risk-free investments. This is true. But the long run can be a long time—and certainly longer than people tend to think during a bull market.

Certainly, if we looked at the performance of stocks, corporate bonds, and three-month Treasury bills since 1972, we would see that stocks have been the best choice. A $10,000 investment in the Standard & Poor's 500 Stock Index would have grown to $226,466 from 1972 through 1997. In contrast, corporate bonds, as measured by the Merrill Lynch Corporate Bond Master Index, would have grown to $93,096; 3-month T-bills would have grown to just $55,648 (see Figure 3.5).

Bear in mind that most of the 1990s were a thundering bull market in stocks. Those 10 years tend to skew the entire picture. If we look at the 10 years that ended in 1982, for example (see Figure 3.6), we get a rather different picture.

After 10 years of investing, the S&P 500 grew to $22,178. But 3-month T-bills grew to $22,870 with virtually no risk.

Over 20-year periods, stocks have won hands down. But you have to be willing to commit your money to the market for at least 10 years, and preferably longer, if you want the best chance of producing the best returns. Not only that, but:

- *Be sure to reinvest your dividends and gains.*
  As we have seen earlier, reinvesting dividends
  and gains is one of the single most important
  ways of boosting your returns.

- *Minimize your taxes.* Taxes pay the national
  debt, keep the country safe, educate children,
  and other worthy things. It's legally and
  morally wrong to evade taxes. But it's not
  wrong to use the tax shelters Congress has
  given you. So whenever possible, keep your
  long-term investments in tax-deferred retirement accounts, such as Individual Retirement
  Accounts or Keogh plans.

- *Diversify.* The S&P 500 Stock Index recovered
  from the 1987 stock market crash within 18
  months. But two of the top stocks of that era,
  IBM and Digital Equipment, took almost a
  decade to recover. In fact, DEC never did. A
  stock portfolio should have at least 10 stocks to
  be reasonably diversified.

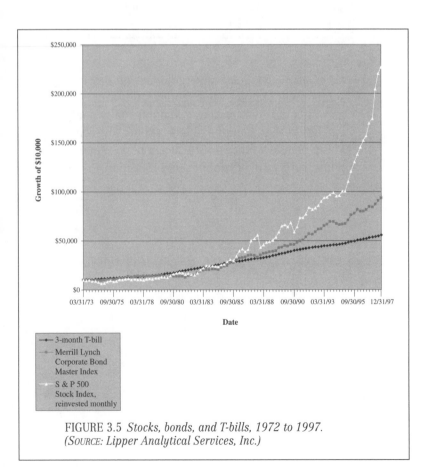

FIGURE 3.5 *Stocks, bonds, and T-bills, 1972 to 1997.*
(SOURCE: *Lipper Analytical Services, Inc.)*

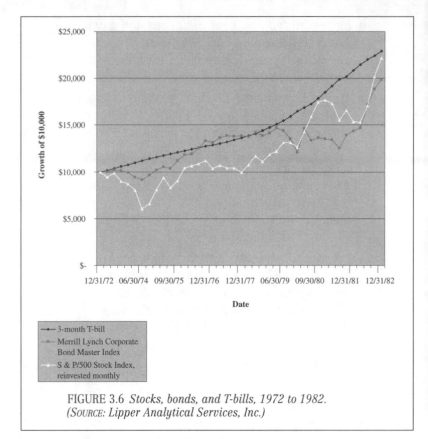

FIGURE 3.6 *Stocks, bonds, and T-bills, 1972 to 1982.*
(*SOURCE: Lipper Analytical Services, Inc.*)

- *Keep your costs low.* Every dollar you pay to someone to manage your money, tally your accounts, or give services you don't really need is a dollar you won't be able to spend yourself. Many people would love to slice a percentage point from your portfolio. Don't let them.

Mutual Advantages

Walk past any newsstand and you'll see two or three magazines that feature mutual funds in their cover stories. *Money* magazine, *Smart Money, Kiplinger's,* and *Worth* all carry several articles on mutual funds in each issue, and hire a small army of reporters and researchers just to cover mutual funds. Then there's *Mutual Funds* magazine, devoted entirely to mutual funds. *USA Today,* the *New York Times* and the *Wall Street Journal* all devote considerable real estate to mutual funds, too.

Why all the interest in mutual funds? It's a big business. One in every three Americans has a mutual fund account. The mutual fund industry now has more than $5 trillion in assets. Americans invested more than $231 billion into mutual funds in 1996—roughly $26 million an hour. In the past decade and a half, mutual funds have become the way Americans save.

WHAT A MUTUAL FUND IS

A *mutual fund,* sometimes called an *investment company,* pools the assets of small investors and invests in stocks, bonds, or other securities.

The securities markets used to be a playground reserved for the very wealthy. Commission structures for stocks, for example, favored those who could buy in *round lots*—that is, lots of 100 shares or more. Individual investors could also expect to pay more to buy bonds than institutional investors. And small investors were shut out of the money market entirely.

Even today, the large investor enjoys considerable advantages over the individual investor. If you buy stocks in *blocks*—10,000 shares or more—you can expect to pay just pennies a share in commissions. In addition, you get investment research from brokerage firms as well as other perks for doing business with the big boys.

More important, it was (and still is) very expensive for a small investor to build a diversified portfolio of stocks independently. Suppose you wanted to invest in the 10 stocks that account for the largest part of the Standard & Poor's 500 Stock Index (S&P 500). Got your checkbook ready? Figure 4.1 shows the bill for all 10 stocks, as of January 16, 1998.

So the basic idea behind a mutual fund is very simple. You may not have enough money to buy 100 shares of 10 S&P 500 stocks, or even 100 shares of General Electric. But if everyone on your block pitched in, you might have enough to buy the 10 biggest components of the S&P 500. Carried further, if your whole town pitched in, you could buy a diversified portfolio of 50 or so stocks, and get the advantage of diversification. So if one of your holdings got shuffled off to Palookaville, profits from the rest of the portfolio would cushion the loss.

Stock	Price	Cost for 100 shares
General Electric	73.38	$ 7,337.50
Microsoft	135.25	13,525.00
Coca-Cola	65.00	6,500.00
Exxon	65.00	6,500.00
Merck & Co.	109.75	10,975.00
Intel	74.81	7,481.25
Royal Dutch Petroleum	51.94	5,193.75
Philip Morris	45.31	4,531.25
Procter & Gamble	79.31	7,931.25
AT&T	65.19	6,518.75
Total		$76,493.75

SOURCE: *Bloomberg Business News.*

FIGURE 4.1 *Cost of the 10 largest S&P 500 stocks, January 16, 1998.*

Pooling assets among smaller investors isn't a new idea. Savings and loan associations (S&Ls), for example, have been pooling depositors' money for years, and using them to make home loans. The associations were also supposed to encourage thrift, which is why Wall Street types often call S&Ls *thrifts*. Credit unions are a similar attempt at cooperative banking.

FUNDS ARE WELL REGULATED— FOR GOOD REASON

The concept of a mutual investment company—a company whose sole purpose is to invest in the stocks and bonds of other companies—goes back to the 1870s in England. Back then, British bonds yielded about 3 percent. American bonds yielded 6 percent. Robert Fleming, a bookkeeper at the English textile firm of Edward Baxter & Son, formed an investment association in 1873 and proposed to put the proceeds into a variety of American railroad bonds. By 1890, about 16 trusts had been formed in England.

The idea of an investment trust took hold more slowly in the United States. The Railway Light and Securities Company, a forerunner of the mutual fund, was started in Maine in 1904. The first modern U.S. mutual fund was the Massachusetts Investment Trust, formed in March 1924 and still going strong to this day.

Funds became popular in 1927, as the great bull market began to head to its unfortunate conclusion. In 1927, for example, the funds had annual sales of $400 million; by 1929, the funds had sold $3 billion. The investment trusts (as they were called then) had 55,000 shareholders in 1927; by 1929, they had 525,000.

But the early funds had huge problems. A fund manager could borrow heavily to buy other stocks—even shares of other funds that had borrowed heavily to buy stocks! Brokerage houses often had far too cozy relationships with funds, and used them as a dumping ground for failed initial public offerings. As a Senate committee later noted, "A veritable epidemic of investment trusts afflicted the Nation."

The Dow peaked at 381 in 1929 and kept falling until 1932, when it bottomed at 41—an 89 percent loss. Bear markets have a way of focusing the public's attention on how the financial system works. A series of post-Depression laws regulate mutual funds, including the following:

- *The Securities Act of 1933.* The Act requires each fund to give investors a prospectus, the legal document that tells investors what a fund invests in.

- *The Securities and Exchange Act of 1934.* The Act puts funds under Securities and Exchange Commission regulation. It also makes them subject to advertising and sales rules established by the National Association of Securities Dealers.

In the late 1930s, Congress held hearings on mutual funds, many of which had fallen even harder than the Dow, thanks to some shady investment dealings on the part of the funds. The result of the hearings was the Investment Company Act of 1940, which put an end to many of the more dubious mutual fund practices of the day. The Act made mutual funds price their shares every day, and standardized the rules for pricing those shares. It also outlawed most securities transactions between a fund and its manager, and it required each fund to have an independent board of directors to act in the shareholders' best interests.

The Act has gone a long way toward protecting investors for more than 60 years. Funds suffered some scandals during the 1960s and early 1970s, and the Act was further amended to prevent shenanigans. Thanks to the 1940 Act, and the diligence of the Securities and Exchange Commission, the fund industry is probably the most scandal-free financial industry in the nation.

HOW A MUTUAL FUND IS ORGANIZED

A mutual fund itself consists of its assets, which are owned by shareholders. A typical fund has no direct employees. Instead, the fund uses affiliated companies to perform the jobs it needs to get done. Let's look at the companies a fund typically employs:

- *Directors.* These oversee the fund operations and are charged with making sure that the fund follows its investment rules and acts in the shareholders' interests. Recently, some boards have come under fire for being too cozy with the interests of the investment advisors, and for being too quick to raise fees. As a shareholder, you should always be careful to vote against fee hikes, unless you genuinely believe it will help the fund.

- *Investment advisor.* This is the group that decides what securities the fund should buy or sell. The fund's manager is technically an employee of the investment advisor, and can be fired by the fund's board of directors for poor performance.

- *Custodian.* This is the company that holds the fund's assets—stocks, bonds, and money market securities. Normally, it's a bank. The fund manager never touches the fund's actual holdings.

- *Administrator.* Oversees the costs for the fund's overall operations, including rent and SEC compliance.

- *Attorney.* Prepares the many legal documents necessary to run a fund.

- *Transfer agent.* Maintains records of shareholder accounts.

KEY CONCEPT HOW A MUTUAL FUND WORKS

Suppose you invest $1,000 in a mutual fund. Let's take a look at what happens to your money.

We'll assume you're buying shares of the T. Rowe Price Growth and Income fund. T. Rowe Price receives your check, reviews your application, and deposits your check. Most funds credit your investment the day it's received, even though the check may take several days to clear. On this particular day, the fund's share price is $89.34 per share. Funds normally deal in round dollar amounts, not in round amounts of shares. So you now own 11.19320 shares of T. Rowe Price Growth and Income. Although some fund companies still issue actual share certificates, most simply enter your name in the shareholder database.

You are now a shareholder in T. Rowe Price Growth and Income, which is a corporation, just like IBM or General Motors. But unlike IBM, whose business is making computers, or GM, whose business is making automobiles, your fund's business is buying and selling stocks. You get a vote in the annual meeting for T. Rowe Price Growth and Income, and you're entitled to the fund's annual reports and semiannual updates.

Most important, you share in the fund's gains and losses. Every day, T. Rowe Price must total up Growth and Income's holdings, subtract any liabilities, and divide that by the number of shares outstanding. The result is the fund's *net asset value,* or share price. When the fund's holdings do well, the fund's price will rise. When the fund's holdings do poorly, the fund's price will fall.

On the day your money lands in Growth and Income, several things happen. First, the portfolio manager gets a report on the fund's holdings. She sees that the fund has received some new money from investors, and that it has also received a dividend payment from one of the fund's stocks. That's $1.2 million of new money.

Furthermore, she reads in *USA Today* that a company whose stocks she owns could report worse-than-expected earnings next quarter. So she decides to sell that stock. She gets $50,000 from the sale of the stock. All told, your manager now has $1,250,000 to invest.

If she found no stocks that she thought were worth buying, she wouldn't just leave the money in a non-interest-bearing checking account. Instead, she would invest the money in the money market: commercial paper, perhaps, or some jumbo bank CDs. It's always better to earn a little money than none at all. Because these investments are easily bought and sold, Wall Street calls them *cash* or *cash equivalents.*

Most managers don't like to park much money in cash, however. (Indeed, Jeff Vinik, a former manager of Fidelity Magellan, the nation's largest stock fund, was roundly criticized for keeping too much of the fund's assets in cash and bonds.) If the market is performing well, a cash-heavy portfolio won't perform as well as one that's 100 percent invested in stocks. And a stock-fund manager, after all, is paid to invest in stocks.

So on this particular day, your manager decides to buy $1,250,000 of BingCo common stock, issued by the popular yet fictional maker of high-performance ball bearings. Your $1,000 is part of that purchase. She writes up the buy order and gives it to her trader.

The trader sees that BingCo last sold for $45. The trader wants to buy the stock as cheaply as possible, so he puts out a bid for $44⅞. Unfortunately, the market is moving up. The best bid he can get for a block—10,000 shares—is $45⅛ from a brokerage house on the West Coast. He takes it. A few minutes later, 5,000 shares are offered at $45. He takes that, too. Later in the day, another block of BingCo is offered by another fund company in Colorado. The trader gets 10,000 shares at $44⅞. Finally, he fills the remainder of the order for $45 a share. Your $1,000 was part of that order.

At the end of the day, T. Rowe Price again tallies up the current market value of its holdings. Unfortunately, stock prices were off mildly this day. Growth and Income's assets are now worth $89.28 per share, a loss of 0.07 percent. Your $1,000 is now worth $999.22, a loss of 78 cents.

 FUNDS CHARGE ANNUAL FEES TO PAY COSTS

As mentioned earlier, mutual funds hire investment advisers to manage their portfolios. Funds incur other expenses as well, including rent, administrative costs, trustee fees, and so forth. To pay these expenses, funds take fees from the fund's assets.

The Securities and Exchange Commission makes funds display their fees on the first page of the prospectus—the legal document that spells out how the fund will operate. The *expense ratio* shows what percent of the fund's assets are taken to pay expenses. It can range from as low as zero percent for funds that temporarily waive fees to more than 2 percent. The average expense ratio for diversified U.S. stock funds is about 1.4 percent, according to Morningstar, the Chicago-based mutual fund trackers. The expense ratio for international stock funds is 2 percent; for government bond funds, 1.2 percent; for municipal bond funds, 1.1 percent.

The expense ratio doesn't include the commissions the fund pays to buy and sell securities. It also doesn't include commissions that investors pay to buy the fund from a broker or financial advisor. But it does show the fund's management and administrative fees, as well as its *12b-1 marketing fees*.

What are those? The name comes from the Securities and Exchange Commission rule that allows the fee. Essentially, a 12b-1 fee goes for advertising and distribution costs, which include advertising and, in many cases, paying the broker who sold you the fund. A 12b-1 fee can range from 0.25 to 1.0 percent.

Expenses are typically taken from a fund's income at regular intervals. All things being equal, it's always best to look for funds with the lowest expense ratios. Look at it this way: Over time, the stock market rises an average of 12 percent a year, if you include reinvested dividends. So a $10,000 investment, on average, should grow to about $300,000 in 30 years.

If you give 1.5 percentage points to your mutual fund's management—and it doesn't earn that money back through shrewd management—then you have lost a substantial amount of money. How much? Let's say you earn 10.5 percent on your $10,000 after expenses over 30 years. Your investment will grow to $200,000—$100,000 less than it would have at 12 percent.

Expenses are a crucial consideration for bond funds, too. For example, suppose the typical bond in your fund's portfolio has a yield of 5 percent—quite possible for a municipal bond fund. If your fund is taking 1.5 percentage points, it's taking 30 percent of your yield.

How can you find out about a fund's expenses? Simply look at the front of the fund's prospectus. The SEC makes funds publish a fee table at the front of the prospectus that spells out their expenses precisely.

BUYING AND SELLING MUTUAL FUNDS

You have two ways to buy mutual fund shares, both of which have advantages and disadvantages:

1. You can buy through a broker, who will generally charge you a commission, or *load,* in industry jargon. Loads can be as little as 1 percent of your fund purchase, or as much as 8.5 percent.
2. You can buy directly from the fund company. Typically, these funds have no sales fee. In industry jargon, these are *no-load* funds.

KEY CONCEPT

Buying through a Broker

For many years, most mutual funds were load funds. If you wanted one, you bought it through a broker—typically for an 8.5 percent load.

And, in fact, most mutual funds are still sold through a broker, although average commissions have fallen dramatically. The loads for bond funds typically range from 3 to 5 percent. The loads for stock funds range from about 4 to 5.75 percent. Of course, there are exceptions—both higher and lower.

For most load funds, you simply pay the commission on your purchase. This is called a *front-end load.* Although a front-end load is expressed as a percentage—a 5 percent load, for example— it's actually the difference between the *bid* price and the *offer* price. The bid price is what the fund company will pay for the shares you're selling. The asked price is what it will charge you to buy shares. The difference is the load. So if a fund has a $9.15 bid price and a $10.00 offer price, the load would be $0.85 per share, or 8.5 percent. On this particular fund, then, you'd pay $850 in commissions on a $10,000 purchase.

On no-load funds, there is no difference between the bid and asked prices.

In an effort to make sales charges more palatable, fund companies have rolled out different types of loads for the same funds. These are designated as different share classes, typically with a letter after the fund's name: Big Growth Fund A, Big Growth Fund B, and so on. Unfortunately, in their rush to make loads more acceptable, they have made the mutual fund universe excessively complicated. The basic share-class breakdown runs as follows:

- Class A shares have the traditional front-end load.

- Class B shares have no front-end load. Instead, they carry a 12b-1 marketing fee. They also carry a redemption charge, sometimes called a *back-end load.* Typically, the back-end load is 6 percent of the fund's assets the first year, 5 percent the second, and so on. The redemption charge usually vanishes after the sixth year, but the 12b-1 charge often lingers on. For this reason, it's typically better for long-term investors to shun B shares and buy A shares, even though they have front-end sales charges. Some funds will now convert B shares to A shares automatically after the redemption charge has vanished. Others don't. You should ask before you buy B shares.

- Class C shares are called *level-load* shares. These typically have no sales charge, but a high 12b-1 fee—sometimes as much as 1 percent a year.

- Class I shares are typically sold to institutions, such as pension or 401(k) plans.

To make matters more confusing, fund companies don't stick to the ABC nomenclature for share classes. Currently, funds offer share classes for nearly every letter of the alphabet. State Street Research, for example, offers A, B, C, and D share classes. Franklin offers I and II share classes. IDS offers A, B, and Y shares.

If you buy a fund with a letter designation, be sure to ask your broker to spell out the commission structure precisely. In the normal load structure, a broker gets the same commission no matter what type of share classes you buy. It's all a matter of how you decide to pay it.

And don't let anyone tell you a B share is no-load. It's not. And if you buy a load fund, you should be getting advice and guidance from your broker. If you're not, you're getting ripped off.

 No-loads Help You Save on Commissions

You buy no-load funds directly from the mutual fund company, so you pay no commission. That can be an enormous savings.

Let's say that you invest $10,000 in a bond mutual fund that charges a 4.5 percent load. Your bill for the bond fund is $450, so you now have $9,550 invested. To break even, you must earn 4.71 percent on your investment. For some bond funds, that's equal to an entire year's interest.

What's the catch? When you buy a no-load, you have to make your own decisions. If you choose a rotten fund, you have no one to blame. (On the other hand, if you choose a brilliant fund, you can lay claim to being a financial wizard.)

You Can Get in for as Little as $50

Most funds have a *minimum initial investment requirement;* That is, they want you to open your account with at least a certain amount of money. For the typical fund, the minimum initial requirement is $1,000 to $2,500. Many funds insist on higher minimums. To open an account at the Vanguard Index 500 Portfolio, you'll need to write a check for $3,000. A few funds require $5,000 or even $10,000 to get in. And institutional funds, which are sold to banks, pension funds, and other big-ticket customers, often require an initial investment of $100,000 or more.

Now, if $3,000 (or even $1,000) sounds too rich for your blood, don't despair. Many funds have significantly lower minimums for Individual Retirement Accounts (IRAs). That's because IRA money is stable, long-term money that often requires very little additional paperwork on the fund's part. A typical IRA minimum is just $500.

You say even $500 is too much? Well, many fund companies now offer automatic investment plans, which let you start with just $50 or $25—provided you allow the fund company to withdraw money from your bank account each month until you reach the fund's ordinary minimum. If you stop the program before you reach the fund's ordinary minimum, the fund has the right to sell your shares and return your money.

So if you're interested in a fund but don't think you have enough to invest, give the fund a call and ask if it has an automatic investment plan. The odds are good that it does.

Incidentally, broker-sold funds often have lower minimums than no-load funds. If you can find a broker who will deal with a small account—and that can be rare—you may be able to find a low-minimum fund through him or her. Of course, you'll have to pay the sales charge. But that's only fair.

Know How to Get Out

Mutual funds are exceptionally liquid—that is, you can convert them to cash quickly, often through a telephone call. But getting out easily means setting up your account properly in the first place.

When you fill out your application, the form will generally ask you if you want telephone switching privileges. This means that you can call your fund and ask them to sell shares of your bond fund and buy shares of another fund within the group of funds. If you don't check the box, you can't do it.

And even though telephone exchange privileges (*switching,* in the vernacular) are widespread, a few funds won't let you redeem shares unless you send them a letter telling them to do so. The Vanguard Index 500 fund, the nation's second-largest stock fund is, one such fund.) So if you think you might need to move money quickly, the time to ask about telephone exchange privileges is before you invest, not after.

If you think you will need the money in an emergency, then you should set up a money market mutual fund at the same time. You may have to invest the minimum in the fund to do so. That way, you can transfer money from your bond fund (or stock fund, for that matter), put it into your money fund, and write a check from your money fund.

You should also check to see if your fund will allow wire transfers directly to your bank. Many times, the fund will need to know your bank's routing number in order to complete the transfer. Sheldon Jacobs, editor of *The No-Load Mutual Fund Investor,* a newsletter, says it's best to give wire transfers a test run at the outset. Sell a small number of shares, instruct your fund to wire the proceeds to your bank account, and see if the money does indeed appear in your bank account. If not, call the fund representative and see what went wrong. It's better to find out before you really need the money.

 Listen to Facts, Not Myths

The debate between no-load and load funds is often acrimonious. First, let's dispel a few myths:

1. *There is no discernable difference in investment performance between load and no-load funds.*   No-load funds don't have better investment returns than load funds. By and large, the two groups have very similar performance. And

why shouldn't they? When you pay a load, the money doesn't go to investment research. It goes to the broker to pay him for his time and effort spent finding funds for you.

2. *There is no large difference between expense ratios at load and no-load funds.* Brokers will sometimes tell clients, "No-load funds aren't free. They have higher expense ratios to make up the difference. They just don't tell you about them." Baloney. No-load funds don't have brokers, so they don't have commissions. But otherwise, load and no-load fund expenses are very similar.

3. *No-load investors always buy at the top of the market, and always sell at the bottom.* In fact, unscrupulous brokers say that Peter Lynch, the superstar former manager of Fidelity Magellan, says most investors in his fund didn't make any money because they sold at the wrong time. There is some evidence that no-load investors trade their holdings more rapidly than load investors. This makes a degree of sense, since load fund investors have to pay another commission to buy a new fund. Whether investment advisers are savvier about moving in and out of the market than individuals is rather debatable. One thing that's not debatable: Peter Lynch never claimed that most investors lost money during his 13-year tenure as manager of Magellan. It's a myth, pure and simple, but unscrupulous people love to repeat it.

4. *Only dummies buy load funds.* Not at all. It's extremely reasonable to seek expert advice on investments, just as you would for legal or medical matters. And many no-load funds are sold through financial advisers who charge a flat fee for their services, rather than a commission. Anyway, if you get advice, you should pay the advisor, and that's what loads are for.

5. *Running your own finances is like performing your own brain surgery.* Well, no. It's quite reasonable for an average person to run his or her own financial affairs. Personal finance isn't brain surgery. But if you think your time is better spent elsewhere, that's a valid point, too.

A Third Route: Mutual Fund Supermarkets

Not too long ago, managing a portfolio of no-load mutual funds could be like administering a small army unit. For example, suppose you owned a Kemper Scudder bond fund, a Fidelity stock fund, and a Dreyfus money market fund. If you wanted to move money from your bond fund to your money market fund, you would have to call Scudder, sell your shares, have the check sent to your bank, wait for the check to clear, and write a check to Dreyfus. (You could probably have the money wired to your bank if you were in a real hurry.) Yeesh.

Fortunately, you can now buy and sell many no-load mutual funds through mutual fund supermarkets—discount brokerage accounts that charge no fee for buying and selling no-loads. All your fund shares will stay on one statement, and you can call just one company when you want to move your holdings around.

Charles Schwab & Co. has one of the largest and best-known no-load mutual fund marketplaces. Its OneSource program offers more than 800 no-load funds. Schwab's archrival, Fidelity Investments, has a similar program called Funds-Network. Other fund supermarkets are offered by discount broker Jack White, American Express, NationsBank, Scudder Investments, Waterhouse Investments, Quick & Reilly, Bear Stearns, Wheat First Butcher Singer, and Smith Barney.

What are the drawbacks?

- Not all funds are available for no fee through the supermarkets. Vanguard funds, for example, aren't available through the Schwab One-Source program You have to pay a $29 commission to buy Vanguard funds through Schwab.

- Most funds that belong to mutual fund supermarkets have slightly higher expense ratios than funds that don't. So you pay for the convenience of mutual fund supermarkets, even if you don't use them.

Most supermarkets will let you buy funds that aren't part of the no-transaction-fee (NTF) deal. But you'll have to pay a commission to buy and sell the funds.

Most supermarkets will charge a penalty if you switch between funds too frequently. Charles

Major Mutual Fund Marketplaces

- *Accutrade.* 800-882-4887. Number of funds: 6,035. NTF funds: 4,150. Minimum transaction fee for funds not in the NTF program: $27.

- *American Express Financial Direct.* 800-297-8800. Number of funds: 200. NTF funds: 200. Minimum transaction fee for funds not in the NTF program: $27.

- *Fidelity FundsNetwork.* 800-544-9697. Number of funds: 3,400. NTF funds: 820. Minimum transaction fee for funds not in the FundsNetwork program: $25.

- *Jack White No Fee Network.* 800-233-3411. Number of funds: 5,900. NTF funds: 1,200. Minimum transaction fee for funds not in the NTF program: $27.

- *Muriel Siebert.* 800-872-0666. Number of funds: 5,500. NTF funds: 660. Minimum transaction fee for funds not in the NTF program: $39.50.

- *NationsBank.* 800-926-1111. Number of funds: 4,000. NTF funds: 350. Minimum transaction fee for funds not in the NTF program: $40.

- *Quick & Reilly.* 800-837-7220. Number of funds: 2,100. NTF funds: 300. Minimum transaction fee for funds not in the NTF program: $25.

- *Schwab OneSource.* 800-435-4000. Number of funds: 2,500. No transaction fee (NTF) funds: 900. Minimum transaction fee for funds not in the OneSource program: $39.

- *Scudder.* 800-700-0820. Number of funds: 6,260. NTF funds: 530. Minimum transaction fee for funds not in the NTF program: $35.

- *Waterhouse Investors.* 800-934-4443. Number of funds: 4,250. NTF funds: 840. Minimum transaction fee for funds not in the NTF program: $25.

- *Wheat First Butcher Singer.* 800-999-4328. Number of funds: 1,400. NTF funds: 1,400. Minimum transaction fee for funds not in the NTF program: none.

Schwab & Co., for example, will slap you with a $39 transaction fee if you trade your fund within 90 days after you buy it. And big, frequent traders are sometimes sent packing.

 You Can Get Funds and Advice from Financial Planners

Brokers aren't the only ones who will choose mutual funds for you. You can also see a financial planner. The best financial planners look closely at your entire financial picture—your debts, your assets, your goals, and your risk tolerance—and find investments that suit you. The worst financial planners are simply brokers whose main objective is to sell you as many funds from their affiliated brokerage as possible.

To make matters more difficult, the financial planning community makes the Balkans look like a model of solidarity. Planners come from all different backgrounds. Some begin as certified public accountants (CPAs) and then go into financial planning. Some start with special financial planning courses. Others start from the life insurance industry.

Here's a quick rundown on the different financial planning designations:

- *Certified Financial Planner (CFP).* This is one of the most common designations for financial planners. The CFP mark (a registered trademark) is given only to those who have passed a 10-hour exam, which is administered by a special CFP Board of Standards. Those who have the CFP designation have to complete 30 hours of training every 2 years to keep the CFP mark.

- *Certified Financial Analyst (CFA).* This is a much more advanced degree than a CFP. People with a CFA have passed rigorous tests administered by the Association for Investment Management and Research (AIMR). They must also have several years of professional experience. Most mutual fund managers and Wall Street analysts are CFAs.

- *Certified Fund Specialist (CFS).* This is a relatively new designation. A person with a CFS must pass a 60-hour course and exam on mutual funds sponsored by the Institute of Certified Fund Specialists. In most cases, you would want someone who had additional professional designations.

- *Chartered Life Underwriter (CLU).* This is a life insurance agent. To get the CLU, he or she must have 3 years' experience and have passed 10 college-level courses on life insurance and financial planning. An agent who completes three more courses can become a Chartered Financial Consultant (ChFC), which is the life insurance industry's version of a CFP. Expect someone with a ChFC to emphasize life insurance when they make your financial plan.

- *Chartered Mutual Fund Consultant (CMFC).* This is a degree in mutual funds, not financial planning. A person with a CMFC has completed a self-study program sponsored by the National Endowment for Financial Education and the Investment Company Institute, the mutual fund industry's trade group. In most cases, you would want a planner with additional certifications.

- *Certified Public Accountant (CPA).* Has passed a national uniform exam for accountants, completed educational courses, and received approval from the state's accounting board. A growing number of CPAs are taking the Personal Financial Specialist (PFS) designation, which means they have passed a personal finance exam sponsored by the American Institute of CPAs. And some CPAs are also Enrolled Agents (EAs), who are entitled to practice before the IRS. To be an EA, they must pass a special test on tax law.

Almost as important as a planner's professional designation, however, is how a planner gets paid. Some planners work on commissions, just like brokers do. Some charge a flat fee. Others charge a fee for their plan, and a commission for the investments they sell.

Fee-only planners typically use no-load mutual funds. They don't take commissions, so there's no reason for them to buy load funds. (Some planners with very large practices can get into load funds without paying the commission, but they are rare.) Many fee-only planners either charge an hourly rate or a percentage of your assets for their services.

Which is better? Planners who take commissions have an incentive to favor funds with higher sales charges. There are many fine funds with high sales charges, but as a financial consumer, you should be more concerned with the best deals for you, not for your financial planner. But a fee-only planner with a 2 percent fee isn't doing you any favors, either: Over the long run, the planner's fees plus the fund's fees can cost as much as paying commissions—or more.

So how do you find a planner? Hit the phones. All the different types of planners have professional organizations that will help you find planners in your area. Some organizations to call are the following:

- The *International Association for Financial Planning,* a trade group for the entire financial planning community, will send you a list of planners in your area. They also have excellent materials on choosing and evaluating a planner. 800-945-4237.

- The *National Association of Personal Financial Advisors,* a trade group for fee-only planners, will provide names of fee-only planners in your area. 888-333-6659.

- The *Institute of Certified Financial Planners* will give you a list of CFPs in your area. They will also verify if a planner really is a CFP. Call 800-282-7526 for the list; call the CFP board at 888-237-6275 to verify a planner's right to hold a CFP designation.

- The *American Institute of Certified Public Accountants* will send you a list of CFPs who are financial planners, too. 800-862-4272

Once you have a list (or two) of planners, start asking questions. Ask for referrals and a sample financial plan they have done for someone else. Most important, ask exactly how they will be paid.

Finally, be suspicious. Don't let anyone have discretionary power over your investments. (That means they can move your money around without asking your permission.) And check their background thoroughly. Start by calling the National Association of Securities Dealers (800-289-9999) to see if they have had any disciplinary action taken against them. Then call your state securities commissioner to check a planner's licenses. If you don't know the number, call the North American Securities Administration Association at 202-737-0900. The Securities and Exchange Commission (800-732-0330) can tell you if your planner is a registered investment adviser.

KEY CONCEPT

MUTUAL FUND TAXES

The tax code lets mutual funds pass their tax liability on to shareholders. That way, the fund doesn't get taxed on its trades. That's good.

Unfortunately, you do. That's bad.

You can owe taxes on your fund in several ways. The first is through income and dividend distributions.

When a fund receives income from a money market investment or a bond interest payment, it must pay out that distribution to shareholders. That income is taxable to you at the same rate you pay taxes on your salary. The maximum federal income tax is currently 39.6 percent.

Similarly, when funds receive a dividend payment from a stock, they must pass that income on to shareholders, too. Dividend income is also taxable at your current tax rate.

Funds must also pass on their accumulated capital gains—the profits from buying and selling securities—to you. The current tax rates on capital gains are as follows:

- *Short-term.* Gains on assets held for more than a year but less than 18 months—15 percent for those in the 15 percent tax bracket, 28 percent for all others

- *Long-term.* Gains on assets held for more than 18 months—10 percent for those in the 15 percent tax bracket, 20 percent for all others.

Your fund will tell you how much of your capital gains distribution is long-term or short-term for tax purposes.

Most funds have capital gains distributions once a year, typically in November or December. Stock funds will usually make their interest and dividend distributions at the same time.

Many new shareholders become alarmed at distribution season because a fund's share price drops dramatically when it makes its distribution. Suppose the Bullmoose fund has a share price of $25 per share. It makes a capital gains distribution of $3 per share and an income distribution of $2 per share. You own 1,000 shares, for a total account value of $25,000.

The day the Bullmoose fund makes its distribution, its share price will drop $5 a share. Your account will look like the following:

1,000 shares of Bullmoose at $20 per share	$20,000
Capital gains distribution	3,000
Dividend distribution	2,000
Total value	$25,000

In short, you still have $25,000. But $5,000 has become taxable.

Funds that pay distributions monthly, such as bond funds, also drop in price when they pay their distributions. The drop is typically smaller than when stock funds pay their annual distributions, however.

 Minimize Taxes with Tax-Deferred Savings

If you're saving for retirement, don't put a penny in a taxable mutual fund account until you have filled all your tax-deferred retirement options. Tax-deferred earnings can build up incredibly quickly.

Your 401(k) corporate savings plan should be your first target. These plans let you put up to $10,000 per year in tax year 1998 into a tax-deferred account, although companies may limit how much you can contribute. Best of all, many companies will match part of your contribution. Free money, in investing, is nearly always a good thing, and for that reason you should invest in a 401(k) first, even if the funds your company offers are mediocre.

If you have additional money you can save, your fund company will be happy to help you open an Individual Retirement Account. You have two choices: the traditional IRA and the Roth IRA. Individuals can contribute a maximum $2,000 of earned income in any combination to a Roth or a traditional IRA. Couples can contribute $4,000. The difference is as follows:

- In some cases, you can deduct your contributions to traditional IRAs. If you are covered by a retirement plan at work and your modified adjusted gross income is less than $25,000 (for singles) and less than $40,000 (for couples), you can deduct your full IRA contribution. If you have no retirement plan at work, you can take the full deduction, no matter what your income. In any event, your earnings are tax deferred until you take withdrawals. In most cases, you have to pay a 10 percent tax penalty, plus income taxes, on any amount you withdraw before age 59½.

- Roth IRAs, named after the Republican senator from Delaware, are never deductible. But all the money is tax-free when you withdraw it. Couples must have an adjusted gross income (AGI) less than $150,000 to contribute the full $2,000 to a Roth IRA. Singles must have less than $95,000 AGI. You can withdraw money without penalty or taxes after 5 years if you are older than 59½, disabled, or making a first-time home purchase. Otherwise, you'll owe the 10 percent penalty, as well as income taxes, on the amount you withdraw.

Which is better? Unless you plan to be in a significantly lower tax bracket when you retire, you're generally better off in a Roth IRA. And the simplicity of the Roth has its own charms, particularly at withdrawal.

Variable Annuities Can Reduce Taxes—but Watch Fees

Variable annuities are a great way to save for retirement. For some people. Sometimes.

Variable annuities let you invest in mutual funds and defer taxes on your earnings, just like an IRA. As with an IRA, you pay a 10 percent tax penalty if you withdraw money before age 59½.

But unlike regular annuities, which give a lifelong set income, variable annuities don't promise a set payoff. Instead, what you get depends on how well your funds perform.

One big difference: If you die, your beneficiaries are guaranteed to get at least the principal you've invested, minus any withdrawals. If the market value of the account is greater than your contributions, your beneficiaries get that.

Most annuities don't require you take distributions before age 85. You can choose several options for taking withdrawals, as follows:

- *Lump sum.* You take your money all at once.
- *Systematic withdrawal.* You take a set amount regularly until your money is gone.
- *Annuitization.* You get a set amount for life. If your money runs out before you die, you still get paid. If you die before your money runs out, or before a minimum guarantee period, your beneficiaries get nothing.

So what are the drawbacks? In a word, *fees.* You will have to pay the following fees:

- *Insurance fees.* To pay for the guarantee of your principal, variable annuities charge annual mortality and expense fees.
- *Management fees.* The funds within the annuity charge management fees, just as mutual funds do.
- *Contract fees.* Many companies charge $25 to $40 a year for serving your account.
- *Surrender fees.* If you move your money to another policy, or withdraw money early, most annuities hit you with surrender fees of up to 10 percent of the amount you withdraw. That's on top of the 10 percent tax penalty you pay on money you withdraw before age 59½.

If you have contributed the maximum to your 401(k) plan, and filled up your IRAs, too, then consider an annuity. Be sure to see how many investment options you're offered—don't settle for less than eight—and exactly how much you'll be charged in fees. Insist on seeing how well the funds have performed versus other funds with similar objectives.

 **HAVE YOUR INCOME AND DIVIDENDS REINVESTED**

Most funds will ask you if you want your dividends and gains reinvested automatically. Unless you really need the income, you should do so. Over time, reinvested dividends and gains make a huge difference in your overall returns.

Consider the Vanguard Index 500 Trust, the nation's second-largest stock mutual fund. If you had invested $10,000 in the fund in October 1982, your investment would have grown to $119,622 in 15 years, according to Morningstar. Had you not reinvested your capital gains and dividends, however, your account would have been $55,782 after 15 years.

Why the big difference? Dividends and gains compound over time, which can turbocharge your growth. Typically, a third to a half of all the gains from the stock market come from dividends. And nearly all the long-term growth from the bond market comes from reinvested interest.

 CLOSED-END VERSUS OPEN-END MUTUAL FUNDS

Mutual funds come in two varieties: open-end and closed-end.

Most mutual funds are *open-end funds:* They continually issue new shares and redeem old ones. When you invest in an open-end fund, the fund creates new shares for you.

Closed-end funds are the oldest variety of mutual fund, although they are much less common now. A closed-end fund, like any other company, issues a set amount of stock, which is traded on the stock exchanges. It uses the money it receives from the sale of the stock to buy and sell stocks and bonds.

Every day, the fund will calculate its *net asset value* (NAV); that is, the value of its holdings divided by the number of shares outstanding. (Funds rarely have much debt, but any debts are subtracted from the value of its holdings; hence the *net* in net asset value.) Suppose a fund had $10 million in assets, and 1,234,500 shares outstanding. Its NAV would be $8.10 per share.

Perversely, a closed-end fund's share price rarely matches its NAV. Most closed-end funds sell at less than their NAV, or a *discount.* Sometimes they sell for more than their NAV, or a *premium.*

Academicians wrangle over why a fund whose NAV is $8.10 should sell for $7.98 or $10.25. The most common explanation for a discount is that investors figure that the fund will never liquidate and deliver that $8.10 to shareholders. So they are only willing to pay less than the fund's NAV. Premiums typically happen when a closed-end fund is the only way to invest in a particular arena, such as a small, developing foreign stock market.

The more likely explanation is this: Closed-end funds are somewhat of a backwater in the stock market, and most investors pay little attention to them. So their shares are often mispriced.

Some funds eliminate the discount by transforming themselves into open-end funds. For example, Stratton Monthly Dividend was a closed-end fund until 1981. Spectra was a closed-end fund until 1996. A fund has to get permission from its board of directors to become open-ended. But when it does, the fund's discount quickly disappears.

Funds can also liquidate themselves to eliminate the discount. Some closed-end funds, in an effort to keep their discounts low, determine the liquidation date when the fund is started.

Why are open-end funds so much more popular than closed-end funds? Open-end funds have no pesky discounts or premiums to worry about. The disadvantage of open-end funds: When investors want their money back, the manager has to sell securities from the fund to pay them. Closed-end fund managers don't have to worry about shareholder redemptions.

 NEVER BUY A CLOSED-END FUND AT A PREMIUM

One of the worst mistakes you can make in investing is to pay too much for something. A closed-end fund that has a premium is, by definition, selling for more than it is worth.

Why would you buy a closed-end fund that's selling for more than the value of its holdings? A couple of reasons.

- *An investment fad.* Every so often, investors get swept away by the potential of a particular investment area. In 1989, for example, the collapse of the Berlin Wall was hailed as an exciting investment opportunity. Closed-end funds that specialized in Germany soared. But two things happened. First, Wall Street rolled out several new closed-end Germany funds, making it unnecessary to pay a premium for existing closed-end Germany funds. Second, investors eventually realized that the payoff for the collapse of Communism would be a long time coming.

- *A new offering.* New closed-end funds often sell for a premium as brokers busily sell them to all and sundry. Almost invariably, the funds fall back to a discount within a few months.

A better strategy is to look for closed-end funds selling at large discounts—and whose discounts are narrowing. To find a fund's discount or premium, pick up a copy of *Barron's,* which has extensive listings of closed-end funds. You can also get closed-end information through Morningstar, the Chicago mutual fund trackers. Its website (http://www.morningstar.net) has monthly information on closed-end funds.

UNIT INVESTMENT TRUSTS (UITs) OFFER DIVERSIFICATION, BUT NO MANAGEMENT

Like mutual funds, unit investment trusts (UITs) are a portfolio of bonds or stocks. But they are a sort of fire-and-forget investment. There's no fund manager. Once the portfolio is formed, it stays the same. During the life of the UIT, you get regular checks for interest or dividends. When the UITs mature, the trustee returns your principal. But the company that forms the UIT—called the *sponsor*—will monitor the portfolio. If one of the UIT's investments is likely to go belly up, the trustee will sell the investment from the trust and return the proceeds to investors.

Most UITs are bond or tax-free muni bond UITs, geared toward investors who want income. The majority are created by big brokerage houses, such as Merrill Lynch and Dean Witter, or by investment management companies, such as John Nuveen and Van Kampen American. Although you can buy intermediate-term bond unit trusts, which mature in 5 to 7 years, most bond UITs mature in 10 to 30 years. Stock UITs typically mature in 1 to 5 years.

Since they are broker-sold, they carry sales charges, or loads. The average stock UIT has a 1 percent upfront sales charge and a 1.75 percent sales charge taken out during the trust's lifetime. Bond UITs typically have up-front loads of 4.5 to 5 percent.

Why buy a UIT?

UITs: Barking with the Dogs

If you like the *Dogs of the Dow* strategy mentioned in Chapter 3, then your broker really has a deal for you.

The Dogs of the Dow are the hottest-selling unit trust at many brokerages. Merrill Lynch was the first to roll out a Dow dogs unit trust, and it is still Merrill's best-selling stock unit trust. Spurred by Merrill's success, firms now are starting unit trusts using the same approach with different indexes and even different stock theories.

You can buy several Dogs of the Dow UITs. Now brokerage firms also are introducing variations on the theme, as follows:

Name	Sponsor	Description
SPOT	Van Kampen American	50 high-yielding stocks from the MorganStanley Capital International USA Index.
Select S&P	Merrill Lynch Industrial Portfolio	15 high-yielding stocks from the Standard & Poor's 500, screened for size and quality.
S&P Quality Equity Portfolio	Nuveen	20 stocks screened for investment quality and stock repurchases by Standard & Poor's.
Strategic 15 & 30 Trust	Van Kampen American	20 highest-yielding stocks of the Dow, Hang Seng, and Financial Times indexes.

Source: *USA Today.*

- *Cost.* You can often buy UIT shares, called *units,* for as little as $100. Their annual fees tend to be far less than those of actively managed open-end funds.
- *Reliability.* If you're an income investor, UITs offer steady yields. Unlike a bond mutual fund, whose interest payments vary, a bond UIT will give you the same interest payment year in and year out—important for people who want a reliable stream of income.
- *Diversification.* Individual bonds can be risky because the issuer can default. But a UIT holds

several securities. So if one defaults, its other
holdings should cushion the blow. Similarly, it's
better to hold a dozen or so stocks than just
one.

- *Discounts.* If you buy your UIT in the secondary market—that is, after its initial public
offering—you can save the money you would
ordinarily give to your broker.

END POINT

Are mutual funds for everyone? Of course not.
Exceptionally wealthy people can live quite comfortably off the interest from municipal bonds.
Very conservative investors may want only federally insured deposits. And those with a more speculative nature may be better served with futures
and options.

For the vast majority of investors, however,
mutual funds are a fine way to save and invest.
Many people can't afford to hire a private money
manager, or even a financial planner. Others simply don't want to spend the time picking individual
stocks and bonds for a portfolio. For those people,
mutual funds are an excellent way to get a diversified portfolio of securities, managed by some of
the best talent Wall Street has to offer.

5

Bond Mutual Funds

If you have read Chapter 2, you're probably all ready to wade into the bond market. You have your calculator ready so you can figure out a bond's yield to maturity. You have spent hours poring over credit reports, searching for a bond that's underpriced relative to its potential to increase its financial health. And you've got a laddered portfolio of bonds of different maturities all ready to go. Now all you need to do is call your broker and check the current bid/asked spreads, right?

No?

You say you have to mow the lawn and fix the roof? You say the kids need to be driven to baseball practice, and your boss makes you work until 8:00 every night? You say you'd rather train rabid ferrets to fetch the newspaper than study bond credit ratings?

Well, cheer up. If you need to invest in bonds, you can get someone else to do the legwork for you: Invest in a bond mutual fund. You'll get a slice of a diversified, professionally managed bond portfolio. You'll be able to buy or sell shares almost any time. And you'll be free to spend your spare time doing the things you want to do, instead of reading about bonds.

The one catch: You have to pick a bond fund that suits your needs. It takes some looking. But it's a lot easier than managing your own bond portfolio.

WHY BOND FUNDS?

You'll probably never hear people talk about bond funds around the water cooler, or at the dinner table, even though more than $700 billion is invested in them. Bond funds, sadly, are just nerds when compared to their more glamorous cousins, stock funds.

Nevertheless, bond funds can be good for you. They can:

- *Protect you against some of the stock market's tumbles.* Let's say you had $100,000 in an average growth stock fund on September 30, 1987. Three months later, your $100,000 would have been worth $78,570. Had you put $70,000 in a stock fund and $30,000 in a government securities fund, however, you would have seen your account fall to $86,589—still a loss, but considerably less than if you had been entirely in a growth fund.

- *Be an important source of investment income.* Throughout most of the stock market's history, the rule of thumb was this: Buy stocks when their dividend yields are greater than the yields on long-term bonds. For much of modern history, a stock's dividend yield was a huge part of returns. Recently, however, dividend payouts have dwindled as companies have focused on pushing their stock prices up. Bond yields are still healthy by comparison, however. So if you need to get income from your portfolio, a bond fund is a good place to look.

- *Provide above-average returns for intermediate-term goals.* You should never invest in the stock market if you don't have the time to make up for losses. If your child is going to college in three years, for example, you don't want to put the tuition money at risk. Bonds can provide better returns than money market funds or bank CDs with less risk than stock funds.

You might not expect a great deal of complexity among bond fund offerings. But Morningstar, the Chicago-based mutual fund trackers, counted 3,700 bond funds in August 1997. That number is certain to grow in coming years.

Obviously, not all bond funds are alike. In order for investors to choose between apple and apples (as opposed to, say, apples and weasels), such fund trackers as Lipper Analytical Services or Morningstar classify funds in one of two ways:

1. By *investment objective*—that is, what the funds say they plan to do. For example, a fund that restricts its investments to AAA-rated corporate bonds would be compared with other funds that invest in AAA-rated corporate bonds.

2. By *portfolio composition*—that is, what funds actually do. For example, Morningstar also ranks bond funds by credit quality and average maturity. So if you're thinking of investing in a fund that invests in short-term municipal bonds, you can compare its performance with other short-term municipal bonds.

Both approaches have merit. Most fund trackers rank funds by investment objective, however, and that's how it will be done here.

Total Return Tells the Total Story

Most people who invest in bond funds are looking for income—a regular series of dividends or interest from their funds. So they buy the funds with the highest yield, or the best yield compared with bank CDs or money market accounts. But that's a terrible way to look for a bond fund.

Instead, you should look at total return—the amount of money you get from a fund's price appreciation, capital gains distributions, and income distributions. For example, suppose you bought your fund at $10 a share. Over the course of the year, the fund paid you $0.51 per share in income, or 5.1 percent. That's nothing to get excited about. But during the course of the year, the fund's share price also rose to $10.50. So your total return—share price plus appreciation—was $1.01, or 10.01 percent. Not bad.

Similarly, suppose your fund had started the year at $10 and paid out $0.95 a share—9.5 percent. Pretty good, eh? But not if the share price fell to $9.50. Then your total return would have been $0.45 a share, or 4.5 percent. Three other things you should know about total return:

1. Total return figures assume that you're reinvesting your dividends and interest in the fund, which is what most investors do. So the total return figure also reflects the power of compounding.

2. Total returns show what you get after the fund has paid expenses. So you don't have to subtract out the fund's expenses from what you see published.

3. Total return figures don't include sales commissions or taxes. So if you're investing through a broker, or investing in a taxable account, your actual returns will be lower than the returns you see published in the newspaper.

 Annualized Returns Can Be Misleading

As if that weren't confusing enough, you can also look at total return in two different ways: cumulative or annualized. A *cumulative* return shows how much an investment has grown over the entire period of time being measured. For example, the average fund that invested in corporate bonds with an A rating or better from Standard & Poor's returned a total of 43.59 percent over the five years that ended November 30, 1997. Put another way, $10,000 invested in the average high-quality corporate bond fund grew to $14,359 over that period, assuming dividends and gains were reinvested.

The *annualized* return expresses the same amount of total return, but shows it as an annual percentage rate, much like a bank CD. In the preceding example, we would say that the high-quality bond funds returned an average 7.5 percent a year for 5 years.

Which is better? Probably cumulative. People tend to associate annual yields with investments that offer guaranteed results—and bond funds certainly don't do that. Also, annualized returns tend to mask the results of long-term poor performance. After all, a 10 percent return from a stock fund over the past 10 years sounds fairly good, right? But that's actually 2 percentage points lower than the stock market's historic average over the past 50 years.

 Performance Figures Can Help You Choose a Fund

Turn the pages of any newspaper or magazine, and you'll find a fund that's touting its performance over the past 1, 3, 5, 10, or 15 years. They can't advertise that record if they haven't earned it. But it's the wrong place to start looking when you're evaluating a fund.

You must first decide if the overall risks and rewards of a particular type of fund suits your goals and your overall investment temperament. If you're saving for the down payment for a house next year, you shouldn't be in any investment where there's any risk of losing money. You won't have time to make up your loss.

Similarly, if you're saving for a long-term goal, such as retirement, you should take some risks. Risky investments offer the chance to earn big returns. And if you're wrong, well, you have plenty of time to make up for your mistakes.

So when you are looking for investments, you first need to see if the investment offers the kind of returns that will get you to your goals. And you also need to make sure that the investment's risks won't keep you up and staring at the ceiling all night.

Your best way to do this is to look at the investment's average performance over time. True, anything can happen in the future, and past performance doesn't guarantee future returns, as the good people at the Securities and Exchange Commission will remind you. But over the long term, past performance can give you some idea of how an investment has done in various market conditions.

Of course, many people would rather do anything than spend a few hours looking at averages and percentages. And there's no need to spend a lot of time doing so. But you should at least be familiar with a fund's category's overall risks and returns. And past performance is the best measure we have.

So for each of the major bond fund categories, certain bits of data will be presented that will help you decide whether the type of fund is suitable for you. The data shows how the average fund has performed over time. We'll start with government securities funds. But first, let's take a look at what government securities funds are.

 GOVERNMENT BOND FUNDS ARE GREAT—BUT NOT GUARANTEED

Government bond funds are the vanilla ice cream of the bond fund world.

A government bond fund invests in a wide range of government securities—Treasury notes and bonds, agency obligations, and mortgage-backed securities. (Typically, there's a limit on what percentage of a government bond fund's portfolio can be in mortgage-backed obligations; otherwise, it would be considered a mortgage fund.)

Because government bonds have very little credit risk, the managers can't boost the fund's yield by buying lower-quality (but higher-yielding) bonds. True, they can buy bonds issued by agencies of the government that don't carry the Treasury's prestigious full faith and credit guarantee. That will push yields up a bit, but not a lot.

Instead, government bond fund managers typically try to play the maturity game. They buy long-term bonds when they think interest rates will fall. That way, they can lock in current high rates for the long term. And, as was noted in Chapter 2, long-term bond prices rise when interest rates fall.

Similarly, if they think interest rates will rise, they buy short-term bonds in the hope of reinvesting money at progressively higher rates. And short-term bond prices don't get clobbered as badly as long-term bond prices when interest rates rise.

As you might expect, government securities funds offer higher returns than money market funds over time, at the expense of higher short-term risk. Over the 10 years that ended September 30, 1997, a $10,000 investment in the average government bond fund would have grown to $21,272, versus $17,067 for the same amount invested in a government-only money market mutual fund, according to Lipper Analytical Services, which tracks the funds.

But government bond funds would have had several losing quarters. After all, the funds themselves are not guaranteed against loss, even though they invest in highly creditworthy bonds. As the price of the fund's holdings rise and fall, so will the fund's share price. The average government bond fund fell 3.14 percent over the three months that ended March 1994, for example. So don't think that because the fund invests in extremely safe investments that the fund itself is bulletproof.

What the Past Can Tell You about Government Bond Funds

Here's where the historical data comes in. But don't worry. We'll walk through it.

Figure 5.1 shows a broad overview of how government securities have fared over the past 25, 15, 10, and 5 years. Use the 25-year averages with several grains of salt—a block, in fact. Only a few bond funds have 25-year records, so a category's 25-year average may consist of just 1 or 2 funds. When this data is presented for other types of funds, you may see *NA* in the 25-year category. That means the category doesn't have a record for the particular period in question, so *NA*—not available—is listed in the table.

The Recent Past Can Be Misleading

As you can see from Figure 5.1, the average government bond fund earned 252 percent over the past 15 years, or about 8.7 percent a year. Now suppose you wanted to buy a retirement home in 15 years. Should you assume that you will earn 8.7 percent a year in a government bond fund? Or suppose you wanted to buy a car in five years. Should you assume that you will earn 6.43 percent a year?

Not necessarily. Sometimes, recent market conditions can skew the picture of a fund group's long-term performance. For example, in the five years that ended in 1997, interest rates were generally falling—a great time for bond prices, although a pretty skimpy time for yields. As an investor, you want to know whether recent history is typical for this kind of investment. If recent returns are low compared with typical returns, this may be a good time to buy government bonds.

Type	25 years	15 years	10 years	5 years
Cumulative, %	753.4	251.78	114.67	36.75
Annualized, %	8.95	8.7	7.9	6.43

SOURCE: Lipper Analytical Services, Inc.

FIGURE 5.1 *Cumulative and annualized returns of government bond funds.*

If recent returns are high, it may not be such a good time.

To get a better idea of a fund's typical 5-year performance, every 5-year period for 25 years was reviewed, at 3-month intervals. In other words, the 5-year period that ended November 30, 1996, was looked at, the 5-year period that ended February 28, 1997, and so on. The median 5-year period—half were higher, half lower—is probably the most typical 5-year return for the funds. To give some idea of the range of 5-year returns, the best and worst 5-year periods were also included.

Naturally, it's quite possible that government securities funds will do better or worse than their median 5-year periods. But looking at highs and lows gives you some idea of the potential risks and rewards over a 5-year period.

As you can see from Figure 5.2, government funds struggled during the period that ended February 28, 1982. That 5-year period was utterly wretched for the bond market. The yield on the benchmark 30-year Treasury bond soared from an average 7.75 percent in 1977 to an average 12.76 percent in 1982. Bond prices plunged. The only saving grace: Yields were so high that they offset the funds' considerable principal losses.

So Figure 5.2 shows us that the 37 percent performance from the typical government bond fund is on the low end of the spectrum. We can't be sure, but expecting a somewhat higher return could be more in line with reality.

Look at Three-Month Performance to Check Volatility

Suppose you're certain that the Great Gods of Investment have cursed you. You know that as soon as you invest, the market will go south. Just how good or bad can short-term performance be

Type	5 years ending	Gain or loss, %
Best	August 1986	119
Worst	February 1982	30
Median		53

SOURCE: *Lipper Analytical Services, Inc.*

FIGURE 5.2 *Best, worst, and median five-year performance.*

Type	3 months ending	Gain or loss, %
Best	August 1974	16.1
Worst	February 1975	−11.39
Median		1.88

SOURCE: *Lipper Analytical Services, Inc.*

FIGURE 5.3 *Best, worst, and median short-term performance.*

in a government bond fund? The numbers in Figure 5.3 will tell you what it was like over the fund group's best and worst quarters. If short-term performance like this would give you the whim-whams, then you shouldn't invest in this type of fund.

As you can see, bond funds have far bigger ups and downs over the short term than they do over the long term. (This is true for most investments, incidentally.) And the most volatile periods were in the 1970s, when interest rates soared and plunged with sickening regularity.

Government securities funds are popular because they have very little credit risk and they sport yields comparable with 10-year Treasury notes. If you're looking for a middle-of-the-road bond fund with few ugly surprises, a government securities fund is one way to go. But don't forget that their short-term performance can be volatile.

 Buy a Top-Performing Fund

Any number of factors can send a fund's performance spiraling. The fund's expenses can be too high. It can take in too much money and not be able to invest it effectively. Or the manager can simply stop investing well. A fund with good performance today may not be tomorrow's top-performing fund.

On the other hand, a rotten fund tends to stay rotten. While a good fund may not stay good, you can bet a poor fund will stay poor. So it makes sense to look for the best-performing funds.

A fund's five-year performance is a decent place to start your examination. It's particularly good for bond funds, because 1994 was a bear market year in the bond market. A fund that can do well in bull and bear markets is probably a good fund. The government bond funds with the best five-year records are shown in the Stellar Performers sidebar.

Because government securities funds are a sturdy and popular type of bond fund, their returns are used here as a benchmark. In the following pages, you will see returns from various types of bond funds. You will also see the returns from government securities funds, so you can compare the two types of funds.

Ginnie Mae Funds

Government securities funds aren't the only funds that invest mainly in government-issued debt. Government National Mortgage Association (GNMA) funds, popularly called Ginnie Mae funds, invest in government-backed mortgages and are some of the most popular bond funds around.

If ever there was an investment that was tailor-made for a mutual fund, it's Ginnie Maes. As you will recall from Chapter 2, Ginnie Mae securities are actually bundles of mortgages insured by the Federal Housing Administration or the Veterans Administration. Ginnie Mae bundles these mortgages together and guarantees timely interest and principal payments. Ginnie Mae's guarantee is backed by the full faith and credit of the U.S. government, just like Treasury bills, bonds, and notes.

But Ginnie Maes are exceptionally irritating securities to own. If you own a home, you know that part of your monthly mortgage payment goes toward interest, and another part goes toward principal. The same is true with mortgages backed by Ginnie Mae. So when you get your payments from Ginnie Mae certificates, part of that payment will be interest, and another part will be principal. When someone moves and repays the loan, you get rather large slugs of principal returned—which you then have to reinvest elsewhere. If you're careless and don't keep track of interest and principal payments, you could spend your entire investment unwittingly. Furthermore, Ginnie Maes are expensive: You typically need $25,000 to buy a Ginnie Mae certificate.

Some Ginnie Mae funds, on the other hand, will let you in for as little as $100. And reinvesting interest and principal is the manager's problem, not yours. So you don't have to worry about where you're going to invest that $12.97 of

Stellar Performers: Top-Performing General Government Bond Funds, Ranked by Five-Year Total Return

	Return, %		
Fund name	1997	1992–1997	Telephone
Rushmore U.S. Government Bond	13.06	50.62	800-343-3355
Federated U.S. Government Bond	11.74	48.94	800-341-7400
Strong Government	9.03	46.40	800-368-1030
Citizens Income	10.48	45.00	800-223-7010
California Investment Trust II: U.S. Government Securities Fund	9.33	44.54	800-225-8778

SOURCE: Lipper Analytical Services, Inc. Dividends and gains reinvested through December 31, 1997.

principal you got from your Ginnie Mae certificate last month.

So what are the drawbacks? First of all, Ginnie Maes are peculiar securities. In Chapter 2 it was noted that long-term bonds are more volatile than short-term bonds. But no one really knows when a Ginnie Mae certificate will mature. In theory, all of the mortgages in one Ginnie Mae pool are of the same maturity. But the average person moves every seven years. So in practice, the average Ginnie Mae certificate has a maturity of 5 to 10 years.

More important, when rates move down sharply, most people refinance their mortgages. Someone holding a Ginnie Mae certificate gets big gobs of principal back then—which must be reinvested at lower interest rates. So unlike most other types of bonds, Ginnie Maes don't perform well when interest rates fall.

And, because Ginnie Maes are still a fixed-income security, they don't perform real well when interest rates rise, either. In fact, the best economic environment for Ginnie Mae funds is when rates stand still—an occurrence about as frequent as a grand alignment of the planets.

So why bother with them at all? Mainly because Ginnie Maes tend to yield more than garden-variety government securities. People who need income can't afford to overlook that. But do the higher yields make up for the other problems Ginnie Maes present? Let's take a look at the numbers in Figure 5.4.

	Cumulative performance, %			
Type	25 years	15 years	10 years	5 years
Ginnie Mae	501.27	303.29	125.03	37.48
Government securities	753.40	251.78	114.67	36.75

	Annualized performance, %			
Type	25 years	15 years	10 years	5 years
Ginnie Mae	7.44	9.74	8.44	6.57
Government securities	8.95	8.70	7.90	6.43

SOURCE: *Lipper Analytical Services, Inc.*

FIGURE 5.4 *Cumulative and annualized returns of Ginnie Mae Funds.*

Best five-year periods		
Type	**5 years ending**	**Gain or loss, %**
Ginnie Mae Funds	August 1986	137
Government securities funds	August 1986	119

Worst five-year periods		
Type	**5 years ending**	**Gain or loss, %**
Ginnie Mae funds	August 1981	−7
Government securities funds	February 1982	30

Median five-year period performance, %		
Type	**25 years**	**10 years**
Ginnie Mae Funds	48	54
Government securities funds	53	50

SOURCE: *Lipper Analytical Services, Inc.*

FIGURE 5.5 *Best, worst, and median five-year performance.*

As you can see, Ginnie Mae funds have beaten government securities funds over the past 5 and 10 years. You can thank the higher yields that Ginnie Maes pay for that.

But as you can see from Figure 5.5, Ginnie Mae funds are slightly more volatile than government securities funds. So the extra return you get from Ginnie Maes comes with extra risk.

So as you can see, the typical return from a Ginnie Mae fund over 5 years is 48 percent—about 8.15 percent a year. Like most bond funds, Ginnie Mae funds' worst period was in the late 1970s and early 1980s, when interest rates skyrocketed (see Figure 5.6). Long-term interest rates fell from about 13.5 percent in 1981 to about 7 percent in 1986, which explains why Ginnie Mae funds—and most other bond funds—did so well then.

In the short term, Ginnie Mae funds are slightly less volatile on the downside than government securities funds. For most people who invest in Ginnie Mae funds, that's a comfort. People who are looking to generate income don't like big swings in their principal—at least big swings downward. The best Ginnie Mae funds are listed in the Stellar Performers sidebar.

Best three-month period		
Type	3 months ending	Gain or loss, %
Ginnie Mae	August 1981	18.57
Government securities funds	August 1974	16.10

Worst three-month period		
Type	3 months ending	Gain or loss, %
Ginnie Mae	November 1981	−7.43
Government securities funds	February 1975	−11.39

Median three-month period performance, %		
Type	25 years	10 years
Ginnie Mae Funds	1.85	2.11
Government securities funds	1.88	1.88

Source: *Lipper Analytical Services, Inc.*

FIGURE 5.6 *Best, worst, and median three-month performance.*

 Don't Buy Treasury Securities Funds

Lipper Analytical Services tracks several funds that invest entirely in Treasury securities. You can safely skip these.

Why? Because if you want a portfolio of Treasury securities, it's very easy to create one yourself (see Chapter 2 for details). A true government securities fund can pick up some extra yield by investing in little-known federal agency obligations. But a Treasury fund manager would be hard-pressed to beat a laddered portfolio of Treasury bills, bonds, and notes.

So if you want to invest only in Treasuries, do yourself a favor and do it yourself. You'll have as much—or more—safety than if you bought them through a fund. More important, you'll save the fund's management fee, which can be 1 percent or more a year. In the bond market, that's serious money.

Intermediate-Term Government Bond Funds

These funds limit the maturity of the bonds their managers buy to three to seven years. Typically,

Stellar Performers: Top-Performing Ginnie Mae Funds, Ranked by Five-Year Total Return

Fund name	Return, % 1997	1992–1997	Telephone
Dreyfus Basic GNMA Fd	9.54	44.16	800-373-9387
Lexington GNMA Income	10.20	42.90	800-526-0056
Vanguard Fxd:GNMA Port	9.47	41.37	800-662-7447
Princor Govt Sec Inc;A	9.69	40.97	800-451-5447
USAA GNMA Trust	9.51	40.94	800-382-8722

SOURCE: Lipper Analytical Services, Inc.

intermediate-term bonds will give you most of the yield of long-term bonds, but about half the price fluctuations.

Sounds good in theory. In practice, most bond funds stay in the 3- to 10-year range, anyway. That's where most of the bonds are. Use these funds if you have a firm belief about keeping your fund's maturity in the middle of the yield curve. Otherwise, a regular government securities fund will serve admirably.

As you might expect, intermediate-term government bond funds compare favorably with regular government securities for the past 5 and 10 years (see Figure 5.7). But their worst five-year periods have actually been worse than government securities funds, as shown in Figure 5.8. Their best five-year periods have been somewhat better than government securities funds, and their ten-year median performance has been better, too.

In the short term, intermediate-term government funds have lived up to their reputations, producing smaller losses than regular government bond funds, and higher overall gains (see Figure 5.9).

If these funds appeal to you, the five top-performing funds as of the end of 1997 are listed in the Stellar Performers sidebar.

Cumulative performance, %				
Type	25 years	15 years	10 years	5 years
Intermediate government bond funds	NA	267.57	114.31	34.46
Government securities funds	753.4	251.78	114.67	36.75
Annualized performance, %				
Type	25 years	15 years	10 years	5 years
Intermediate government bond funds	NA	8.99	7.90	6.08
Government securities funds	8.95	8.70	7.90	6.43

SOURCE: *Lipper Analytical Services, Inc.*

FIGURE 5.7 *Cumulative and annualized returns of intermediate-term government bond funds.*

Best five-year periods		
Type	5 years ending	Gain or loss, %
Intermediate government bond funds	November 1977	126
Government securities funds	August 1986	119

Worst five-year periods		
Type	5 years ending	Gain or loss, %
Intermediate government bond funds	February 1980	19
Government securities funds	February 1982	30

Median five-year period returns, %		
Type	25 years	10 years
Intermediate government bond funds	48	56
Government securities funds	53	50

SOURCE: Lipper Analytical Services, Inc.

FIGURE 5.8 *Five-year rolling returns of intermediate-term government bond funds.*

Best three-month period		
Type	3 months ending	Gain or loss, %
Intermediate government bond funds	November 1979	12.23
Government securities funds	August 1974	16.10

Worst three-month period		
Type	3 months ending	Gain or loss, %
Intermediate government bond funds	February 1980	−10.63
Government securities funds	February 1975	−11.39

Median three-month period performance, %		
Type	25 years	10 years
Intermediate government bond funds	2.00	1.90
Government securities funds	1.72	1.88

SOURCE: Lipper Analytical Services, Inc.

FIGURE 5.9 *Best, worst, and median three-month performance.*

Stellar Performers: Top-Performing Intermediate-Term Government Bond Funds, Ranked by Five-Year Total Return

| | Return, % | | |
Fund name	1997	1992–1997	Telephone
Pegasus Bond A	9.63	47.55	800-688-3350
Fidelity US Bond Index	9.55	43.44	800-544-8888
Vanguard Index Total Bond	9.44	42.99	800-662-7447
Nationwide Government Bond	9.48	40.71	800-848-0920
Dupree International Bond	9.39	39.67	800-866-0614

SOURCE: Lipper Analytical Services, Inc.

CORPORATE BOND FUNDS RANGE FROM CLASS TO TRASH

Corporate bonds often have higher yields than government bonds, so it's no surprise that corporate bond funds often have somewhat higher returns than government bond funds.

Let's take a look at two types of corporate bond funds: those that invest in bonds rated A or better by Standard & Poor's, and those that invest in bonds rated BBB or better. A-rated bonds, as you may recall, are highly rated. BBB is the lowest investment-quality grade that many institutional buyers, such as pension funds, can purchase.

First, here are the historical returns. Once again, government securities funds have been included as a baseline comparison (see Figure 5.10).

No surprises here. Low-rated corporate bond funds have fared better than the higher-grade bond funds for all periods except the past 25 years. The reason: The period from 1972 through 1977 was wracked by high interest rates and recession—a dreadful time for low-rated bonds. Since then, however, the bond market has rewarded those who have taken the risk of investing in lower-quality bonds.

Type	Cumulative performance, %			
	25 years	15 years	10 years	5 years
Corporate debt, A-rated	678.46	318.65	138.06	43.59
Corporate debt, BBB-rated	663.55	330.37	145.61	50.96
Government securities	753.40	251.78	114.67	36.75

Type	Annualized performance, %			
	25 years	15 years	10 years	5 years
Corporate debt, A-rated	8.52	9.98	9.03	7.48
Corporate debt, BBB-rated	8.47	10.17	9.36	8.54
Government securities	8.95	8.70	7.90	6.43

SOURCE: Lipper Analytical Services, Inc.

FIGURE 5.10 *A-rated versus BBB-rated corporate bond funds.*

Best five-year periods		
Type	**5 years ending**	**Gain or loss, %**
Corporate debt, A-rated	August 1986	135
Corporate debt, BBB-rated	August 1986	139
Government securities funds	August 1986	119

Worst five-year periods		
Type	**5 years ending**	**Gain or loss, %**
Corporate debt, A-rated	August 1981	13
Corporate debt, BBB-rated	August 1981	10
Government securities funds	February 1982	30

Median five-year period returns, %		
Type	**25 years**	**10 years**
Corporate debt, A-rated	55	58
Corporate debt, BBB-rated	53	61
Government securities funds	53	50

SOURCE: *Lipper Analytical Services, Inc.*

FIGURE 5.11 *Five-year rolling returns of corporate bond funds.*

Best three-month period		
Type	**3 months ending**	**Gain or loss, %**
Corporate debt, A-rated	May 1980	13.07
Corporate debt, BBB-rated	November 1982	13.55
Government securities funds	August 1974	16.10

Worst three-month period		
Type	**3 months ending**	**Gain or loss, %**
Corporate debt, A-rated	February 1980	−6.29
Corporate debt, BBB-rated	February 1980	−7.49
Government securities funds	February 1975	−11.39

Median three-month period performance, %		
Type	**25 years**	**10 years**
Corporate debt, A-rated	2.09	2.18
Corporate debt, BBB-rated	2.14	2.11
Government securities funds	1.72	1.88

SOURCE: *Lipper Analytical Services, Inc.*

FIGURE 5.12 *Best, worst, and median three-month performance of corporate bond funds.*

Now let's take a look at various five-year periods in all three types of funds (see Figure 5.11). As you would expect, corporate bonds in general have greater extremes in their five-year performance. And low-quality corporate bonds have even greater extremes. But overall, they have produced superb returns over the past 25 years.

Our indicators of short-term volatility don't hold any big surprises, either. You would expect funds that invest in lower-grade bonds to have greater volatility than those that invest in high-grade corporate bonds. And that's exactly what happens (see Figure 5.12). Some things in life are wonderfully predictable.

During most periods, corporate bond funds offer a good deal of extra value over government securities funds. The five best high-rated corporate bond funds are listed in the Stellar Performers sidebar. Their slightly less reputable cousins are listed in Figure 5.13.

JUNK FUNDS OFFER HIGH YIELDS, BUT TRASHY CREDIT

Now we come to junk bonds, which the mutual fund industry prefers (understandably) to call *high-yield bonds*. Junk bonds have high yields because they have poor credit ratings. They run a higher risk of default than A-rated bonds or even BBB-rated bonds. So investors demand higher yields to compensate for the risks they take (see page 58, Chapter 2).

Junk bonds got most of their bad reputation in the late 1980s and early 1990s, when they produced dreadful returns. First, the economy was sliding into recession. As the economy went south, so did junk-bond prices. After all, a company with poor credit in an economic recovery is likely to have absolutely dreadful credit in a recession. And the default rate among junk-bond issuers did rise substantially during the 1990 recession.

But junk got hit with a double whammy. At the height of the economic boom three players dominated the junk-bond market: savings and loan institutions, insurance companies, and mutual funds. As the boom turned to bust, however, several key players dropped out. Many S&Ls went bankrupt in the late 1980s, and those that didn't dropped their junk bonds in a hurry in the reces-

| | Returns, % | | |
Fund name	1997	1992–1997	Telephone
Alliance Bond			
Corporate Bond A	11.81	80.07	800-227-4618
Strong Corporate Bond	11.86	70.56	800-368-1030
Federated Bond Fund F	10.92	57.93	800-341-7400
Managers Bond A	10.42	57.45	800-835-3879
Ivy Bond A	11.87	57.13	800-456-5111

SOURCE: *Lipper Analytical Services, Inc.*

FIGURE 5.13 *Top-performing lower-quality corporate bond funds, ranked by five-year total return.*

sion. Insurers, too, began to send junk bonds to the trash heap because several large (and questionably solvent) insurers were caught with overly large junk holdings. That left mutual funds to do all the buying—and when investors started fleeing junk-bond funds, there were precious few buyers. Some junk funds, in fact, had to sell their better bond holdings to meet redemptions, because they simply couldn't sell their speculative holdings. What was left was utter garbage.

So in November 1990, junk funds had their worst three-month period since the dark days of the 1973 to 1974 recession. The average junk fund tumbled 8.48 percent. At the bottom of the 1990 bear market in junk, the average junk fund had earned just 19 percent over the previous 5 years, or about 3.5 percent a year. That's dreadful for bonds whose interest payment averaged more than 12 percent a year during the period.

Nevertheless, junk funds provide splendid returns during periods of economic recovery—which is most of the time. And their high yields do provide some cushion against losses. Let's take a look at junk bonds by the numbers (see Figure 5.14). Their returns are compared with other corporate funds and, of course, with the ubiquitous government securities funds.

Obviously, junk-bond investors have enjoyed far higher returns than have those who bought less risky funds. And surprisingly, their highs and lows (see Figure 5.15) have not been as onerous as you would think.

Note that junk-bond funds' worst five-year period was better than the worst five-year period

Stellar Performers:
Top-Performing High-Quality Corporate Bond Funds, Ranked by Five-Year Total Return

Fund name	Return, % 1997	1992–1997	Telephone
Smith Barney Investment Grade A	17.12	70.19	800-451-2010
Vanguard Fixed Income: Long-term Corporate	13.79	57.67	800-662-7447
Bond Fund Of America	9.24	49.47	800-421-4120
FPA New Income	8.31	48.31	800-982-4372
John Hancock Sovereign Bond	9.64	48.24	800-225-5291

SOURCE: Lipper Analytical Services, Inc.

	Cumulative performance, %			
Type	25 years	15 years	10 years	5 years
Corporate debt, A-rated	678.46	318.65	138.06	43.59
Corporate debt, BBB-rated	663.55	330.37	145.61	50.96
Corporate junk bonds	867.82	396.07	178.25	71.60
Government securities	753.40	251.78	114.67	36.75

	Annualized performance, %			
Type	25 years	15 years	10 years	5 years
Corporate debt, A-rated	8.52	9.98	9.03	7.48
Corporate debt, BBB-rated	8.47	10.17	9.36	8.54
Corporate junk bonds	9.46	11.16	10.69	11.37
Government securities	8.95	8.70	7.90	6.43

SOURCE: *Lipper Analytical Services, Inc.*

FIGURE 5.14 *Cumulative and annualized performance of junk-bond funds.*

for all but government securities funds. Even in the 1990 recession, junk funds' high yields provided a cushion against severe losses. Incidentally, group averages can sometimes hide big losses among individual funds. Dean Witter's junk fund, for example, posted a 40.1% loss in 1990, compared with a 9.8 percent loss for the average junk fund. And, as can be seen, the best period for junk funds was only slightly better than the best period for BBB-rated funds. But the typical five-year period was far better.

Does this mean you should dump all your other bond funds and jump on the junk wagon? No. But it does mean that junk funds are probably not as risky as is generally believed. But you'll have to be able to overcome the panic you feel when you see short-term results like the ones in Figure 5.16.

So if you need extra yield, junk funds will give it to you. But you'll get extra volatility in with the bargain. In fact, many observers have noted that junk bonds bear a closer resemblance to stocks than bonds. And if you're looking at price fluctua-

Best five-year periods		
Type	5 years ending	Gain or loss, %
Corporate debt, A-rated	August 1986	135
Corporate debt, BBB-rated	August 1986	139
Corporate junk bonds	February 1987	141
Government securities funds	August 1986	119
Worst five-year periods		
Type	5 years ending	Gain or loss, %
Corporate debt, A-rated	August 1981	13
Corporate debt, BBB-rated	August 1981	10
Corporate junk bonds	November 1990	19
Government securities funds	February 1982	30
Median five-year period performance, %		
Type	25 years	10 years
Corporate debt, A-rated	55	58
Corporate debt, BBB-rated	53	61
Corporate junk bonds	67	68
Government securities funds	53	50

SOURCE: Lipper Analytical Services, Inc.

FIGURE 5.15 *Best, worst, and median five-year performance of junk-bond funds.*

tions, that's quite true. The top of the trash heap is shown in the Stellar Performers sidebar.

MUNICIPAL BOND FUNDS—TAX FREE

Municipal bonds have one overwhelming charm: Income from muni bonds is free from federal taxes. And if you buy a muni bond issued within your home state, the income is free from both federal and state taxes.

This book deals primarily with muni bond funds that buy bonds in every state. The interest from these funds is free from federal income

Type	3 months ending	Gain or loss, %
Best	February 1976	14.21
Worst	August 1974	−9.75
Median		3.12

SOURCE: Lipper Analytical Services, Inc.

FIGURE 5.16 *Best, worst, and median three-month periods for junk bonds.*

Stellar Performers: Top-Performing High-Yield Bond Funds, Ranked by Five-Year Total Return

Fund name	Return, % 1997	Return, % 1992–1997	Telephone
Fidelity Spartan High Income	15.90	97.28	800-544-8888
Morgan Stanley High Yield A	15.87	93.35	800-282-4404
Mainstay High Yield Corporate Bond B	11.55	90.57	800-624-6782
Seligman High Income Bond A	14.20	90.06	800-221-2783
Value Line Aggressive Income	14.14	87.27	800-223-0818

SOURCE: Lipper Analytical Services, Inc. Dividends and gains reinvested through December 31.

taxes, and a portion may be free from state income taxes, too. But there is a tax-free muni bond fund for nearly every state in the Union, so if you're in a state with high state income taxes, such as California or New York, then it makes sense to look into a state tax-free fund.

The tradeoff: Muni yields are lower than those of fully taxable bonds. Typically, a municipal bond (or muni bond fund) pays about 85 percent of the interest paid by a Treasury bond. So muni bond funds are best suited to investors in the upper tax brackets. (To figure out whether a muni bond fund is a worthwhile investment, follow the formula in Chapter 2 on pages 62 to 63.)

Lipper Analytical Services classifies municipal bond funds in much the same way as it does government and corporate bonds: by the credit quality of the bonds the fund may buy, as well as by the maturity of those bonds.

The benchmark here for munis will be Lipper's General Municipal Bond category. These funds invest in municipal bonds around the country. The bonds they buy can vary in credit quality and maturity, but most invest in high-quality, intermediate-term munis. They are the hamburgers of the municipal bond fund menu: You might get different trimmings from fund to fund, but the basics are pretty much the same in all the funds.

There's not enough data for a 25-year benchmark for muni funds. So the funds' average performance over the past 15, 10, and 5 years are used. Figure 5.17 shows how general munis have fared.

As you'll notice, munis have returned somewhat more than government securities funds. And that makes perfect sense. After all, the U.S. government doesn't guarantee municipal bonds. Munis can be backed by the taxing power of the states, but many aren't (see Chapter 2, pages 60 to 61). And there have been several famous cases of municipal bond defaults, most notably Orange County, California, in 1994 and the Washington Public Power Supply in the early 1980s. So investors have demanded a higher return from munis than they would from government bonds.

You'll also notice that muni bond funds are far more volatile than government bond funds. This, too, makes sense. As returns increase, so does risk. The top general muni funds are shown in the Stellar Performers sidebar.

Insured Muni Funds Might Not Be Worth the Cost

Muni bond funds are aimed at people with a fair amount of money. After all, you have to be in a relatively high tax bracket to make buying munis worthwhile. (The wee folk can actually do better in taxable bonds, even after taxes.) People with a fair amount of money, quite sensibly, don't like to lose money. So many municipal bonds are insured by private insurance companies, such as the Municipal Bond Insurance Association (MBIA) and the American Municipal Bond Assurance Corporation (AMBAC). Because these companies are extremely sound, Wall Street credit ratings agencies, such as Standard & Poor's, gives these bonds their top ratings.

So a number of municipal bond funds invest only in insured municipal bonds. But investors sometimes think that their bond funds are insured, too. That's not the case. Although the fund may never lose a cent because a bond in its portfolio defaulted, its share price will still vary. Why? Because changes in interest rates will affect the fund just as profoundly as it would a government-guaranteed bond fund.

Cumulative and annualized performance, %			
Type	15 years	10 years	5 years
Cumulative	301	121	39
Annualized	9.67	8.24	6.74

Best, worst, and median five-year performance*		
Type	5 years ending	Gain or loss, %
Best	August 1986	140.3
Worst	August 1981	−18.46
Median		49.1

Best, worst, and median three-month performance*		
Type	3 months ending	Gain or loss, %
Best	February 1986	11.24
Worst	August 1981	−9.48
Median		2.24

*May 1976 through November 1997.
SOURCE: Lipper Analytical Services, Inc.

FIGURE 5.17 *General municipal bond funds.*

Stellar Performers: Top-Performing General Municipal Bond Funds, Ranked by Five-Year Total Return

Fund name	Return, % 1997	1992– 1997	Telephone
Smith Barney Managed Munis A	10.92	55.98	800-451-2010
Excelsior Tax-Exempt Long-term	9.44	52.57	800-446-1012
Eaton Vance Muni Bond LP	14.12	47.82	800-225-6265
Eaton Vance National Muni B	12.89	47.60	800-225-6265
Nuveen Flagship All-America Muni A	10.86	46.82	800-621-7227

SOURCE: Lipper Analytical Services, Inc.

But insurance comes with a cost: Insured muni bonds yield less than uninsured bonds. After all, if the bond defaults, the insurer will step in and pay interest and principal to bondholders. And the insurers are so sound that investors figure the chance of losing money because of default is very slim indeed.

Because insured muni bonds yield less than their uninsured brethren, it makes sense that mutual funds that invest in insured muni bonds yield less than those that don't. Over time, that lower yield hurts the performance of insured muni funds, as seen in Figure 5.18. Here again, the past five years have seen fairly low average yields—and low total returns from muni bond funds. Figure 5.19 shows that muni funds' most recent returns are well below the median five-year returns from munis.

The indicators of short-term volatility don't hold any big surprises, either. You would expect funds that invest in lower-grade bonds to have greater volatility than those that invest in high-class bonds. And that's exactly what happens (see Figure 5.20).

Don't Overlook State Tax-Free Funds

"Gosh," you might be saying to yourself after reading the Stellar Performers sidebar, I'm a left-handed pipefitter who lives in Kentucky. Is there a muni bond fund for me?"

Well, there are no funds that cater specifically to left-handed pipefitters. But there are several

Cumulative performance, %			
Type	15 years	10 years	5 years
Insured muni funds	273.04	117.78	37.56
General muni funds	300.52	121.13	38.65
Annualized performance, %			
Type	15 years	10 years	5 years
Insured muni funds	9.17	8.08	6.57
General muni funds	9.67	8.24	6.74

SOURCE: *Lipper Analytical Services, Inc.*

FIGURE 5.18 *Insured municipal bond funds.*

Best five-year periods*		
Type	5 years ending	Gain or loss, %
Insured muni funds	February 1987	125.33
General muni funds	August 1986	140.30

Worst five-year periods*		
Type	5 years ending	Gain or loss, %
Insured muni funds	August 1982	1.49
General muni funds	August 1982	−0.84

Median five-year period* returns, %		
Type	15 years	10 years
Insured muni funds	51.33	54.24
General muni funds	55.10	49.12

*August 1982 through November 1997.
SOURCE: Lipper Analytical Services, Inc.

FIGURE 5.19 *Five-year rolling returns for muni funds.*

Kentucky tax-free funds. In fact, there are tax-free
funds for nearly every state in the Union. And
some of the larger states, such as New York and
California, have subvarieties of tax-free funds,
such as insured or intermediate-term tax-free
funds.

By and large, if you need tax-free bonds, it
makes great sense to choose a state tax-free fund.

Best three-month period*		
Type	3 months ending	Gain or loss, %
Insured muni funds	February 1986	11.52
General muni funds	November 1981	11.64

Worst three-month period*		
Type	3 months ending	Gain or loss, %
Insured muni funds	August 1981	−10.22
General muni funds	May 1987	−4.29

Median three-month period* performance, %		
Type	15 years	10 years
Insured muni funds	2.36	2.10
General muni funds	2.40	2.26

*November 1977 through November 1977.
SOURCE: Lipper Analytical Services, Inc.

FIGURE 5.20 *Lower-grade bond performance.*

Stellar Performers: Top-Performing Insured Municipal Bond Funds, Ranked by Five-Year Total Return

Fund name	Return, % 1997	1992–1997	Telephone
Executive Insured Tax-Exempt	10.29	53.85	800-423-4026
Alliance Insured National Muni	9.66	44.16	800-227-4618
Vanguard Muni Insured National	8.65	42.94	800-662-7447
Nuveen Insured Muni Bond	8.57	42.41	800-351-4100
Fidelity Spartan Insured Muni	9.54	41.59	800-544-8888

For example, suppose you are in the 36 percent federal tax bracket. A muni fund yielding 5 percent would be the equivalent of a 7.8 percent taxable yield. But suppose you are in the 8 percent tax bracket in your home state. A single-state muni fund yielding 5 percent would be the equivalent of an 8.9 percent taxable yield.

So before you invest in a national muni fund, ask the fund representative if the fund company offers a single-state muni fund in your state. The odds are good that they do.

BEWARE OF NOVELTY BOND FUNDS

DANGER!

Bonds are not meant to be exotic, exciting, or even particularly interesting. Although there may be a new type of bond hitherto undiscovered by the mutual fund industry, it's not likely. And if you begin to see fund companies touting an exotic type of bond fund, you can generally bet it will leave a deep, smoking crater in the near future.

Consider international bond funds. The argument: Many of the world's bonds are traded abroad. Many of these bonds yield more than U.S. bonds. As an investor, you should be exposed to international bond funds for higher yields and greater diversification.

In 1997, these funds posted extremely impressive gains—at least until the Southeast Asian economies began to falter and overseas currencies began going south. Then the funds posted ugly losses in the latter part of 1997: The average international bond fund fell a whopping 11.75 percent.

You see, all gains from abroad must be translated back into U.S. dollars. Investors can either gain or lose from exchanging currency. In 1997, they lost. One can make a reasonable argument that you should be exposed to international stocks. After all, many of the world's best companies are headquartered abroad. But it's hard to make a compelling argument that you need to be exposed to international debt. An AAA-rated Swiss bond probably doesn't have that much more potential than a AAA-rated U.S. bond. And the Swiss bond carries currency risk, which the U.S. bond doesn't.

AVOID FUNDS WITH
ABOVE-AVERAGE EXPENSES

DANGER! Although it's perfectly possible to make a great deal of money in the bond market, you don't hear of many people who have made their fortunes in the bond market. The bond market is a game of inches: A good fund manager will get an extra half a percent here and there to propel that fund to the top of the ratings.

Therefore, it makes great sense to look for bond funds with rock-bottom expenses. After all, every dollar you send to the mutual fund company is one that you don't get in your own pocket. With few exceptions, there's no reason to buy a bond fund whose expense ratio is 1 percent or higher. If possible, look for funds with expense ratios of even less than that.

One alternative: The Vanguard Group of mutual funds has a series of bond index funds whose expenses are low enough to crawl under a snake. Unlike many funds, which aim to beat a particular index, these funds simply strive to match their index. Because matching an index doesn't keep an army of analysts busy all day, the funds offer an exceptional value.

For example, the Vanguard Bond Index: Long-Term Bond fund, which tries to match the performance of the Lehman Brothers Mutual Fund Long Government/Corporate Index, has an expense ratio of just 0.20 percent, versus 1.09 percent for the average corporate bond fund. On a $10,000 investment, you're paying Vanguard $20, versus $109 for the average corporate bond fund.

The tradeoff: Your Vanguard fund won't ever beat the Lehman Brothers Mutual Fund Long Government/Corporate Index. It will come very close to matching it. On the other hand, relatively few mutual funds beat the index, either. So all in all, it's a very good deal. (For more information on the Vanguard bond index funds, call 800-662-7447.)

BEWARE OF FUNDS WITH
ABOVE-AVERAGE YIELDS

DANGER! Every so often, you'll find a bond fund with yields that are spectacularly above average. Normally, these funds attract huge amounts of money. The manager appears in print and on tele-

vision, explaining modestly that his or her investment technique really isn't any riskier than any
other fund.

Hogwash.

As you look over the figures and sidebars in the
preceding pages, you'll note that the difference
between various classes of bonds isn't that dramatic, with the exception of junk-bond funds. And
as was mentioned, there's good reason for that:
Junk bonds carry so much credit risk that they are
not terribly different from stock funds.

So how do you get extremely high yields from
bond funds?

- *Cut expenses.* This, in general, is a noble
  thing for fund companies to do. But fund companies sometime waive expenses for a year or
  so and then reinstate them—a form of the old
  bait-and-switch routine that banks used to do
  for certificates of deposit. Funds that have low
  expenses—and keep them low—are very good
  indeed. But they are rare, too.

- *Buy junkier bonds.* There is nothing wrong
  with this, either, so long as management warns
  you that it can take big positions in junk. The
  trade-off for the extra yield, however, is greater
  short-term volatility.

- *Buy long-term bonds.* Long-term bonds react
  more violently to interest rate changes. It's a
  good technique if your manager can predict
  interest rates. Most can't.

- *Invest in exotic securities called derivatives.*
  Derivatives are like nitroglycerine. In the right
  hands, derivatives can add performance and
  take away risk. In the wrong hands, derivatives
  can blow your fund's portfolio apart.

Derivatives are investments whose value is
derived from another security, or even an index,
such as the London Interbank Offered Rate
(LIBOR). Futures and options are derivatives. But
so are other exotic investments, with such names
as *inverse floaters, strips,* and *structured notes.* In
1994, several bond funds suffered extremely heavy
losses because of their investments in derivatives.

For example, consider the Piper Jaffray Inter-
mediate Bond fund. In 1993, the fund rose 15.6
percent, versus 10 percent for the average inter-
mediate investment-grade debt fund—the best in
its category. The fund's manager used derivatives,

which investors liked during the ride up. But the ride down was like being in the gondola of the *Hindenburg.* The fund fell 28 percent in 1994, versus a 3.7 percent loss for the average fund in its category.

So there's nothing wrong with choosing a top-performing fund. But funds that are real outliers are disasters in the making. Be extremely wary when looking at a bond fund with performance substantially above the rest of the pack. A good bond fund makes small gains over time—not big gains all at once.

 BOND FUNDS WON'T PROVIDE FIXED PAYMENTS

Here's the biggest drawback to bond funds: Every time you get an income distribution from your bond fund, it won't be the same as the one you got previously. It may be larger. It may be smaller. But if it's the same, it's pure coincidence.

Bond funds have to pay out what they get in income, and that amount will vary month by month, depending on the fund's investment portfolio. If you need to know how much money you will be getting from your investments every month, you won't get much satisfaction from a bond fund.

If you really must have a set amount of money from your investments each month, consider investing in a bank CD (Chapter 1), a unit investment trust (Chapter 3), or in individual bonds (Chapter 2). If you're content with a variable yield, however, a bond fund will suit you perfectly.

 **BOND FUNDS CAN HELP SMOOTH OUT A STOCK PORTFOLIO**

So why buy a bond fund? One of the best reasons is this: Ideally, bond funds and stock funds move in opposite directions. A bond fund will often cushion the blow of a major stock market meltdown.

Let's suppose you decided to invest $10,000 in an average growth fund on September 30, 1987. Three months later, your investment would have been worth $7,857—a 21.43 percent loss, thanks to the Crash of 1987.

But let's suppose you had split your initial investment between stocks and bonds. You put

$7,000 in a stock fund and $3,000 in a bond fund. By December 31, 1987, your stock fund would have sagged to $5,500. But your bond fund would have risen to $3,159. (Interest rates fell in the wake of the crash, pushing bond prices up.) Your total account would have been worth $8,659—a 13 percent loss, but far better than if you had been only in stocks.

If you're a long-term investor with 20 years or more before you will need the money, then you're better off staying 100 percent in stock funds. Over time, stocks tend to produce higher returns than bonds do. A $10,000 investment in the typical growth fund on September 30, 1977, would have grown to about $213,000 by September 30, 1997. A 70 percent investment in stock funds and a 30 percent investment in bond funds, however, would have grown to only $180,000.

If you're a more conservative investor, however, adding bonds reduces your risk significantly. If you lie awake at night over your investments, adding bonds will generally increase your portfolio's overall stability. The traditional mix is 60 percent stocks and 40 percent bonds. But that's up to your individual investing tolerance.

END POINT

Bond mutual funds are good for providing income, and are a good way to balance your overall portfolio. But you can usually get better returns over long periods of time in the stock market—which is the subject of the next chapter.

Stock Mutual Funds

At work you get a friendly notice from your Human Resources department. Your company's pension plan, never generous to begin with, is shrinking further. To make up for your incredible shrinking pension, however, your company is offering even more choices for your 401(k) plan. Now you have a growth fund, a growth and income fund, an international fund, a small-company growth fund, and a real estate fund. Your company is thinking of adding even more.

You groan. After all, your life is complicated enough without having to figure out the difference between a half-dozen stock mutual funds. You don't know how much of your money you should have in stock mutual funds, much less which ones are best.

Well, there are worse things in the world than having to learn about stock mutual funds. Imagine having to rely on only a small pension and Social Security when you retire. Corporate America has increasingly turned the job of managing retirement money to individuals. And, if you're investing for the long term, that means creating a portfolio of stock mutual funds. Learning about stock funds is no longer optional. It's essential.

This chapter is designed to help you construct a portfolio of stock funds that can help you meet your long-term goals. We'll start by figuring out how much of your total portfolio you should have in stocks. From there, we will work on constructing a group of core holdings—long-term funds with good track records. We'll also tell you how to add other funds to the mixture to tilt your portfolio toward areas that you think will be rewarding in the future.

STOCK FUNDS LET YOU LEAVE THE DRIVING TO SOMEONE ELSE

For many people, investing in individual stocks is a pleasure. They like to pore over annual reports looking for hidden assets, investigate new companies, and chart the meanderings of the Standard & Poor's 500 Stock Index (S&P 500). For them, chasing the perfect stock is more than saving and investing: It's a hobby, too.

But for many more people, investing is one more detail in a life that's already crammed with too many details. There are cars to wash and children to fuel up. There is work, and housework, and yardwork, too. And there's just not enough time.

Why not have someone pick stocks for you? You could hire a professional money manager. But most money managers won't look at your account unless you can write a check for $100,000. And even then, they would prefer that you brought $500,000 to the table.

But for an average of $150 a year on a $10,000 account, you can hire some of the best money managers in the nation. We'll explain later why you should begrudge even that $150 a year. But remember that you probably pay more than $150 a year for cable television, fast-food hamburgers, or soda.

More important, you get a degree of diversification you probably couldn't get yourself. Sure, you could create a portfolio of 10 or 15 blue-chip stocks over time. And if you traded at a deep-discount online brokerage or if you created a portfolio of dividend reinvestment plan stocks, you could keep costs to a minimum.

But if one of your stocks went seriously wrong, you'd pay even more dearly. For example, suppose you had 10 stocks. Nine earned 10 percent. One fell 30 percent. Your overall return would fall to 6 percent. If two stocks fell 20 percent, your return would fall to 4 percent. You could do better at a bank, with less risk.

Stock funds have their drawbacks. Most funds probably won't beat the S&P 500. If that's your goal, you might be better off picking stocks your-self. And stock funds aren't necessarily invest-ments that you can buy and forget. You have to pay some attention to them and check up on them two or three times a year. But if you're looking for a low-cost, low-maintenance way to invest in the stock market, then a stock mutual fund will gener-ally do the trick.

FIGURE YOUR ASSET ALLOCATION

Before you start looking at individual stock funds, or even individual types of stock funds, you need to ask yourself how much money you should invest in the stock market. Unless you pick a very poorly performing fund—and there are a few—this is your single most important decision. Financial planners call it *asset allocation*. It's a decision you'll have to make for your 401(k) retire-ment portfolio, your children's education portfolio, and any other stock portfolio you care to create.

Why is asset allocation so important? Take a look at Figure 6.1, which shows how $10,000 would have grown over the 10 years that ended December 31, 1997, using different asset alloca-tions. (The S&P 500 with dividends and gains reinvested is used for the stock index.)

Asset allocation	Growth of $10,000
0% T-bills, 100% stocks	$52,443.26
10% T-bills, 90% stocks	48,910.05
20% T-bills, 80% stocks	45,376.84
30% T-bills, 70% stocks	41,843.63
40% T-bills, 60% stocks	38,310.42
50% T-bills, 50% stocks	34,777.21
60% T-bills, 40% stocks	31,244.00
70% T-bills, 30% stocks	27,710.79
80% T-bills, 20% stocks	24,177.58
90% T-bills, 10% stocks	20,644.37
100% T-bills	17,111.16

Source: Lipper Analytical Services, Inc.

FIGURE 6.1 *Ten-year growth from December 31, 1986, to December 31, 1997.*

As you can see, the difference between a portfolio of T-bills and a portfolio of stocks is dramatic. In fact, even a 10 percent allocation of T-bills would have reduced your returns by 7 percent.

Many financial experts use tables like Figure 6.1 to show that you must have most of your portfolio in stocks. But before you go out and mortgage the house to buy stock funds, you should realize that the table is misleading on two counts. First, the 10 years that ended December 31, 1997, contained some of the strongest years in stock market history. Let's see the results if the period from December 31, 1964, through December 31, 1974, is used (see Figure 6.2).

Even though stocks performed well throughout much of the 1960s, your best investment from 1964 through 1974 was the lowly Treasury bill. Any amount you added in stocks simply decreased your returns. Of course, the next 10 years would have been far more lucrative—and the 10 years after that would have been absolutely astounding.

The point is that any statistical figures you see for the next 5 or 10 years will be tilted towards stocks. Before you throw aside all caution, you should be aware that any large returns come at the expense of higher risks. And the risks are such decades as 1964 through 1974.

Asset allocation	Growth of $10,000
0% T-bills, 100% stocks	$11,305.31
10% T-bills, 90% stocks	11,882.68
20% T-bills, 80% stocks	12,460.04
30% T-bills, 70% stocks	13,037.41
40% T-bills, 60% stocks	13,614.78
50% T-bills, 50% stocks	14,192.15
60% T-bills, 40% stocks	14,769.52
70% T-bills, 30% stocks	15,346.89
80% T-bills, 20% stocks	15,924.25
90% T-bills, 10% stocks	16,501.62
100% T-bills	17,078.99

SOURCE: Lipper Analytical Services, Inc.

FIGURE 6.2 Ten-year earnings from December 31, 1964, to December 31, 1974.

CONCEPT

Time Is Your First Consideration

The 1964 to 1974 period looks so awful now because it ended with a dreadful bear market—the worst since the Great Depression. Odds are good that your 10-year period won't end with a bear market. In fact, the odds are very good indeed that your stock investment will outperform an investment in bonds or money market funds. But you need to give your stock investment plenty of time—more than 10 years, if at all possible.

Just how important is time for a stock investment? Let's see how the Standard & Poor's 500 Stock Index has performed during 12-month periods since December 31, 1962. Each 12-month period was started at 3-month intervals: the first at December 31, 1962, the second at March 31, 1962, and so on. Total: 137 time periods in 35 years. During that time, the S&P 500 has:

- Posted gains 110 times, or 80 percent of the time.

- Beaten inflation 98 times, or 72 percent of the time.

- Beaten 3-month Treasury bills 90 times, or 66 percent of the time.

The picture improves if we use 10-year holding periods. In 101 10-year periods since 1962, the S&P 500 has:

- Posted no losses.

- Beaten inflation and T-bills 70 times, or 69 percent of the time.

So over a 10-year period, your odds are extremely good—far better than what you'd get in Las Vegas. But this is your retirement savings we're talking about, not a casino. If you want to improve your odds, you need to have a time period longer than 10 years. If we look at 20-year time periods, the S&P 500 has beaten inflation and T-bills in all 60 periods.

So if you want to invest rationally, then you need to figure how much risk you can take. And your first question should be how much time you have to invest before you need to tap your savings. A rough guideline follows:

- If you have more than 10 years before you will need to spend your money, keep 80 to 100 percent in stock funds. Any money not in stocks should be in bond funds.

- If you will need your money in 5 to 10 years, keep 60 to 70 percent of your money in stock funds; keep the rest in bond funds.
- If you will need your money in less than five years, keep half in money market funds and the rest in bond funds.

Bear in mind that this is a starting point. You'll need to refine your asset allocation as you get older and your goals change.

 Keep an Emergency Fund

There are two other points to consider before you decide how much money you want to invest in stock funds. The first is an emergency fund in a safe investment, such as a bank certificate of deposit or a money market mutual fund. If you don't have an emergency fund, you'll need to get one. If you get laid off, or if you encounter a sudden large expense, you don't want to blow your investment plans to flinders. The question is: How much of an emergency fund do you need? Probably less than you may think.

You'll often read that you need six months' salary in money market funds before you invest any money elsewhere. For many couples, 6 months' salary is $50,000 or more. That's too much money to leave cooling its heels in a money market fund.

In fact, it's just too much money, period. First of all, your emergency fund should be based on your net salary, not your gross. You have probably already paid taxes on your emergency savings. So if you gross $100,000 a year, you certainly don't need $50,000 in the bank.

Furthermore, you have an emergency fund to pay expenses. So it's more accurate to have an emergency fund equal to several months' expenses, not salary. This means that you don't have to count your 401(k) savings plan contribution or other nonessential expenses.

Finally, you have to gauge whether you'll really need six months' of salary to see you through. Are jobs difficult to get? Does your spouse work? Do you have other sources of funds, such as a paid-up life insurance policy or a family trust that you can tap?

Most people will be able to get by with an emergency fund equal to two or three months' expenses. There's no need to have a $50,000 kitty in the bank before you start investing.

Know Your Risk Tolerance

The trickiest part of the asset allocation equation is this: You need to keep a portfolio that will not keep you awake at night.

If you skip back to Figure 5.1 on page 137, you'll see that those investors who have done the best over the past 10 years are those who have had the most money in the stock market. As was mentioned earlier, it's misleading to some extent because it looks back over one of the best investment periods in history. It's also misleading because it doesn't reflect the amount of risk that each portfolio contains.

For example, a portfolio that was 50 percent in stocks and 50 percent in T-bills would have earned less money than one that was 100 percent in stocks. But a 50/50 split between stocks and T-bills is also half as risky as a portfolio that's 100 percent in stocks.

And that, in turn, can make a dramatic difference in a downturn. In the third quarter of 1990, for example, a $10,000 investment in the S&P 500 would have shrunk to $8,627, thanks to the bear market sparked by Iraq's invasion of Kuwait. A 50/50 split between stocks and T-bills would have shrunk to $9,407, however—a far smaller loss.

So you also have to decide how aggressive you want to be with your savings. As was mentioned way back in Chapter 1, your potential rewards increase with the amount of risk you take. So if you choose to reduce the amount of stocks in your portfolio because they scare you, bear in mind that you may have to save more money to make up for potentially lower returns.

Start with a Core Portfolio

Professional money managers often use a strategy called the *tilt fund*. Essentially, the manager puts most of the fund's assets—60 to 70 percent—in large, well-known stocks, such as those that comprise the Dow Jones Industrial Average or the Standard & Poor's 500 Stock Index. The goal of this part of the portfolio is to simply mirror the market.

The rest goes into an area that the manager thinks will do well, such as technology, health-care, or real-estate funds. So the fund is tilted toward a particular sector. The worst case: The fund underperforms the S&P 500 modestly. The best case: It beats the S&P 500.

This is a good strategy for individual investors, because it requires relatively little monitoring. Once you have set up your core holdings, you shouldn't have to fiddle with it very often. You should monitor it continually, of course, but you shouldn't have to switch funds very often. That's a good thing. Excessive trading can gener-ate taxes, which erode your overall return. And after all, mutual funds aren't speculative invest-ments. If you want something you can trade frequently, trade stocks, options, or futures.

Using this strategy, you would create a core group of funds—two or three, perhaps—that will more or less mirror the market. You don't want any big surprises from these funds. These funds will be 60 percent or more of your portfolio.

The rest will tilt your portfolio toward an area that you think will do well over the next 18 months or longer. Health care is a likely area, because of the aging of 77 million baby boomers. So you might add a health care fund to your core portfolio, tilting it toward that sector. Technology is another perennial favorite.

You can also tilt your portfolio to make it more conservative. Adding a utility fund, for example, will give your portfolio a higher dividend yield. Adding a real estate fund could offer some infla-tion protection.

In any event, the key is to not tilt your portfolio too far, unless you're extremely young, aggressive, or both. A portfolio that's 70 percent in a fund that duplicates the S&P 500 and 30 percent in a health care fund should be aggressive enough for most people.

KEY CONCEPT: CHOOSE YOUR CORE HOLDINGS

Once you have decided how much you want to have in stock mutual funds, your next task is to choose your core holdings. These are highly diversified funds that concentrate on stocks of large or midsized companies.

You have four basic choices:

1. *Index funds,* which mirror the performance of stock market indexes, primarily the S&P 500 or the Wilshire 5000.

2. *Growth funds,* which invest in stocks whose share price management thinks is likely to rise. These funds pay little or no attention to dividends.

3. *Growth and income funds,* which also look for companies whose share price is likely to rise. But these funds also look for dividend income as a secondary consideration.

4. *Equity-income funds,* which keep at least 65 percent of their investments in dividend-paying stocks.

Let's examine each category.

 ### Index Funds for Low-Cost Core Holdings

Most stock mutual funds don't beat the Standard & Poor's 500 Stock Index, even though the aim stated in their prospectuses is to do so. And the problem is actually somewhat worse than it seems, because of something called *survivorship bias.*

In the mutual fund industry, good funds flourish, while bad funds just fade away. Eventually, their records disappear entirely. Ever heard of the Sherman Dean Fund? How about 44 Wall Street? They were awful funds. Sherman Dean rose a paltry 123 percent over the 15 years that ended in 1990, versus 584 percent for the average stock fund and 610 percent for the S&P 500. The snake-bit 44 Wall Street fund managed to fall 15 percent over the same period.

When Lipper Analytical Services calculated the 5-year performance of the average general stock fund in 1990, it showed a 54.5 percent gain. By mid-1997, Lipper's database showed a 58.9 percent rise. That better record is thanks to the demise of such funds as 44 Wall Street and Sherman Dean. Their records are no longer reflected in the returns for that period.

So why have funds lagged the S&P 500 so badly? For years, fund managers had a ready answer: We have to charge expenses to pay our salaries. And besides, you can't buy the index.

But now you can. The typical index fund can mirror the S&P 500 and keep its expense ratio below 0.4 percent—$40 on a $10,000 account. That's because an index fund really needs little management. In the case of an S&P 500 index fund, the fund simply buys all the stocks in the S&P 500 in proportion to the index itself. A computer can handle most of the fund's day-to-day operations, which helps keep expenses to a bare minimum. The Vanguard Index 500 fund, for example, charges just 0.2 percent of assets every year, which is about as low as humanly possible (see the Stellar Performer sidebar).

Other advantages of indexing are the following:

- S&P 500 index funds have been most popular because the S&P 500 has performed so well over the past 5 years. But indexing works equally well for other broad market indexes. For example, the Vanguard Extended Market Index fund mirrors the more broadly based Wilshire 4500 index, which is the Wilshire 5000 without the stocks of the S&P 500. The Vanguard Total Market Index mirrors the Wilshire 5000.

- Index funds do very little trading. Because of this, they tend to have small capital gains payouts and, thereby, are very tax-efficient.

So what are the drawbacks?

- Index funds tend to keep only a tiny portion of their portfolios in money market securities, or cash. That's great in a rising market. But when the stock market gets clobbered, you can expect an index fund to get clobbered harder than the average stock mutual fund.

- Index funds will never beat their indexes. If you want something with the chance of beating the S&P 500, you have to choose an actively managed fund.

- Index funds for small, inefficient markets tend not to do as well as actively managed funds. One reason it is hard to beat the S&P 500 is that these are very widely followed companies. Toss a nickel in the air on Wall Street and it's likely to hit an analyst who follows General Electric or IBM. There's very little about these companies that an enterprising fund manager could discover before the rest of the Street. But a good manager in, say, small-company stocks or emerging markets stocks can find out information before the rest of the herd—and beat the index.

S&P 500 Index Funds

Before looking at performance notes for S&P 500 index funds (see Figure 6.3), you should know that annualized returns are not being considered here. There's a reasonable argument for using annualized returns for bond mutual funds, because many people compare them with bank CDs. But there's no particular reason for using annualized returns for stock funds, so they are omitted here.

	Total return, %				
Name	1 year	5 years	10 years	15 years	25 years
S&P 500 index funds	32.60	146.20	385.72	979.17	New

Rolling five-year returns since December 31, 1976		
	5 years ending	Percent change
Best	June 1987	232.59
Worst	June 1982	39.77
Median		99.61

Rolling three-month returns since December 31, 1976		
	3 months ending	Percent change
Best	March 1987	20.45
Worst	December 1987	−22.77
Median		4.55

Top-performing S&P 500 index funds			
	Return, %		
Fund name	1997	1992–1997	Telephone
Vanguard Index: 500 Port	33.19	150.10	800-662-7447
Fidelity Sparat US Equity Index	33.04	148.62	800-544-8888
SEI Index S&P 500	33.07	148.58	800-342-5734
SSGA S&P 500 Index	33.10	148.38	800-647-7327
Pegasus Equity Index	33.00	148.33	800-688-3350

SOURCE: Lipper Analytical Services, Inc. Dividends and gains reinvested through December 31, 1997.

FIGURE 6.3 *Performance of S&P 500 index funds.*

Stellar Performer: The Vanguard Index 500 Portfolio

The Vanguard Group developed the index fund—and, some say, perfected it, too.

The Vanguard Index 500 fund was the first fund to mimic the S&P 500. Manager George Sauter pioneered the computer programs that run the fund, and has created several newer and younger index funds as well. (As if to prove his own versatility, Sauter also runs an actively managed fund, Vanguard Horizon Aggressive Growth).

You won't get any surprises from this fund. Sauter doesn't try anything fancy: no options, no overweighting favored sectors, and no second-guessing. You'll get the S&P 500 index for just $20 a year on a $10,000 account.

Of course, you won't get any exposure to small-company stocks, either. The S&P 500 isn't the same thing as the entire stock market. And you'll get one of the largest stock mutual funds in the known universe. At $48 billion, the fund is approaching the size of its arch-rival, the actively managed $63 billion Fidelity Magellan fund.

Vanguard has pulled out all the stops to keep expenses down. So don't expect to pick up the phone and ask to switch your Vanguard Index 500 account to a money fund. Vanguard requires that redemptions be by mail only.

Nevertheless, if you want an S&P 500 index fund with skinflint pricing, the Vanguard Index 500 fund is for you. The particulars follow.

Vanguard Index 500 Fund

Minimum investment: $3,000; $1,000, for IRAs.

Expense ratio: 0.20 percent, or $20 on a $10,000 investment.

Sales charge: None.

Performance:

| | Return, % | | | | |
Name	1 year	3 years	5 years	10 years	15 years
Vanguard Index 500 Fund	33.19	124.94	150.10	416.39	979.17
Average stock mutual fund	24.29	95.01	118.40	346.64	692.44

Telephone: 800-662-7447.
Website: http://www.vanguard.com.

SOURCE: Lipper Analytical Services, Inc.

Growth Funds for Growth or Value

A growth fund's job is to beat the Standard & Poor's 500 Stock Index over time, by investing in stocks with above-average potential for price appreciation.

But that covers a galaxy of different management styles. Growth funds—and their kindred, aggressive growth funds—are a holdover from an older time, when wealthy investors would entrust their money to a money manager and let him invest it in whatever way he wanted.

Growth-fund managers today tend to be more closely confined to particular management styles. Financial planners and 401(k) administrators don't like surprises from money managers. And they have a point: Consistency is a good thing. But as was said in Chapter 3, you could line up all the money managers in the world and they still wouldn't come to a conclusion about the best way to beat the S&P 500. So there are a plethora of management styles from which to choose. Here's a rundown of the strategies growth fund managers use in their quest to beat the S&P 500.

Growth investors, as noted in Chapter 3, make their own earnings estimates and try to figure out what companies should have above-average earnings over the next 3 to 18 months. Look for classic growth funds from Fidelity Investments, the Janus Group of funds, the Alger funds, Stein Roe, and T. Rowe Price.

Momentum investors are a subset of the growth investing category. They use three different strategies. Some fund managers stick to one discipline; others use a blend of all three.

1. *Earnings momentum.* These managers look for companies whose earnings are increasing rapidly. Typically, the stocks have annual earnings increases of 30 percent or more. Because these stocks don't go unnoticed on Wall Street, they often have high prices, and high price-to-earnings ratios (the stock price divided by earnings per share.)

2. *Estimate revision.* These managers look for stocks of companies whose earnings estimates are continually revised upward by analysts. Because they have high expectations, these stocks also tend to have high prices.

Stellar Performer: G. Kenneth Heebner's CGM Capital Development

G. Kenneth Heebner may be the archetypal growth fund manager. Heebner runs a tightly concentrated portfolio of 30 to 35 stocks, and often sells the entire portfolio 3 times in a year. Depending on his reading of the market, CGM Capital Development will be in stocks of small, growing companies one year, and large, dividend-paying companies the next.

Although Heebner is always looking for stocks with above-average earnings growth, this former economist for Kroger often has an opinion on the overall direction of interest rates and the economy, as well. This top-down approach hasn't been without the occasional disaster: The fund suffered a 23 percent loss in 1994 when Heebner bet the portfolio on industrial cyclical stocks.

Nevertheless, his good years more than make up for his bad years. In 1991, the fund rocketed 99 percent; in 1995, it soared 41 percent. Over the past 10 years, a $10,000 investment in CGM Capital Development didn't beat the S&P 500—it stomped it flat. CGM Capital Development turned $10,000 into $70,764 over the 10 years that ended in 1997, despite 1994's big loss. The S&P 500, in contrast, would have turned $10,000 into $55,287.

CGM Capital Development, alas, is closed, and is likely to remain so. But Heebner also offers CGM Mutual, a balanced fund, and CGM Focus, a new growth fund. Like CGM Capital Development, it will have a tightly concentrated portfolio. But it will invest in larger stocks as the fund grows. The particulars on CGM Focus follow.

CGM Focus Fund

Performance: New.

Minimum initial investment: $2,500; $1,000 for IRAs.

Sales charge: None.

Expense ratio: Not available.

Telephone: 800-345-4048.

Website: http://www.cgmfunds.com.

3. *Earnings surprise.*   These managers buy stocks of companies whose earnings come in far higher than Wall Street expects.

Earnings momentum funds include funds from American Century/Twentieth Century, AIM, PBHG, and the Van Wagoner funds. In general, they fare best in the early stages of a bull market, when investors are willing to pay a high premium for stocks with exceptional growth. As you might expect, when they fall, they fall hard.

Value investors look for stocks of companies that have been unfairly beaten up by Wall Street. Value investors include the Mutual Series and Franklin funds, Neuberger & Berman, and Merrill Lynch funds. Value investors can be lumped into two groups:

1. *Absolute value managers* are the Orthodox version of the school of value investing. They have strict limits on how cheap a stock must be before they buy it. If they can't find any stocks that meet their limits, they simply keep their money in money market securities, or cash. Some have criticized absolute value managers for being closet market timers. This isn't really fair, however. They have their rules, and they abide by them. Some absolute value managers include the top-performing (but closed) FPA Capital fund, Clipper, and Longleaf Partners funds.

2. *Relative value managers* are the Reformed school. They tend to stay 100 percent invested in stocks. But they choose the stocks that are least overvalued. Acorn fund is one such relative value fund; Strong Schafer Value is another.

Growth at a reasonable price (GAARP) is a growth and value blend. Funds that look for the world according to GAARP include the Davis/Venture funds and the American funds.

Which is best? It depends on when you ask. In the early part of the 1990s, growth investors, and particularly momentum investors, left all other funds crawling in the dust. In 1995, however, the funds started turning south and value investors took the lead.

Generally speaking, you want growth funds at the beginning of a bull market, and value funds toward the end. If you happen to know when the beginning and end of a bull market are, however, you're smarter than nearly everyone on Wall

Street. So your best solution is to use two or three top-rated growth funds with differing styles for your core holding.

Figure 6.4 will give you some idea of how growth funds have fared recently, and how that performance squares with the typical growth fund performance.

 Growth and Income Funds for a More Conservative Approach

As was noted in Chapter 3, dividends account for a third or more of the returns from stocks over the long haul. But growth funds really don't care about dividends. They want capital appreciation, and that's it.

Growth and income funds take a more measured approach. They, too, want the share prices of their stocks to rise. But they also try to generate a reasonable level of income. In most cases, that's about equal to the dividend yield of the S&P 500. Because companies that pay dividends tend to be fairly large, mature companies, most equity-income funds invest exclusively in large-company stocks.

But it never hurts to ask. Some equity-income funds mix growth stocks for the growth compo-

Cumulative returns, %, 1972 to 1997					
Name	1 year	5 years	10 years	15 years	25 years
S&P 500 Index funds	32.60	146.20	385.72	979.17	New
Growth funds	25.17	117.02	349.74	710.95	2013.93

Rolling five-year returns, 1972 to 1997		
	5 years ending	Gain or loss, %
Best	June 1987	192.47
Worst	December 1977	−4.31
Median		99.99

Rolling three-month returns, 1972 to 1997		
	3 months ending	Gain or loss, %
Best	March 1975	22.88
Worst	September 1974	−22.08
Median		4.57

SOURCE: Lipper Analytical Services, Inc. Dividends and gains reinvested through December 31, 1997.

FIGURE 6.4 *Performance of growth funds.*

Stellar Performer: Top Growth Funds 1992 to 1997

Fund	Return, % 1997	1992– 1997	Telephone
Legg Mason Value Trust Prime	37.05	201.24	800-577-8589
Torray Fund	37.12	190.02	800-443-3036
Mairs & Power Growth	28.65	189.47	800-304-7404
Vanguard PRIMECAP	36.83	188.39	800-662-7447
Merrill Growth Fund; A	18.69	183.76	800-637-3863

SOURCE: Lipper Analytical Services, Inc. Dividend and gains reinvested through 12/31/97.

nent and low-quality bonds for the income component. That's probably more risk than you're bargaining for.

Nevertheless, dividends give many growth and income funds a slight edge over their more aggressive cousins, the growth funds (see Figure 6.5).

Equity-Income Funds for the Most Conservative Core Holdings

What's the difference between a growth and income fund and an equity-income fund? It's a matter of degree, really. If a growth and income fund gives a nod to dividend income, an equity-income fund embraces dividend income wholeheartedly.

If you are a conservative investor and want the most dividend income from your core holdings, an equity-income fund is for you. One particularly attractive subdivision of the equity-income universe is the *rising dividend* fund. These funds follow a strategy outlined in Chapter 3: They buy only stocks of companies that have raised their dividends for five consecutive years or more.

Cumulative returns, %, 1972 to 1997					
Name	1 year	5 years	10 years	15 years	25 years
S&P 500 Index funds	32.60	146.20	385.72	979.17	New
Growth funds	25.17	117.02	349.74	710.95	2013.93
Growth & Income funds	26.99	125.24	325.72	741.02	1966.55

Rolling five-year returns, 1972 to 1997		
	5 years ending	Gain, %
Best	June 1987	200.34
Worst	December 1977	11.82
Median		91.59

Rolling three-month returns, 1972 to 1997		
	3 months ending	Gain or loss, %
Best	March 1975	21.95
Worst	September 1974	−19.67
Median		3.84

SOURCE: Lipper Analytical Services, Inc. Dividends and gains reinvested through December 31, 1997.

FIGURE 6.5 *Growth and income funds returns.*

Stellar Performer: Top Growth and Income Funds, 1992 to 1997

| | Returns, % | | |
| | 1997 | 1992– 1997 | |
Name	1997	1997	Telephone
Excelsior Value & Restructuring	33.58	232.84	800-446-1012
SAFECO Equity No Load	24.21	179.89	800-426-6730
Enterprise Growth & Income Y	27.65	165.40	800-432-4320
T Rowe Price Dividend Growth	30.77	163.46	800-638-5660
Dodge & Cox Stock	28.40	160.61	800-621-3979

SOURCE: Lipper Analytical Services, Inc. Dividends and gains reinvested through December 31, 1997.

These funds don't necessarily have higher yields than other funds. But their holdings tend to be some of the most stable and profitable companies in the nation. For example, the T. Rowe Price Dividend Growth Fund had the stocks shown in Figure 6.6 among its 10 largest holdings at the end of January, 1997.

Although equity-income funds are conservative, you shouldn't immediately dismiss them. As was noted in Chapter 3, dividends can be a huge part of your fund's total return over time. Not only do they boost your returns in a bull market, but they cushion a bear market's claws. Let's say you invested $100 in a small-company stock fund at the end of August 1987. Your timing was awful: The Dow Jones Industrial Average peaked on August 25. If you had invested in the average small-company growth fund, which pays virtually no dividends, your $100 would have become $67.99 at the end of November 1987. By comparison, you would have had:

- $70.33 in the average S&P 500 fund.
- $74.47 in the average growth and income fund.
- $78.17 in the average equity-income fund.

Dividends weren't the entire reason these funds held up well during the crash of 1987: In a panic, investors dump more speculative stocks and buy stocks of strong, established companies, which normally pay dividends.

Dividends also help your investments recover faster after a downturn (see Figure 6.7). Let's return to the $100 you invested in August 1987. If you had chosen an S&P 500 index fund, you would have waited 21 months, until May 1989, before you had $100 in your account again.

Stock name	Dividend, %
Fannie Mae	1.55
Mobil	3.33
SBC Communications	1.2
Allied Signal	2.35
Mellon Bank	2.19
Philip Morris	3.86

SOURCE: T. Rowe Price, Bloomberg Business News.

FIGURE 6.6 Holdings of the T. Rowe Price Dividend Growth Fund.

Fund name	Total return, %		Telephone
	12 months	5 years	
T. Rowe Price Dividend Growth	30.77	Tk	800-638-5660
Dean Witter Dividend Growth B	25.66	Tk	800-869-3863
Hancock Sovereign Investor A	29.14	Tk	800-225-5291
Franklin Rising Dividends I	32.35	Tk	800-342-5236
Kayne Anderson Rising Dividends	30.99	New	310-556-2721
Hancock Dividend Performers	34.33	New	800-225-5291
Franklin Rising Dividends II	31.72	New	800-342-5236
Fidelity Dividend Growth	27.90	New	800-544-8888

SOURCE: Morningstar, Lipper Analytical Services, Inc.

FIGURE 6.7 *Rising dividend funds.*

But funds with more generous dividend payouts recovered more rapidly (see Figure 6.8). Equity-income funds, for example, broke even five months earlier, in January 1989. And utility funds, which traditionally offered high yields, had recovered by August 1988.

Cumulative total return, %, 1972 to 1997					
Name	1 year	5 years	10 years	15 years	25 years
S&P 500 Index funds	32.60	146.20	385.72	979.17	New
Growth funds	25.17	117.02	349.74	710.95	2013.93
Growth & Income funds	26.99	125.24	325.72	741.02	1966.55
Equity Income funds	27.44	120.51	285.54	638.79	2264.64

Rolling five-year returns, 1972 to 1997		
	5 years ending	Gain or loss, %
Best	June 1987	184.13
Worst	June 1977	38.87
Median		88.59

Rolling three-month returns, 1992 to 1997		
	Date	Gain or loss, %
Best	12/31/74 to 3/31/75	19.23
Worst	9/30/87 to 12/31/87	−17.1
Median		3.99

SOURCE: Lipper Analytical Services, Inc. Dividends and gains reinvested, through December 31, 1997.

FIGURE 6.8 *Equity income funds returns.*

Stellar Performer: Top Equity-Income Funds, 1992 to 1997

Fund name	Returns, % 1997	Returns, % 1992–1997	Telephone
Kemper-Dreman High Return	31.93	169.85	800-621-1048
PIMCo Renaissance A	35.92	155.85	800-426-0107
Fidelity Equity-Income	29.98	152.15	800-544-8888
T. Rowe Price Equity-Income	28.82	148.29	800-638-5660
Prudential Equity-Income A	36.41	145.29	800-225-1852

SOURCE: *Lipper Analytical Services, Inc. Dividends and gains reinvested, through December 31, 1997.*

So don't think that equity-income funds are only for people over 80 years old. They make great sense over the long term.

INTERNATIONAL FUNDS—NOT THE BEST COURSE

If you frequently talk to financial advisers you'll hear them urge you to put 20% of your portfolio in international stock funds.

People who have followed that advice have watched their funds lag, albeit with a certain international je ne sais quois. For example, in 1997, international funds rose just 5.49 percent, versus 24.29 percent for the average stock mutual fund.

But one year's performance could be a fluke. Suppose we looked at the five-year performance of international funds versus growth funds. Not being content with the last five years' performance, let's look at every five-year period of the past decade at three-month intervals (see Figure 6.9). That's 21 five-year periods.

Cumulative returns, %, 1972 to 1997					
Name	1 year	5 years	10 years	15 years	25 years
S&P 500 index objective	32.60	146.20	385.72	979.17	New
Growth funds	25.17	117.02	349.74	710.95	2013.93
International funds	5.49	78.45	153.44	614.94	1008.09

Rolling five-year returns, 1972 to 1997		
	5 years ending	Gain or loss, %
Best	September 1987	333.09
Worst	December 1977	−11.78
Median		70.91

Rolling three-month returns, 1972 to 1997		
	3 months ending	Gain or loss, %
Best	March 1975	21.77
Worst	September 1974	−20.78
Median		3.76

SOURCE: *Lipper Analytical Services, Inc. Dividends and gains reinvested through December 31, 1997.*

FIGURE 6.9 *International funds performance.*

Growth funds beat international funds every time.

You can make the argument that you need international funds to diversify your portfolio. But think for a minute about why you diversify. Ideally, you want something that charges when the rest of your portfolio is in retreat.

And at least at first, international stocks would work. If you compare the Morgan Stanley Europe, Australia, and Far East Index with the Standard & Poor's 500 Stock Index, you see that the two are not very closely correlated. The two indexes have a correlation coefficient of 0.6 over the past five years. A correlation of one means that the two move perfectly in tandem. So the two are not well correlated.

But there's a catch. Major foreign markets often rise when the New York Stock exchange rises. But when U.S. stocks tumble, so do foreign stocks. What good is that?

And when foreign stocks rise, they don't necessarily rise as much, thanks to the currency effect. A U.S. mutual fund may hold stocks that are denominated in foreign currencies. But every day, the fund must value its holdings in U.S. dollars. So suppose your fund owns a French stock that didn't change in price from one day to the next. If the French franc fell 2 percent, your fund would value the stock at 2 percent below its price the day before. You see, for everything to go perfectly in an international fund, you need foreign markets to rise and foreign currencies to rise against the dollar. That does happen from time to time, but it's rather rare.

So keeping a set percentage of your portfolio in overseas stocks really doesn't make sense. Instead, you should keep a percentage of your portfolio in foreign stocks when you have a strong opinion on foreign markets—and on the direction of the U.S. dollar. As an alternative, a few funds specialize in stocks of U.S. companies that get a significant percentage of their earnings from overseas. One such fund is Fidelity Export; another is Papp America Abroad. But if you decide to buy international funds, consider it an intelligent speculation, not a cure for volatility.[1]

GLOBAL FUNDS—A COMPROMISE

If you feel that you need some international exposure to your portfolio, but you can't decide exactly how much, then consider investing in a global fund. These funds can invest almost anywhere in the world where stocks are traded—including the United States. In short, you leave the task of evaluating world markets to your fund manager.

Of course, managers' opinions will vary widely. In the beginning of 1998, for example, GAM Global had 48.6 percent of its assets in the United States and Canada, and another 21.3 percent in Europe, according to Morningstar, the Chicago fund-trackers. Janus Worldwide, however, had 60.7 percent of its assets in Europe, and just 11.9 percent in the United States and Canada.

What are the drawbacks to global investing? As you can see from Figure 6.10, the international component to global funds has acted as a drag the past few years. On the other hand, global funds

Cumulative returns, %, 1972 to 1997					
Name	1 year	5 years	10 years	15 years	25 years
S&P 500 index objective	32.60	146.20	385.72	979.17	New
Growth funds	25.17	117.02	349.74	710.95	2013.93
International funds	5.49	78.45	153.44	614.94	1008.09
Global funds	12.89	92.90	200.90	733.40	2205.61

Rolling five-year returns, 1972 to 1997		
	5 years ending	Gain, %
Best	September 1987	261.61
Worst	December 1977	15.87
Median		103.15

Top global funds, 1992 to 1997			
	Returns, %		
		1992–	
Fund name	1997	1997	Telephone
GAM Global A	35.02	204.83	800-426-4685
Janus Worldwide	20.48	146.98	800-525-8983
Idex Global A	20.39	141.93	800-851-9777
Templeton World I	19.12	137.22	800-292-9293
Oppenheimer Global A	21.82	130.66	800-525-7048

SOURCE: *Lipper Analytical Services, Inc. Dividends and gains reinvested through December 31, 1997.*

FIGURE 6.10 *Global funds performance.*

have very good median performance, particularly when compared with international funds.

One other danger: Expect relatively high expenses on global funds. The typical global fund charges 2.1 percent a year in expenses, versus about 1.6 percent for the average diversified U.S. stock fund. That's steep. Try to choose a fund with below-average expenses.

AGGRESSIVE GROWTH FUNDS DON'T ALWAYS GROW

Aggressive growth funds look for price appreciation any way they can get it. The typical aggressive growth fund trades far more actively than the average growth or growth and income fund. One way of measuring trading is called *portfolio turnover*. It refers to the amount of the portfolio that gets traded in a 12-month period. The average stock fund has an 83 percent turnover rate; the average aggressive growth fund has a 137 percent turnover rate. Strong Discovery fund, an aggressive growth fund, had a mind-boggling 793 percent turnover rate in 1997, according to Lipper Analytical Services.

Aggressive growth funds also use other strategies to boost performance. Some dabble in small-company stocks; others look for companies with rapidly accelerating earnings. Yet others buy some of their stocks on margin, or make short sales.

Yet for all of their gyrations, most aggressive growth funds simply increase risk and expenses without increasing performance. As you can see from Figure 6.11, aggressive growth funds tend to have worse periods of poor performance than the average fund. But over the past 10 years, all that risk hasn't been rewarding. The average aggressive growth fund has risen 310 percent, versus 325.72 percent for the average equity-income fund.

Expenses make the situation worse. The typical aggressive growth fund carries a 1.83 percent expense ratio. And that doesn't cover the cost of all that trading, because brokerage expenses aren't part of a fund's expense ratio.

If you choose an aggressive growth fund, monitor it carefully. If it shows signs of faltering, sell it promptly. Your aggressive growth fund manager would do the same.

Name	Cumulative returns, %, 1972 to 1997				
	1 year	5 years	10 years	15 years	25 years
S&P 500 index funds	32.60	146.20	385.72	979.17	New
Growth funds	25.17	117.02	349.74	710.95	2013.93
Aggressive growth funds	20.28	107.35	305.60	591.44	1605.46

Rolling five-year returns, 1972 to 1997		
	5 years ending	Gain or loss, %
Best	June 1983	229.79
Worst	December 1977	−13.24
Median		102.3

Rolling three-month returns, 1972 to 1997		
	3 months ending	Gain or loss, %
Best	December 1982	24.24
Worst	December 1987	−22.14
Median		4.37

Top aggressive growth funds, 1992 to 1997			
	Returns, %		
Fund name	1997	1992–1997	Telephone
Fidelity New Millenium	24.63	193.53	800-544-8888
First Eagle Fund	29.46	174.52	800-531-5142
Gabelli Value	48.23	175.25	800-227-4618
Westwood Equity	29.57	169.40	800-338-2550
Spectra	24.69	160.80	800-237-0132

SOURCE: Lipper Analytical Services, Inc. Dividends and gains reinvested through December 31, 1997.

FIGURE 6.11 *Aggressive growth funds performance.*

SMALL-COMPANY GROWTH FUNDS NEVER MEET EXPECTATIONS

Another favorite mantra of financial advisers is "Buy small-company stocks for the long term. Small-company stocks always do better than large-company stocks over the long term."

The source of that advice is a celebrated study by Ibbottson and Associates, a respected financial research company based in Chicago. The oft-cited study showed that small-company stocks have outperformed their larger brethren since 1926.

Small-company mutual funds, however, haven't outperformed large-company funds over the past 15 or 20 years. One reason: The typical stock in a small-company fund's portfolio has a market capitalization of $875 million. The Ibbottson study looked at stocks with market caps of $200 million to $300 million. That's tiny—so tiny, in fact, that stocks in the $200 million to $300 million capitalization range are called *microcaps*.

If you look at small-company stock fund performance since 1972, you'll see that it's pretty much a coin toss whether they beat large-company stocks.

If we throw out results from the 1970s, growth funds are clear leaders, however. Why kick out the 1970s? The 1970s had a very different investment climate, including high interest rates and high inflation. And the mutual fund industry was tiny. Just 11 small-company funds have records from 1972 through 1982, versus 92 growth funds.[2]

As you can see in Figure 6.12, the maxim that small-company stocks always do better in the long run is, sadly, not true. Nevertheless, if you want to seek higher highs (and you're willing to brave the lower lows), then consider tilting a long-term portfolio toward small-company stock funds. The best time to tilt your portfolio toward small-company funds is when the economy is growing strongly and interest rates are falling. Rising interest rates are poison for small companies, which tend to be heavy borrowers—and whose loans are typically floating-rate notes.

SMALL IS ALWAYS BETTER FOR SMALL-COMPANY STOCK FUNDS

If you decide to buy a small-company stock fund, look for one whose assets are below $1 billion. Although size can actually be an advantage for large-company stock funds, it's a handicap for small-company funds.

The rules that govern mutual funds say that a diversified fund can't own more than 10 percent of a company's outstanding stock. And most funds make sure that no one holding is much more than 5 percent of the fund's total assets.

For most funds, those aren't terribly onerous restrictions. But suppose a small-company fund manager likes the shares of BingCo, the fabled

Cumulative returns, %, 1972 to 1997					
Name	1 year	5 years	10 years	15 years	25 years
S&P 500 index funds	32.60	146.20	385.72	979.17	New
Growth funds	25.17	117.02	349.74	710.95	2013.93
Small-company stock funds	20.63	116.48	369.06	594.47	2009.54

Rolling five-year returns, 1972 to 1997		
	5 years ending	Gain or loss, %
Best	December 1980	255.97
Worst	December 1977	2.19
Median		105.32

Rolling three-month returns, 1972 to 1997		
	3 months ending	Gain or loss, %
Best	March 1975	28.36
Worst	December 1987	−23.91
Median		4.17

Five best small company funds, 1992 to 1997			
	Returns, %		
Fund name	1997	1992–1997	Telephone
Baron Asset	33.89	177.75	800-992-2766
Lord Abbett Developing Gr A	30.78	172.92	800-874-3733
Franklin Small Cap Grth I	15.78	169.08	800-342-5236
Enterprise Small Company Growth	7.33	164.21	800-432-4320
Govett Smaller Companies A	−16.52	159.80	800-821-0803

SOURCE: *Lipper Analytical Services, Inc. Dividends and gains reinvested through December 31, 1997.*

FIGURE 6.12 *Small-company stock funds performance.*

ball-bearing company. BingCo's total outstanding stock is worth $500 million. A fund with $400 million in assets could buy $20 million of BingCo with no problem. The purchase would be 4 percent of the stock's capitalization, and 5 percent of the fund's assets.

Now suppose the fund has $5 billion in assets. The manager decides to buy BingCo. The manager can't put 5 percent of the fund's assets in BingCo. That would be $250 million, or half the company's stock. The most the manager could buy would be

$50 million. But $50 million is just 1 percent of the fund's assets. The manager will have to find another 99 stocks he or she likes as much as BingCo to keep the fund's performance above average.

Interestingly, a study by Charles Schwab & Co., the discount brokerage, found that new small-company funds tend to fare better than older ones, at least for the first year or two of their existence. This may be, in part, because the funds are small and maneuverable—and because their managers are eager to prove themselves.

ADD SECTOR FUNDS FOR SPICE

International, global, aggressive growth, and small-company stock funds are all diversified. But if you want to really tilt your fund, the mutual fund industry has a wide array of nondiversified funds, called *sector funds,* from which to choose.

How do you choose among all the different sectors? There's no exact answer. Probably the best route is to use sectors as a way to play long-term trends. For example, there are some 77 million baby boomers in the United States, many of whom will be passing the half-century mark in the next few years. Whatever you may think of the boomers, they tend to move in great herds—and move certain stock sectors, too. If you want to play the aging of the baby boom, you might consider the following:

- *Health funds.* These funds invest in health care stocks, such as pharmaceutical manufacturers, hospitals, and medical technology. They also invest in biotechnology companies. The baby-boomer angle: As boomers get older, they will need more health care.

- *Financial services funds.* These funds invest in banks, brokerages, and insurance companies. Just like their parents, boomers have begun to save as they have gotten older. And as they begin to approach retirement age, their saving rate will probably approach a frantic pace.

- *Technology funds.* Technology funds invest in disk-drive, computer, and telephone manufacturers. Boomers love technology—and as they age, they will become increasingly dependent on it.

Over the past five years, the leader in this boomer trio has been financial services funds, which have risen 202 percent. Health care funds, stricken by the controversy over government health care, have risen 112 percent. Technology funds are up 133 percent. A mixture of all three would have returned 149 percent.

You can also try a technical approach, which means that you try to look at current price trends and ride them as long as possible. A crude but reasonably effective system: Buy the top-performing sector fund each year.

This was tested on Fidelity's Select funds because they are all in one fund family and are easy to track (see Figure 6.13). The approach is guaranteed to lead to occasional disasters. For

Name	1 year	5 years	10 years	15 years	25 years
Balanced funds	18.94	86.34	233.84	563.65	1459.51
China region funds	−23.47	19.33	New	New	New
Emerging market funds	−2.35	40.53	New	New	New
European region funds	15.76	126.38	169.17	New	New
Financial services funds	45.23	214.49	670.91	1260.26	1892.87
Global funds	12.89	92.90	200.90	733.40	2205.61
Gold funds	−42.33	4.03	−30.05	−21.81	263.79
Health funds	21.15	117.57	567.82	1267.96	New
Japanese funds	−15.43	−6.50	11.23	255.14	668.18
Latin American funds	25.27	72.09	New	New	New
Microcap funds	29.78	105.09	278.64	622.19	New
Midcap funds	19.72	105.11	354.67	582.95	1989.54
Natural resources funds	0.06	99.99	158.49	426.69	1451.29
Pacific except Japan funds	−35.45	6.55	32.23	310.03	New
Pacific funds	−27.62	18.35	48.88	785.64	New
Real estate funds	22.39	86.12	207.06	421.22	824.02
Science and technology funds	9.66	156.84	508.89	688.16	1459.50
Utility funds	25.69	86.37	255.27	651.55	1037.87

SOURCE: Lipper Analytical Services, Inc. Dividends and gains reinvested through December 31, 1997.

FIGURE 6.13 *Sector funds performance.*

example, you would have started 1988 with 1987's best Select, which was Select American Gold. The fund fell 12.5 percent in 1988.

But the system has hit several home runs. For example, Fidelity Select Biotechnology was the top-performing Select in 1990. It soared 99 percent in 1991.

A $10,000 investment in the system in January 1988 would have grown to roughly $90,000 by 1997, versus $50,500 for the same amount invested in the Standard & Poor's 500 Stock Index. The calculation doesn't account for taxes or the Selects' 3 percent sales charge. And it ignores the fact that it can be difficult (although not impossible) to find the best Select on December 31 and switch by the first trading day of the year.

Using only 10 years' results, you can't overlook the possibility of sheer dumb luck, either. Nevertheless, strong investment trends often last more than a year, and this might help you identify some of the larger trends. And you don't have to restrict yourself to Fidelity funds. There are plenty of non-Fidelity sector funds, some of which don't carry a 3 percent sales charge.[3]

 Sectors Don't Stay the Same

We usually talk about industry sectors as if they were eternal. There's some reason for this. Unless someone discovers the Fountain of Youth, health care will pretty much be concerned with drugs, hospitals, and insurance companies. And autos will be autos, at least until someone discovers a reliable form of teleportation.

But some sectors do change radically over time. That's not always bad. But it illustrates why you can't just invest in a sector fund and forget about it. Let's look at two changing sector funds, utilities and gold.

Utilities funds invest in electric power utilities, gas companies, telephone companies, and water companies. Back in the 1920s, electric utilities were exciting growth companies. After all, not everyone had electric power back then, and the companies' growth rates were phenomenal.

But for the past several decades, utilities stocks—and the mutual funds that invest in them—have been reserved for people whose idea of excitement is alphabetizing the spice rack. They were known for above-average dividends and steady but unremarkable earnings growth. That's changing, however.

Utilities still have above-average dividend yields. The Standard & Poor's Electric Utilities Index has a dividend yield of 5.7 percent. The S&P Utilities Index, which includes gas and telephone utilities, has a 5 percent yield. That may not sound like much, but it's fabulous in these days of miserly dividends.

Even though they still sport high yields, utilities are undergoing a remarkable transformation. Electric utilities are being deregulated, which means they can compete with each other for business. Competition typically helps drive prices down, and proponents of deregulation say that consumers will see their electric bills drop by 15 to 40 percent.

That's great for consumers. For investors, however, deregulation means increased uncertainty. After all, a company that has fared well without competition may not do well when other companies start vying for its business. Do you remember when airlines were deregulated? Several major lines prospered, while the others went into a protracted death rattle.

Wall Street hates uncertainty. When a sector begins to change, traders often batter the stocks. As a result, the average utilities fund lagged badly from 1995 through 1997, rising just 33 percent, versus 67 percent for S&P 500 index funds.

For mutual fund investors, the tumult in the utilities industry means having to choose utility funds much more carefully than before. One could argue, in fact, that past performance means less than ever when choosing a utility fund, given the changing nature of the industry.

Nowadays, utilities fund managers are doing far more than calculating yields and reviewing state regulations. In fact, your fund could look more like an international fund or a growth fund now. Here's what utilities managers are doing these days:

- *The global play.* These funds salt their U.S. holdings with electric, telephone, and cellular telephone utilities in emerging markets. These have huge growth prospects. Typically, telephone companies in emerging markets leapfrog in technology—they install cellular phones rather than string copper wire. But these are stocks that operate in places like Indonesia and Brazil, so they also have higher risks than the average utility fund. Check the prospectus to see what percentage of the fund can be in foreign holdings, particularly emerging markets.

- *The growth play.* These funds look for stocks that are more likely to boost their earnings than increase their dividends. The prospectus will say that income is a secondary consideration.

- *The income play.* Some funds still look for dividends. To find them, look for funds whose objectives emphasize current yield, not growth of principal.[4]

Gold could be another changing sector. Ancient financial wisdom holds that gold is the ultimate weapon against inflation. To give you an idea of the stable purchasing power of gold, an ounce of gold has been able to buy a good men's suit since colonial days.

Why is gold valued as an inflation hedge? Inflation is the progressive devaluation of paper money. The government can print more money, but it can't make more gold. So when inflation rises, gold does, too.

Gold funds, which invest mainly in the stocks of gold-mining companies, were exceptionally popular in the late 1970s and 1980s. In fact, United Services Gold Shares was the top-performing no-load fund three times—in 1979, 1982, and 1989.[5]

But inflation has been whipping gold for more than 10 years. Consumer prices, as measured by the consumer price index, have risen 40 percent over the 10 years that ended in 1997. But gold, the inflation hedge of choice, has fallen from $484 an ounce on December 31, 1987, to $289 an ounce at the end of 1997. Gold funds, which invest mainly in the stocks of gold-mining companies, are down an average 13.7 percent over the past 10 years.

Should you invest in gold funds? One would suspect that gold, which has been a universally recognized investment since the dawn of civilization, probably hasn't fallen into the trash bin of investments. But unless you have a strong feeling that inflation will be increasing, there's no need to include it in your portfolio.

There's a Sector for All Seasons

If you can think of an industry, there's probably a sector for you (see Figure 6.13). A rundown of some of the more prominent sector and specialty funds we haven't dealt with yet follows:

- *Balanced funds.*   The classic balanced fund has 60 percent of its investments in stocks, and 40 percent in bonds. This was long considered the optimum mix. Stocks rose when the economy was strong; bonds rose when the economy was weak. And since the economy rises more than it falls, a 60/40 split was considered the best. These are best for conservative investors who want an all-in-one investment.

- *Emerging markets funds.*   These funds invest in stocks traded in small or developing countries, such as Brazil, the Philippines, Thailand, or Russia. These countries tend to have much higher gross domestic product growth than the United States, and can often produce extremely good returns. Unfortunately, they can also go down just as rapidly, as anyone who invested in Latin America in 1994, or Asia in 1997, can attest. These are best reserved for the most aggressive portion of your international portfolio—as are funds that specialize in China, Latin America, or the Pacific Rim countries except Japan.

- *European, Japanese, and Pacific funds.*   These funds are for those investors who have strong opinions about these regions and feel they want more concentration than a diversified international fund would give them.

- *Microcap funds.*   These funds invest in the stocks of companies that have market capitalizations of $300 million or less. These funds do extremely well when small-company stocks are in vogue. One reason: The stocks are so thinly traded that the funds' own buying pushes up their prices. In a downturn, they tend to get hurt badly because the market for many microcaps doesn't just turn down—it vanishes.

- *Midcap funds.*   These are growth funds that specialize in stocks of companies with $1 billion to $5 billion in market cap.

- *Natural resources funds.*   These funds invest in stocks of oil producers and refiners, mining com-

panies, and timber companies. These funds fare
well in inflationary times, because raw materials
prices sometimes lead the inflationary charge.

- *Real estate funds.* These funds invest primarily in real estate investment trusts (REITs)—
  companies whose main line of business is
  buying and selling real estate. Most real estate
  funds can also invest in stocks of homebuilding
  and construction companies, as well as stocks
  of mortgage lenders. Real estate funds typically
  offer above-average dividend yields, as well as
  a degree of protection from inflation.

BEWARE OF FAD FUNDS

DANGER! The fund industry, like any other industry, is
prone to fads. But fund fads not only make you
feel silly when they're over—they make you
poorer, too.

You should be extremely wary whenever you
see many fund companies trotting out a new type
of fund. For example, many fund companies
launched emerging markets funds in 1993, following their spectacular successes in 1993. But many
emerging markets collapsed in 1994.

New funds are a good contrary indicator for a
particular sector. Normally, the fund industry will
see that one particular type of fund is doing well.
After a while, other fund companies will want
their own version of the fund. But this takes time.
The fund has to get approval from the Securities
and Exchange Commission to sell shares to the
public. And it also must get approval from state
regulators.

So by the time all the new funds come on the
market, 12 to 18 months have passed, and the
investment trend is over.

You should also beware of funds whose main
claim to fame is an affinity group. Funds aimed at
Lutherans, for example, may or may not be good.
But whether or not they are good has nothing to
do with being Lutheran.

SOCIAL INVESTMENT FUNDS CAN BE GOOD AND DO GOOD

A growing number of funds now add social
screens. They won't invest in companies that

manufacture tobacco, for example, or companies that make weapons. Others are proactive as well, investing in funds with clean environmental records or with histories of good employee–management relations.

For a long time, many of these social investment funds had dreadful records. Fortunately, social investing has attracted some very good mutual fund managers in the past few years. So if your religious or personal beliefs lead you to shun certain industries, you should be able to find a decent fund that reflects those views.

A word of warning: Different groups have different views about particular industries. MMA Praxis Growth, for example, is aimed at Mennonites, a pacifist religious group. The fund holds no defense stocks. Dreyfus Third Century, however, does allow defense stocks. So read the prospectus carefully before you invest.

The top social investment funds are listed in Figure 6.14. Because so many are new, they are ranked by three-year performance.

Fund name	Objective	Returns, % 12 months	3 years	Telephone
Domini Social Equity	Growth and income	36.21	30.91	800-762-6814
Dreyfus Third Century	Growth	29.37	29.75	800-373-9387
Ariel Appreciation	Growth	37.95	28.44	800-292-7435
Aquinas Equity Income	Equity-income	27.85	27.82	800-423-6369
Aquinas Equity Growth	Growth	28.97	27.35	800-423-6369
Neuberger & Berman Social Responsibility	Growth	24.41	27	800-877-9700
MMA Praxis Growth	Growth	29.20	26.07	800-977-2947
Ariel Growth	Small-company	36.44	25.93	800-292-7435
Bridgeway Social Responsibility	Growth and income	26.85	24.3	800-661-3550
Citizens Emerging Growth	Aggressive growth	17.69	23.56	800-223-7010

SOURCE: Morningstar. Dividends and gains reinvested through December 31, 1997.

FIGURE 6.14 *Top 10 social investment stock funds, 1994 to 1997.*

YOU DON'T NEED 30 FUNDS

Many mutual fund investors seek diversification by investing in a dozen or more core funds, and then adding another dozen or two sector funds. In the end, however, all they end up doing is getting average performance—and high fees.

Most core funds—S&P 500 funds, growth funds, growth and income funds, and equity-income funds—are highly correlated. That is, when one drops, so do all the others. So having a dozen core funds doesn't make a lot of sense. Three or four will do just fine.

Similarly, if you add a half dozen sector funds to tilt your portfolio, you're more likely to tilt your portfolio back toward the average, rather than tilt it in one direction. One or two sector funds is probably plenty at any given time.

 REBALANCE ONLY WHEN NECESSARY

If you have split your overall portfolio between stocks, bonds, and money market funds, you probably feel the need to check your asset allocation from time to time. This is generally acknowledged to be a Good Thing to Do.

But don't fiddle with your asset allocation unless it's seriously out of whack—say, by more than 10 percentage points between stocks, bonds, and money market funds. If you continually rebalance, you'll be tossing money that's performing well into parts of your portfolio that are lagging. That's good in theory. But because the stock market tends to perform well most of the time, you'll be selling shares far too soon.

Instead, try rebalancing only when your portfolio is seriously out of balance. A 10 percentage-point rebalancing strategy lets your best investments grow, and gives you a reasonable cut-off point for taking profits.

END POINT

Stock mutual funds, like stocks, have two extremely dangerous periods: the top and the bottom. At the top, it is almost physically painful not to be overinvested. Everyone else is making more money than you are; conditions seem fine, even though the market is overvalued; and the market just keeps steaming ahead. It's at this point that people invest too much in a particular sector or in stock mutual funds in general. Then the market plunges.

Which brings us to the other most dangerous time in the stock market: Prices are falling; your portfolio loses money every day; and everyone else is fleeing. Like as not, if you pull your money out now, you'll be doing so at the bottom.

Being a successful investor means overcoming your natural urges to be too greedy in a bull market and too terrified in a bear market. It's not easy. Some suggestions:

- *Invest automatically.* Make investing a monthly habit by having your investment come out of your paycheck. There's not a financial institution in the world that wouldn't be happy to tap your paycheck every month.

- *Invest regularly.* If you put a set amount into a stock or bond fund every month, you have the advantage of dollar cost averaging. You'll buy more shares when the market is low, and fewer when the market is high. Over time, you'll reduce your overall cost per share.

- *Remember that bear markets are buying opportunities.* If you keep a small buying reserve in a money market mutual fund, you'll protect yourself when the market goes down. More important, you'll have money to buy stock funds when everyone else is selling them.

- *Don't be afraid to sell.* Fund companies would have you believe that you should sell only when the sun has burned itself into a fist-sized lump of coal. But you should sell shares if you will soon be needing your money, or if your fund hasn't been performing well. Give your fund six months to a year if it's not meeting your expectations. (Be sure to compare your fund with similar funds to make a fair comparison.) If the fund isn't performing as you expected, sell it.

Scary Stuff:
Precious Metals, Futures, and Options

On your way home from work, you stop to admire a gold ring in a jeweler's window.

At the grocery store, you pick up some orange juice and a few ears of corn. Before you head for home, you fill up your tank with gas.

Gold, orange juice, corn, and gas are all commodities: basic goods and materials that are traded every day for cash. But they are also traded on the commodity futures exchanges around the world.

When we think of commodities, we think of a bunch of 25-year-old lunatics shoving and shouting in the trading pits. That's not entirely wrong. But futures serve a higher purpose than relieving speculators of money. They take risk from those who don't want it and give it to those who do. Without futures, farming would be more difficult than it is, and international trade would be nearly impossible.

But are they good investments? That depends. In some cases, commodities, options, and precious metals make good investments—and can actually reduce the risk in your portfolio. But for most people, these are investments best left to others.

 **GOLD IS THE OLDEST FORM OF MONEY**

Gold has been the monetary standard since the dawn of civilization. People have long valued its beauty, its resistance to rust, and its malleability.

Because it is so prized, gold's purchasing power has remained relatively stable over the years. In Colonial times, an ounce of gold would buy a good men's suit; it still does today. (We're talking a good suit here, not a great suit.)

Some of the first U.S. gold coins were minted privately in Gainesville, Georgia, in 1830. Georgia was the site of the first major gold rush in the United States. Miners there had problems trading their gold for U.S. currency. So Templeton Reid, an assayer, set up shop there. He bought the miners' gold and privately minted gold coins.

Although his efforts eventually failed, the U.S. government stepped in and established mints in Dahlonega, Georgia, and Charlotte, North Carolina, where the miners could exchange their gold fairly. The U.S. circulated gold coins until 1934. At least in theory, some U.S. currency could be exchanged for gold until 1971, when the United States officially went off the gold standard.

Gold still has a reputation for being a store of value, particularly in inflationary times. But lately, gold hasn't lived up to its reputation. Inflation has risen over the past 10 years, but the price of gold has fallen. No one is exactly sure why gold and inflation have moved out of synch. A few suggestions:

- *Better mining techniques.* Gold mining still isn't easy. But new mining techniques can remove gold from ore that previously wasn't worth bothering with. This has helped increase production, which, in turn, has kept gold prices down.

- *More exploration.* New gold finds in Africa, Latin America, and Australia have also helped push more gold onto the market, keeping gold prices down. In recent years, emerging countries have been willing to open vast pit mines when the price of gold gets high enough. This, too, keeps a lid on prices.

- *Russia.* Shortly after the breakup of the Soviet Union, Russia sold massive amounts of gold to shore up its finances. Russia is still one of the leading gold producers.

- *Central banks.* Although most gold is held in private hands, most countries have large reserves of gold that they buy and sell opportunistically.

Wall Street expert Peter Bernstein suggests a further, more fundamental reason for gold's poor performance. He studied the price of gold from 1800 to 1934. During that period, much of the nation's business was conducted in gold coin, and paper currency's value was based on gold. But the United States suffered several large bouts of inflation from 1800 to 1934. Inflation rose sharply after the Civil War, for example, as well as after the Alaskan gold rush and World War I. And the United States had two massively deflationary periods between 1800 and 1934—one in the 1830s and another in the 1930s. He suggests that the nation was able to stay on the gold standard not because gold stabilizes prices, but because prices were relatively stable. And when gold prices fluctuated wildly, as they did after the Civil War, the United States went off the gold standard.

Others say that, at least for the moment, gold has been demonetized—that is, its value as a medium of exchange has been superseded by the U.S. dollar, currently the world's strongest currency. In recent years, in fact, gold has tended to rise when the dollar falls, and vice versa. Should the world (or at least the United States) threaten to fall apart, gold could well regain its importance. On the other hand, if the world falls apart, you'll have other things to worry about besides inflation.

Choose Coins over Bars

You can buy gold in two major forms, bars and coins. Bars have a simplicity about them that's alluring. A stack of gold bars in the basement is a sure-fire way to impress the guests. But there are problems with gold bars, too.

For one thing, bars sometimes have to be assayed, or tested for weight and purity, when you sell them. This depends on who made the bars. If the bars were made by a well-known metals company, such as Engelhard, then they probably won't have to be assayed. If your brother-in-law made them from the gold he panned in the Rockies last year, then you have to get them assayed. Needless to say, this adds to your overall expense. Also, the Fort Knox–style bars are exceptionally heavy. If you plan to flee the country with gold bars, don't forget to bring a forklift.

Gold coins, on the other hand, typically don't have to be tested for weight and purity. U.S. Gold Eagle coins, for example, are universally accepted for weight and purity. You can also buy gold bullion coins from Canada (Maple Leaf), South Africa (Kuggerand) and China (Panda).

U.S. gold coins are sold through dealers, rather than through the U.S. mint. You should shop carefully before you buy, and get several quotes from various dealers. Each dealer has a different markup for the coins, and some offer bulk discounts.

 ## Buy Rare Coins Only if You Love Them

Coin collecting is a great hobby that has, unfortunately, fallen on hard times in recent years. As an investment, however, it's just too hard for the average person to make money.

In the late 1970s and early 1980s, rare coins were one of the hottest investments around. Financial planners often recommended rare coins as part of a diversified portfolio; rare coin galleries sprang up in the more fashionable downtown areas across the country.

The reason, of course, was that prices were soaring. The Brasher Doubloon, one of the earliest and most sought-after Colonial coins, sold for $430,000 in July 1979 and then sold again for $729,000 in November 1979. Prices for Franklin half-dollars and Morgan silver dollars soared, too.

Part of the reason rare coins fared so well was because the price of gold and silver was skyrocketing, too. Gold was on its way to $800 an ounce, and some were predicting that gold would hit $3,000 an ounce. Silver rocketed to $50 an ounce.

But metals prices aren't the only factor that determines a rare coin's value. First is the overall rarity of the coin. There are far fewer Brasher Doubloons than there are, say, 1955 nickels.

Finally, there is the coin's condition. Rare coins are graded on a special scale that starts at Mint State 60 and ends at Mint State 70. Generally speaking, these are coins in exceptional condition. They have either been struck especially for collectors (called *proofs*), or they have never been circulated. Exceptionally rare circulated coins are sometimes traded, too.

Tiny differences—and differences of opinion—separate one mint condition from another. It takes a trained eye to judge whether an MS-65 coin is worthy of the grade. The difference between MS 65 and MS 64 could mean thousands of dollars.

To prevent arguments over a coin's grade, independent companies have several appraisers evaluate a coin and agree upon its grade. Once the grade is certified, the coin is encased in Lucite, or *slabbed,* as they say in the trade. The coin then has the advantage of a (relatively) indisputable grade. The Lucite prevents any deterioration from handling. But be careful: If you buy a coin, make sure the deal has a return period—and that you get a second opinion during that period.

You should also be aware that if you buy from a dealer, you are paying a markup price. You will have to overcome that markup to make a profit. In some cases, that can be a very big markup indeed, so you have to shop carefully. Many coin investors find they can get the best prices at auction.

Most people collect coins because rare coins have a striking beauty that many current coins don't. It's hard to be unimpressed when gazing at an uncirculated walking Liberty half-dollar or a double eagle—the classic $20 gold piece. And that's probably the best reason to buy rare coins. If you're savvy enough to pick up a great coin at a discount, good for you. But otherwise, the odds are stacked against you.

Always Take Physical Possession of Coins and Metals

DANGER!

Here's the easiest way to get ripped off: Let someone store your gold or coins for you.

Owning gold has problems. If you keep it in the house, you have to keep it in a safe place. That means buying a safe, a gun, a dog, or all three. At the very least, it means making sure that your insurance will cover it.

You can also keep your gold in a safety deposit box, although that increases your investment

Getting Help

American Numismatic Association (ANA).   A nonprofit organization of collectors, but many dealers are also members. The ANA provides many educational programs for both novice and experienced collectors. If you have a complaint about an ANA member, you can write to the Association at 818 North Cascade Avenue, Colorado Springs, CO 80903.

Industry Council for Tangible Assets (ICTA).   A national trade association of coin and precious metals dealers. ICTA urges its members to subscribe to a program of binding arbitration administered by the American Arbitration Association (AAA). It also keeps records of other programs of arbitration or mediation its members adhere to. If you have a question whether or not an ICTA member subscribes to the AAA program or another, you may write to ICTA at 666 Pennsylvania SE, Washington, D.C. 20003.

Professional Numismatists Guild (PNG).   An organization of coin dealers and numismatists. Membership in PNG is selective; to qualify, a dealer must have a minimum number of years' experience and meet a minimum net worth requirement. The PNG also requires its members to submit to binding arbitration in order to resolve complaints filed by consumers or other dealers. If you have a complaint against a PNG member, you can write to PNG at 3950 Concordia Lane, Fallbrook, CA 92028.

SOURCE: *The Federal Trade Commission and the American Numismatic Association.*

costs. And if the safety deposit boxes are robbed, you won't be covered under federal deposit insurance.

Con artists often offer to store the gold or coins for you. It's the perfect crime: By the time the victim wants the gold back, the con artist may have been gone for a year or more.

If you decide to buy gold, make sure you have a safe place to keep it. Even though it costs extra, your bank's safety deposit box is probably the best place. But don't let a stranger store it for you. As one state securities administrator said, "If you're stupid, you'll buy gold from an out-of-state dealer you've never heard of. And if you're really stupid, you'll let him store it for you."

OTHER METALS DON'T WEAR AS WELL AS GOLD

In February 1998, legendary investor Warren Buffett announced he had bought 20 percent of the year's production of silver—a staggering 130 million ounces.

Buffett's a long-term investor, so it could be years before we know whether he made a profit on the trade. Silver is an exceptionally tricky commodity to play—as are most other metals besides gold.

For one thing, silver and other metals are used less for monetary purposes and more for industrial purposes. Current U.S. coins contain little silver, for example. So unlike gold, which is bought and sold for its intrinsic value, the price of silver is determined mainly by the supply-and-demand equation. And since silver is primarily a by-product of mining other metals, mainly gold and lead, it's hard to get a handle on the supply-and-demand dynamics of the metal. If you're going to dabble in metals, stick with gold.

METALS SCAMS ABOUND

Mark Twain once defined a gold mine as "a hole in the ground with a liar standing next to it." It's not a bad definition.

There are several great gold mining companies, such as Coeur d'Alene Mines, Battle Mountain Gold, and Echo Bay Mines. The stocks of these companies are all traded on the stock exchanges and make interesting investments when the price of gold is rising. After all, suppose a company's cost of producing an ounce of gold is $200. If gold rises from $300 an ounce to $350 an ounce, the company's profit margin has increased from $100 an ounce to $150 an ounce, a 50 percent increase. Someone who owns the metal has gained only 17 percent.

But many investors get sucked into buying shares of small, worthless mining companies that own nothing but a printing press and a couple of slick sales reps. What will they do to prove there's gold in them thar hills? Anything it takes to separate you from your money. One favorite trick is to stuff shotgun shells with gold dust and blast the walls of an old mine—a trick called *salting the mine.* Your best bet: Stick with real, reputable, and actively traded mining stocks, such as those listed on the New York Stock Exchange.

Another trick that makes its way through all the five-star boiler rooms is the sale of strategic metals. These are supposedly rare metals, such as titanium and indium, which are used in making new Air Force bombers or cruise missiles or ultra-sensitive, top-secret intelligence equipment. The pitch: The government is buying these metals to make a new kind of weapon. The price has nowhere to go but up.

A few years ago, the metal of choice was indium. Scamsters would sell the metal for $90 an ounce and whisper that it was on its way to $300, thanks to its vital role in the nation's defense. But indium is actually a fairly common metal that sells for $5 to $7 an ounce on a good day. Because the scamsters typically offered to store the indium for the victims, the victims never even got possession of the overpriced metal. And, of course, by the time the victims discovered they had been scammed, the money was long gone.

 SPOT MARKETS VERSUS FUTURES MARKETS

Every day, tons of raw materials change hands in the international markets. The *spot market* is where materials trade for cash, and the materials are then delivered immediately. When you buy an ounce of gold from a dealer, you're participating in the spot market. A farmer who takes grain to the silo and gets a check for the amount delivered is participating in the spot market, too.

The *futures market* involves the promise to make or take delivery of a commodity at a specific price and a specific time in the future. Although the futures market is generally viewed as a place to take wild, speculative gambles—which it is—the futures market is also a place where people can reduce risks. In fact, that's why the futures markets originated. Let's look at some examples.

Example 1: The Farmer

Suppose you are a farmer, and you know that you can reasonably expect to produce 10,000 bushels of wheat in September. It's April now. You need to get $3.00 a bushel to pay your costs and make a decent profit—about what wheat is selling for now. If wheat rises to $3.50 by September, you're in tall cotton. But if wheat falls to $2.50, you'll be out of business.

You decide to make a deal with the local silo. You'll agree to deliver 10,000 bushels of wheat in September for $3.00 a bushel. You're giving up the chance to make more, but you're also giving up the possibility of making less. Technically called a *forward contract,* this is the essence of a futures contract.

Example 2: The Baker

Suppose you are a large commercial baker. You know that you will need 50,000 bushels of wheat in 3 months. The current price is $3.50 a bushel, up from $3.00 last month.

Rather than risk paying more than $3.50 a bushel, you contract with a grain dealer to accept delivery of 50,000 bushels of wheat in 3 months at $3.50 a bushel. If wheat falls to $3.00 a bushel, you've lost the chance to cut costs. But you've avoided having to pay more than $3.50 a bushel.

These are simplified examples of how futures contracts work. Now let's look at some of the details.

A FUTURES CONTRACT IS JUST THAT—A CONTRACT

A *commodities futures contract* is an agreement to make delivery or take delivery of a specific amount of a commodity at a specific price at a specific time. In essence, commodities futures contracts are standardized versions of the forward contracts that we've used in the preceding examples. A standardized corn contract would provide the following specifications:

- The amount, typically 5,000 bushels.
- The price.
- The type and grade.
- Form of delivery.
- Location of delivery.[1]

Contracts also specify the date for making or taking delivery. Most futures contracts are for one year. When the contract expires, a new one for one year later takes its place. The contract closest to expiration is called the *near* contract.

Finally, contracts tell you how they are traded. For example, they tell you the increments in which the contract trades. Heating oil contracts trade in 25-cent increments per ton, or *ticks*. Some futures markets also have daily limits on how much the commodity can rise or fall. This, too, is spelled out in the standard contract.

The advantage to a standardized contract is that it makes for a much more liquid market. For example, it might be difficult to find a buyer for 3,291 bushels of corn delivered to Des Moines. Because commodities contracts are standardized, people around the world know exactly what they're getting—which makes the contracts far more appealing.

KEY CONCEPT   Anatomy of a Trade

Let's say it's September, and you buy a contract requiring you to deliver 5,000 bushels of corn at a specific location—an approved ware-house in Chicago—for $3 a bushel in December. In commodities terms, you are *long* December corn.

You buy your contract through a commodity broker, who collects a commission for the transac-tion. You must also put down a margin deposit. This is not like the margin requirements for the stock market. Instead, it's a good-faith deposit. You can put down cash (in the form of a check) or Treasury bills. Normally, the deposit is about 5 percent of the value of the contract. Since your contract is for 5,000 bushels of corn at $3 a bushel, the total contract value is $15,000. Your deposit would be $750, or 5 percent of $15,000.

The broker then forwards your order to the commodities exchange clearinghouse. Techni-cally, your contract is between you and the clear-inghouse, not between you and the person on the other end of the trade. If something goes wrong, you won't have to track down a farmer in Des Moines. The clearinghouse takes care of the problem.

From the clearinghouse, the trade then moves to the exchange. These are the famous commodity pits, where contracts are bought and sold by *open outcry*—that is, by a group of people standing in the pits and shouting orders. Because it can be so noisy in the pits, traders use an elaborate system of hand signals to trade.

Once your order is filled, your account will be valued every day. This is called *marking to market*. Let's say that the next day, corn closes at $3.03 a bushel. You have gained $0.03 a bushel, or $150. Your account will then be credited with $900—your initial $750, plus the day's $150. Your gain is just 1 percent of the value of the contract. But it's a 20 percent gain on your $750.

The commodities markets match buyers with sellers, so the $150 you gained would have come from the account of the person on the other side of the trade. The exchange clearinghouse takes care of that, too.

What's worst that could happen? Plenty. Let's say that corn falls to $2.95 a bushel. You have lost a nickel a bushel, or $250. That's just 1.7 percent of the value of the contract, but a third of your margin.

If your margin falls below a certain level, your commodity broker will call you and ask you to add more money to the account, or your position will be liquidated. In the very worst case, you can hold your contract until it expires, in which case you will have to buy 5,000 bushels of wheat for $3 per bushel. If wheat is then selling for $2 a bushel, you have 5,000 bushels of very expensive wheat. It doesn't happen often, but it does happen.

 Opposite Trades Cancel

Unlike the stock market, where you are buying and selling interests in a company, the futures markets is a market of traded promises. So to get out of a position, you simply perform a trade that's the opposite of your current position.

Let's say you bought a contract to buy December corn, you made some money, and you want to get out. You don't sell your contract. Instead, you tell your broker to sell a contract with the same expiration date. In this case, you would sell a contract for December corn. In the eyes of the exchange, the two cancel out, and your position is closed. The difference between the two transactions is your profit or loss.

Bear in mind that it's equally easy to bet that commodity prices will fall as it is that they will rise. If you think corn prices will fall, for example, you tell your broker to sell a corn contract. To get out of the position, you buy a corn contract that expires on the same date.

FUTURES MARKETS ARE NO LONGER JUST A HILL OF BEANS

Most people think of agricultural goods when they think of futures trading. In fact, foodstuffs are just a small percentage of the futures market.

The futures market can be divided into four parts:

1. *Agricultural.*   These include grains, such as corn, wheat, barley, rough rice, soybeans, flax seed, and oats, as well as broiler chickens, pork bellies, orange juice, coffee, cocoa, and cattle.

2. *Metals.*   Gold, lead, nickel, tin, silver, platinum, palladium, copper, and aluminum all trade on the metals exchanges.

3. *Energy.*   The energy exchanges include oil, unleaded gasoline, heating oil, natural gas, and propane.

4. *Financial futures.*   These are the biggest futures markets these days. You can buy futures contracts for the Standard & Poor's 500, the S&P 400, the Value Line Composite Index, most currencies, and Treasury bills, notes, and bonds.

HOW FUTURES ARE PRICED

Futures contracts, like most other investments, are priced by a combination of logic and speculation.

The logical part works like this: Suppose you are a miller and know you have to buy 5,000 bushels of wheat in 3 months. Wheat now costs $3 a bushel, so the entire amount would cost $15,000. You could buy the wheat now, but you would lose the potential to earn interest on that $15,000 for 3 months. If Treasury bills are yielding 5 percent, your potential earnings from the T-bills would be one-quarter of the annual interest, or $187.50. (5 percent of $15,000 is $750; 0.25 percent of $750 is $187.50.) This is called the *cost of carry.* Naturally, the longer the time period, the higher the cost of carry. So in a perfect market, the price of a futures contract that expires in three months would be the current price minus the cost of carry.

In a normal market, the futures prices of contracts that are further from the expiration date are less than ones that are closer to the expiration date. That's because the cost of carry increases.

But as we all know, markets are not entirely rational. In some exceptional markets, the price of the near-term contract is higher than the cost of contracts that expire later. This indicates extreme bullishness: Traders are convinced the price will go higher and are willing to disregard the cost of carry.[2]

WHY TRADE FUTURES?

The basic use of futures is to speculate on the future prices of various goods. If you think prices will rise, you go long; if you think prices will fall, you go short. You might be saying to yourself, "This is an unbelievably risky way to invest. Why the heck should I expose myself to this kind of risk?" And you're quite right. The average investor in the futures market loses early and often.

Hedging Can Make Sense

Futures do have a legitimate investment use, called *hedging.* Suppose you have a $500,000 stock portfolio. You're worried that the stock market might go down. But you don't want to sell your stocks.

Instead, you can go short one S&P 500 futures contract worth $500,000. (The dollar value of an S&P 500 futures contract is the index value times 500. So if the index is at 1,000, an S&P 500 futures contract would be worth $500,000.) If you're wrong and the market marches upward, your losses on the futures will wipe out any profit you make from your stocks. But if you're right, your gains in the futures will wipe out your losses.

Hedging isn't an exact science. Most investors' portfolios don't resemble the S&P 500. But if done properly, a hedge will keep your losses from being catastrophic.

Managed Futures Spread the Risk

Commodities do have an additional virtue. Several studies have shown that small investments in commodities can actually help reduce risk in stock portfolios. The most famous study, by professor John Lintner of Harvard University, concluded that adding a small percentage of managed commodities to a stock portfolio increased returns without increasing risk.

And this makes a degree of sense. After all, commodity prices tend to rise when inflation rises. Stock prices tend to fall when inflation rises. For example, in 1987, the Standard & Poor's 500 Stock Index rose just 5.3 percent, assuming dividends and gains were reinvested. But the average commodity pool tracked by *Managed Account Reports,* a New York–based newsletter, gained 57.8 percent.[3]

But how do you get exposure to commodities without trading futures? One compromise is the *commodity trading pool.* These are somewhat like mutual funds that invest in commodities. But the analogy is far from perfect.

Commodity pools are actually limited partnerships, because the laws that govern mutual funds don't allow funds devoted to commodity trading. A limited partnership consists of a general partner—in this case, the commodity trading advisor—and a group of limited partners. The limited partners have very little say in the running of the partnership. But in return, their liability is limited to the amount they invest.

Most commodity pools have a limited formation period, during which investors may contribute money. The typical minimum is $5,000 or more, and some even allow $2,000 Individual Retirement Account contributions.

Unlike real estate partnerships, which usually don't let you withdraw money, a commodity pool will often let you withdraw money monthly or quarterly.

What are the advantages?

- *Diversification.* Commodity trading advisors typically invest in a wide array of futures contracts, from hog bellies to interest-rate futures. Some pools do specialize in certain kinds of futures markets, however.

- *Professional management.*   Do you have time to quit the day job and trade futures? No? Then it's probably a good idea to hire a manager to do it for you.

- *Limited losses.*   In all cases, your losses are limited to the amount you invest. Some funds will voluntarily liquidate if losses exceed 50 percent, limiting your losses to a bit more than that after fees. And still others will guarantee the return of your principal if you keep your money in the funds for five years or more. (They do so by investing the bulk of their assets in zero-coupon bonds.)

The disadvantages:

- *High volatility.*   No matter how much diversification and professional management you get, a futures pool is going to be more volatile than a stock mutual fund.

- *Huge fees.*   If you think mutual fund fees are bad, wait until you see commodity trading pool fees. Start with sales fees of 1 to 5 percent. Then add management fees of 2 to 3 percent, plus 20 percent of the profits. Brokerage fees will add another 5 percent or more to the fund's expenses. Overall, expect fees to be about 15 percent a year.

Are they worth it? It depends. If you're an aggressive investor with a large, well-diversified portfolio, adding a commodity pool may improve your returns. But you'll have to do a fair amount of searching. There are some 300 commodity trading advisors registered with the Commodity Futures Trading Commission, the regulatory arm of the federal government that oversees the commodity markets. If you choose one, look for the following:

- *A long-term record.*   Experience counts in commodity trading. You want a survivor.

- *Easily understandable trading methods.*   Can the fund's advisor explain how he or she trades so that you can understand it? If not, move on.

- *Consistent returns.*   Managers who soar 100 percent in one year and then plunge 50 percent the next year really aren't worthwhile. For example, suppose you invest $50,000 with a manager and in the next year, he or she doubles your money to $100,000. The following year, your account falls back to $50,000. You would have been better off investing in Treasury bills.[4]

 OPTIONS: THE RIGHT TO BUY A SECURITY AT A SPECIFIC PRICE

An *options contract* is the right, but not the obligation, to buy or sell a stock at a specific price for a set period of time. Options to buy a stock are called *calls;* options to sell a stock are called *puts*.

What makes the futures market so risky is the requirement that you make or take delivery at the contract's expiration date, if you haven't closed your position out. The futures market is rife with legends of speculators who have woken up as the proud possessors of several trainloads of coal or soybeans.

The options market is also risky, but somewhat less risky than the futures market. In the options market, your potential returns are unlimited, while your losses are limited to the amount you invest.

 **Options Increase Your Purchasing Power**

Let's say that you have been watching the stock of BingCo, the ubiquitous yet imaginary maker of high-performance ball bearings. You think the stock will rise to $60 per share, up from its current $45.

You can simply buy the stock, which would cost you $4,500 for 100 shares.

But suppose BingCo has listed options available. You decide to buy BingCo call options. These allow you to buy 100 shares of BingCo at $45 a share for the next 3 months.

The call options will typically cost a fraction of what it would cost to buy the actual shares. Let's say the call option costs $450. If BingCo soars to $60 a share as you predicted, you could force the writer of the options to sell you 100 shares of BingCo at $45 a share. You could then turn around and sell those shares in the open market for $60. This is called *calling away* the stock. You could also simply sell the call option, whose price would have increased, too.

The advantage: leverage. Suppose you had called away the BingCo stock. You would have invested $450 for the options. But by the time the trade was complete, you would have gained $1,500. Subtract the $450 cost of the options, and your total gain would have been $1,050—more than double your original investment.[5]

The opposite transaction would have worked like this:

Suppose you have seen BingCo trading at $60 a share. You suspect that the bottom will fall out of the ball-bearing market. Rather than sell the stock short, you decide to buy a BingCo put for $600. That is, you have the right to force the writer of the put to buy BingCo stock from you at $60 a share for the next 3 months.

As you predicted, BingCo's stock drops like a rock to $45 per share. You exercise your option— called *putting it to* the writer of the option. You buy 100 shares of BingCo on the open market, which he must buy for $60 per share. You have made $15 per share, or $1,500, less the $600 investment, or $900. Of course, the put option's price has probably risen by $900, so you could simply sell the put.

The Strike Price

KEY CONCEPT Most of the major stocks traded today also have options traded on them. In fact, a stock will often have several options traded. Let's say BingCo is trading at $45 a share, and you are interested in buying a BingCo call. You see that BingCo has three options trading, all with different strike prices. The *strike price* is the price at which you may purchase BingCo stock. You can buy BingCo options at $40, $45, or $50.

The $40 option is called an *in-the-money* option. If you called away the stock, you'd pay $40 per share and could then sell it at a $5 per share profit. The $45 is an *at-the-money* option, since it's at the same price as BingCo stock. And the $50 option is an *out-of-the-money* option, since you would lose money if you bought the stock at $50 and sold it at $45.

Naturally, the reverse would be true of put options. A put on BingCo at $40 would be an

Future Tense: Words of the Futures Markets

arbitrage   The simultaneous purchase and sale of similar commodities in different markets to take advantage of price discrepancy.

arbitration   The procedure of settling disputes between members, or between members and customers.

basis   The difference between the current cash price and the futures price of the same commodity. Unless otherwise specified, the price of the nearby futures contract month is generally used to calculate the basis.

bid   An expression indicating a desire to buy a commodity at a given price; opposite of **offer.**

broker   A company or individual that executes futures and options orders on behalf of financial and commercial institutions and/or the general public.

cost of carry   For physical commodities such as grains and metals, the cost of storage space, insurance, and finance charges incurred by holding a physical commodity. In interest rate futures markets, it refers to the differential between the yield on a cash instrument and the cost of funds necessary to buy the instrument.

cash market   A place where people buy and sell the actual commodities; that is, grain elevator, bank, and so forth. See **spot** and **forward contract.**

clearinghouse   An agency or separate corporation of a futures exchange that is responsible for settling trading accounts, clearing trades, collecting and maintaining margin monies, regulating delivery, and reporting trading data. Clearinghouses act as third parties to all futures and options contracts—acting as a buyer to every clearing member seller and a seller to every clearing member buyer.

commodity   An article of commerce or a product that can be used for commerce. In a narrow sense, products traded on an authorized commodity exchange. The types of commodities include agricultural products, metals, petroleum, foreign currencies, and financial instruments and indexes, to name a few.

Commodity Futures Trading Commission (CFTC)   A federal regulatory agency established under the Commodity Futures Trading Commission Act, as amended in 1974, that oversees futures trading in the United States. The commission is comprised of five commissioners, one of whom is designated as chairman,

(Continued)

(Continued)

all of whom are appointed by the President subject to Senate confirmation. It is independent of all cabinet departments.

commodity pool An enterprise in which funds contributed by a number of persons are combined for the purpose of trading futures contracts or commodity options.

commodity trading advisor A person who, for compensation or profit, directly or indirectly advises others as to the value or the advisability of buying or selling futures contracts or commodity options. Advising indirectly includes exercising trading authority over a customer's account as well as providing recommendations through written publications or other media.

crop (marketing) year The time span from harvest to harvest for agricultural commodities. The crop marketing year varies slightly with each agricultural commodity, but it tends to begin at harvest and end before the next year's harvest; for example, the marketing year for soybeans begins September 1 and ends August 31. The futures contract month of November represents the first major new-crop marketing month, and the contract month of July represents the last major old-crop marketing month for soybeans.

customer margin Within the futures industry, financial guarantees required of both buyers and sellers of futures contracts and sellers of options contracts to ensure fulfilling of contract obligations. Margins are determined on the basis of market risk and contract value. Also referred to as *performance-bond margin.*

daily trading limit The maximum price range set by the exchange cash day for a contract.

expiration date Options on futures generally expire on a specific date during the month proceeding the futures contract delivery month. For example, an option on a March futures contract expires in February but is referred to as a March option because its exercise would result in a March futures contract position.

Forex market An over-the-counter market where buyers and sellers conduct foreign exchange business by telephone and other means of communication. Also referred to as *foreign exchange market.*

forward (cash) contract A cash contract in which a seller agrees to deliver a specific cash commodity to a buyer sometime in the future. Forward contracts, in contrast to futures contracts, are privately negotiated and are not standardized.

(Continued)

(Continued)

futures contract   A legally binding agreement, made on the trading floor of a futures exchange, to buy or sell a commodity or financial instrument sometime in the future. Futures contracts are standardized according to the quality, quantity, and delivery time and location for each commodity. The only variable is price, which is discovered on an exchange trading floor.

futures exchange   A central marketplace with established rules and regulations where buyers and sellers meet to trade futures and options on futures contracts.

hedging   The practice of offsetting the price risk inherent in any cash market position by taking an equal but opposite position in the futures market. Hedgers use the futures markets to protect their business from adverse price changes.

inverted market   A futures market in which the relationship between two delivery months of the same commodity is abnormal.

leverage   The ability to control large dollar amounts of a commodity with a comparatively small amount of capital.

long   One who has bought futures contracts or owns a cash commodity.

maintenance   A set minimum margin (per outstanding futures contract) that a customer must maintain in a margin account.

managed futures   Represents an industry comprised of professional money managers known as **commodity trading advisors** who manage client assets on a discretionary basis, using global futures markets as an investment medium.

margin call   A call from a clearinghouse to a clearing member, or from a brokerage firm to a customer, to bring margin deposits up to a required minimum level.

marking-to-market   To debit or credit on a daily basis a margin account based on the close of that day's trading session. In this way, buyers and sellers are protected against the possibility of contract default.

National Futures Association (NFA)   An industrywide, industry-supported, self-regulatory organization for futures and options markets. The primary responsibilities of the NFA are to enforce ethical standards and customer-protection rules, screen futures professionals for membership, audit and monitor professionals for compliance with general and financial rules, and provide for arbitration of futures-related disputes.

(Continued)

(Continued)

offer   An expression indicating one's desire to sell a commodity at a given price; opposite of **bid.**

offset   Taking a second futures or options position opposite to the initial or opening position.

open interest   The total number of futures or options contracts of a given commodity that have not yet been offset by an opposite futures or option transaction nor fulfilled by delivery of the commodity or option exercise. Each open transaction has a buyer and a seller, but for calculation of open interest, only one side of the contract is counted.

open outcry   Method of public auction for making verbal bids and offers in the trading pits or rings of futures exchanges.

original margin   The amount a futures market participant must deposit into a margin account at the time an order to buy or sell a futures contract is placed. Also referred to as *initial margin.*

pit   The area on the trading floor where futures and options on futures contracts are bought and sold. Pits are usually raised octagonal platforms with steps descending on the inside that permit buyers and sellers of contracts to see each other.

price limit   The maximum advance or decline from the previous day's settlement permitted for a contract in one trading session by the rules of the exchange.

settlement   The last price paid for a commodity on any trading day. The exchange clearinghouse determines a firm's net gains or losses, margin requirements, and the next day's price limits, based on each futures and options contract settlement price. If there is a closing range of prices, the settlement price is determined by averaging those prices. Also referred to as *settle* or *closing price.*

short   One who has sold futures contracts or plans to purchase a cash commodity. (Verb) Selling futures contracts or initiating a cash forward contract sale without offsetting a particular market position.

spot   Usually refers to a cash market price for a physical commodity that is available for immediate delivery.

tick   The smallest allowable increment of price movement for a contract.

SOURCE: *Chicago Board of Trade.*

out-of-the-money put. You would buy the stock at $45 and then put it to the writer of the option at $40. A $45 put would still be *at the money.* And a put at $50 would be *in the money.* You could buy the stock at $45 and make the writer of the option sell it at $50.

CONCEPT   Time and Sentiment Guide Options Prices

In a perfect world, options prices should be easy to set. Suppose once again that BingCo stock is at $45. You decide to buy a BingCo $40 call option. This entitles you to buy 100 shares of BingCo at $40 per share.

In that perfect world, your call option's price should be quoted at 5. The cost of the option would be $500, because you multiply the price of an option by 100 shares of stock to get its price. The $500 is equal to its *intrinsic* value—that is, the $500 profit you would make if you called 100 shares of the stock at $40 and sold it at $45. But the world isn't perfect, and your option actually costs 7, or $700. What's going on?

Two things. One, options prices typically are higher when they have been recently issued. They fall as they come closer to their expiration dates. After all, the more time you have, the more likely the stock is to rise further.

Second, BingCo is a very volatile stock, and many other traders think the stock could spike up, too. So they have bid the option up to $7. Options traders would say that the option is selling at a $7 premium, even through $5 is its intrinsic value.

If you buy the call for $7, you would have to pay $700 for the option. In order for you to hit a *breakeven* price, the stock would have to rise to $47 a share. That is, you would have to call 100 shares of stock for $40 a share, or $4,000. You would then sell the shares for $47 a share, or $4,700. You paid $700 for the option, so you would break even.

Writing Options: Sometimes Prudent

So far, we have discussed only the buyer of puts and calls. But there's a person on the other side of the trade, called the *writer* of the options.

Let's say you own 100 shares of BingCo. You don't want to sell the stock, but you'd like some income. And you wouldn't mind a bit of protection against the stock falling.

So you decide you'll sell an option on 100 shares of your stock. Because you actually own the stock, this is a *covered call.* BingCo is selling at $50 a share, so you sell the call with a strike price of $50. A buyer pays $500 for the option.

You hope that the stock's price will stay steady or even fall a bit. If it stays steady, there's no reason for the buyer to call away the stock. You'll get to pocket the $500. If the stock price falls, you'll have $500 to offset your losses.

The worst case: The stock rises to $60 a share and gets called away. You'll get $5,000 for the sale, but you'll have to figure out somewhere else to invest it.

Because most options expire worthless, covered calls are a useful way to get extra investment income and protect yourself from a slide in stock prices. At worst, you'll have to sell your stock for a below-market price.

Naked Puts and Calls: Terrible Idea

If selling covered calls can be prudent, selling *naked puts* can be awful. When you sell a naked put, you don't have the stock to sell to the owner of the option. If it is exercised, you have to buy the stock at current prices and sell it to the option owner for below-market prices.

Similarly, if you sell naked puts, you'll have to buy stock from an options holder for less than its current market value. Do you need this?

 **WHY INVEST IN OPTIONS?**

- *Sheer speculation.* Options have the potential to give you a great deal of return on relatively small investments. And they limit your losses.

- *Hedging.* Like futures, options are also useful for hedging. Suppose you have 5,000 shares of General Motors. You like the stock, but you're worried that it could fall in the short term. You

Option Clause: Words of the Options Markets

at the money   An option is at the money if the strike price of the option is equal to the market price of the underlying security.

call   An option contract that gives the holder the right to buy the underlying security at a specified price for a certain, fixed period of time.

covered call option writing   A strategy in which one sells call options while simultaneously owning an equivalent position in the underlying security; or in which one sells put options and simultaneously is short an equivalent position in the underlying security.

equity options   Options on shares of an individual common stock.

exercise settlement amount   The difference between the exercise price of the option and the exercise settlement value of the index on the day an exercise notice is tendered, multiplied by the index multiplier.

exercise   To implement the right under which the holder of an option is entitled to buy (in the case of a **call**) or sell (in the case of a **put**) the underlying security.

expiration cycle   Relates to the dates on which options on a particular underlying security expire. A given option, other than **LEAPS,** will be assigned to one of three cycles: the January cycle, the February cycle, or the March cycle.

expiration date   Date on which an option and the right to exercise it cease to exist.

hedge   A conservative strategy used to limit investment loss by effecting a transaction that offsets an existing position.

holder   The purchaser of an option.

in the money   A call option is in the money if the strike price is less than the market price of the underlying security. A put option is in the money if the strike price is greater than the market price of the underlying security.

intrinsic value   The amount by which an option is **in-the-money.**

LEAPS   Long-term Equity Anticipation Securities; long-term stock or index options. LEAPS, like all options, are available in two types, **calls** and **puts,** with expiration dates up to three years in the future.

(Continued)

(Continued)

margin requirement (for options)   The amount an uncovered (**naked**) option writer is required to deposit and maintain to cover a position. The margin requirement is calculated daily.

naked call writing   A short call option position in which the writer does not own an equivalent position in the underlying security represented by the option contracts.

naked put writing   A short put option position in which the writer does not have a corresponding short position in the underlying security or has not deposited, in a cash account, cash or cash equivalents equal to the exercise value of the put.

open interest   The number of outstanding option contracts in the exchange market or in a particular class or series.

out of the money   A call option is out of the money if the strike price is greater than the market price of the underlying security. A put option is out of the money if the strike price is less than the market price of the underlying security.

premium   The price of an option contract, determined in the competitive marketplace, which the buyer of the option pays to the option writer for the rights conveyed by the option contract.

put   An option contract that gives the holder the right to sell the underlying security at a specified price for a certain fixed period of time.

strike price   The stated price per share for which the underlying security may be purchased (in the case of a **call**) or sold (in the case of a **put**) by the option holder upon exercise of the option contract.

time value   The portion of the option premium that is attributable to the amount of time remaining until the expiration of the option contract. Time value is whatever value the option has in addition to its **intrinsic value.**

underlying security   The security subject to being purchased or sold upon exercise of the option contract.

writer   The seller of an option contract.

SOURCE: *Chicago Board Options Exchange (www.CBOE.com).*

could buy GM puts, which would rise in value if GM stock fell, thus protecting your investment.

- *Hedged speculation.* Options aren't an all-or-nothing proposition. Some investors put 90 percent of their money in ultrasafe T-bills and the rest in calls. For example, suppose you have $60,000 to invest, and are thinking of investing in BingCo, the fictional ball-bearing maker. But you are uneasy putting all $60,000 into one company. You could:

> Put 90 percent of your money in Treasury bills.
>
> Put 10 percent of your money in BingCo call options.

The interest from your T-bills will decrease the cost of the call options. If the call options rise above breakeven, you'll get the benefit of the appreciation of BingCo stock. If the options expire worthless, you'll lose only the cost of the option, less the interest from the T-bills.

 OPTIONS AREN'T FOR INDIVIDUAL STOCKS

Options come in staggering variety. Here are just a few of the options available:

- *Futures options.* These give you the right, but not the obligation, to buy a futures contract at a set price. They offer the volatility of futures contracts, with some loss protection. After all, your losses are limited to the amount you invest.

- *LEAPS.* These are long-term options. Typically, an option has a three-month lifespan. LEAPS last for three years.

- *Stock index options.* If you want to speculate on the direction of the stock market as a whole, you can use stock index options. Currently, options are available on the Standard & Poor's 500 Stock Index, the New York Stock Exchange Index, the Standard & Poor's 100 Stock Index, the Major Market Index, and several others. Because it's difficult to deliver all the components of the S&P 500, all these index options have cash settlement.

- *Treasury bond options.* These allow you to speculate on the direction of interest rates.

END POINT

Although you often hear about investors losing vast sums in the futures and options market, you rarely hear about the pension funds, farmers, and banks that have saved vast amounts of money through hedging.

In fact, speculation is simply the way that risk is moved from people who don't want it to the shoulders of people who do. There's nothing intrinsically wrong with speculative investments.

But the basic rule for precious metals, commodities, and options is *caution*. Sure, you can make tons of money in the futures market. But you can lose it, too. And if you can't lose the money you invest, you're better off investing elsewhere.

The best way to double your money quickly is to fold it in half and put it in your back pocket. It's far better to save more and watch your money grow slowly through intelligent investment, rather than put it all at high risk.

NOTES

CHAPTER 2

1. Robert Zipf, *How the Bond Market Works,* 2nd ed. (New York: New York Institute of Finance, 1998), pp. 8–10.

2. Edward Renshaw, *The Practical Forecaster's Almanac* (Homewood, Ill.: Business One Irwin, 1992), pp. 50–51.

3. *Frequently Asked Questions (FAQ) About Savings Bonds,* Federal Reserve Bank of New York (10 October 1997): www.ny.Frb.org/pihome/sug_bnds/.

4. *Standard & Poor's Ratings Definitions,* Standard & Poor's Corp. (12 October 1997): www.Ratings.Standardpoor.com.

5. Jerome Cohen, Edward Zinbarg, and Arthur Zeikel, *Investment Analysis and Portfolio Management* (Burr Ridge, Ill.: Irwin, 1987), p. 412.

6. Robert Zipf, *How the Bond Market Works,* 2nd ed. (New York: New York Institute of Finance, 1998), p. 135.

CHAPTER 3

1. Richard Teweles, Edward Bradley, and Ted Teweles, *The Stock Market,* 6th ed. (New York: John Wiley & Sons, 1992), pp. 25–26.

2. "Directory of Dividend Reinvestment Plans," *American Association of Individual Investors Journal* (June 1997).

3. James Kim, John Waggoner, and Paul Wiseman, "Growling on Wall Street: Bull market slowed by a bear hug?" *USA Today* (April 4, 1994), p. 1b. Copyright 1994, *USA Today*. Reprinted with permission.

CHAPTER 6

1. John Waggoner, "Global investing no cure for volatility," *USA Today* (December 12, 1997), p. 3b. Copyright 1997, *USA Today*. Reprinted with permission.

2. John Waggoner, "Growth funds make better investment bet," *USA Today* (September 19, 1997), p. 3b. Copyright 1997, *USA Today*. Reprinted with permission.

3. John Waggoner, "3 ways to tackle sector-fund maze," *USA Today* (November 14, 1997), p. 3b. Copyright 1997, *USA Today*. Reprinted with permission.

4. John Waggoner, "Changing times spice up utility stock funds," *USA Today* (October 3, 1997), p. 8b. Copyright 1997, *USA Today*. Reprinted with permission.

5. Sheldon Jacobs, *The Handbook for No-Load Mutual Fund Investors* (Irvington-on-Hudson, N.Y.: The No-Load Mutual Fund Investor, Inc., 1997), p. 9.

CHAPTER 7

1. Anne E. Peck, "Futures—Agricultural Commodities," *The Complete Guide to Investment Opportunities* (New York: Free Press, 1981), p. 261–262.

2. Stuart R. Veale, ed., *Stocks Bonds Options Futures: Investments and Their Market* (New York: New York Institute of Finance, 1987), pp. 192–194.

3. Mark J. Powers, *Starting Out in Commodities Trading* (New York: McGraw-Hill, 1993), p. 35.

4. Mark J. Powers, *Starting Out in Commodities Trading* (New York: McGraw-Hill, 1993), p. 37.

5. Stuart R. Veale, ed., *Stocks Bonds Options Futures: Investments and Their Market* (New York: New York Institute of Finance, 1987), pp. 155–157.